Overnight

University of Plymouth Library
Subject to status this item may be renewed
via your Voyager account
http://voyager.plymouth.ac.uk
Exeter tel: (01392) 475049
Exmouth tel: (01395) 255331
Plymouth tel: (01752) 232323

OVERSEAS CHINESE AND TRADE BETWEEN THE PHILIPPINES AND CHINA

OVERSEAS CHINESE AND TRADE BETWEEN THE PHILIPPINES AND CHINA

The Intertwining of Family, Social, and Business Interests in Promoting Trade

R.N.W. Hodder

The Edwin Mellen Press
Lewiston•Queenston•Lampeter

Library of Congress Cataloging-in-Publication Data

Hodder, R.N.W. (Rupert Hodder)
  Overseas Chinese and trade between the Philippines and China / by R.N.W. Hodder.
    p. cm.
  Includes bibliographical references and index.
  ISBN-13: 978-0-7734-5793-5
  ISBN-10: 0-7734-5793-3
    I. Title.

hors série.

A CIP catalog record for this book is available from the British Library.

The Edwin Mellen Press   The Edwin Mellen Press
        Box 450   Box 67
    Lewiston, New York   Queenston, Ontario
    USA 14092-0450   CANADA L0S 1L0

                The Edwin Mellen Press, Ltd.
                Lampeter, Ceredigion, Wales
                UNITED KINGDOM SA48 8LT

            Printed in the United States of America

For

Dr. Mario Borillo (1955-2003), surgeon, who gave his life to others;
and for his father, Angel (1925-2002).

salahat nang ginawamo maraming salamat

安姹悲

大雪下了，扫出寻她
这路连到山上，山上都是松柏，
她是花一般，　这里如何住得，
不如回去寻她，
啊回来还是我家

鲁迅

TABLE OF CONTENTS

Chapter 5 – Political Transformation? China

Chapter 6 – Political Transformation? The Philippines

Chapter 7 – Conclusions

LIST OF ILLUSTRATIONS

List of Figures

List of Tables

COMMENDATORY PREFACE

The Philippines occupies a vital strategic position between Southeast Asia and the Pacific. The significance of this fact is growing with China's huge economy and its status in the world. Yet the Philippines nation remains weak economically, and its polity seems unprepared to restore to its people the economic strength and self-confidence they must have if they are to play a crucial role in the region and globally in this new century. How this might be done is of crucial interest to the Philippines, the region and the world.

Rupert Hodder's book on the political economy of the Philippines and its trade with China is a timely and most interesting contribution to this discussion. It is scholarly, original in its approach, rich in ideas, and possesses many levels of debate.

Its central theme is that social relationships are the basis of economic and political life; and that the quality and efficacy of those institutions can alter dramatically following very subtle changes in attitudes towards social relationships. The organisation of business may help to stimulate those attitudinal changes that can lead to a more general formalisation of the political economy. The organisation of political institutions, too, may contribute to shifts in attitude. In the details of this argument the book provides a new dimension, and greater specificity, to the suggestion that trade and institution-building can foster political, economic and social change for the better.

Another theme taken up by this book is that the details and differences in institutions and practice across varied cultural, social, political, and economic contexts are aspects of an underlying commonality among peoples. Behind this discussion lies yet another. It asks the reader not to take for granted even the most conventional and familiar understandings of the social world. This is necessary to maintain intellectual development, and to preserve a tolerance and flexibility in everyday life.

Layered upon these debates is an appreciation of the practice of economic and political life. It asks academics to consider the impact which their ideas can have upon the people they analyse. It acknowledges that there are within government and business in the Philippines women and men of integrity and ideals who are genuinely committed to improve the lot of Filipinos. And it suggests a broad strategy to encourage these hopeful tendencies. At the same time, the book warns against blindly sacrificing the social emphasis of Filipino society for the Puritanism of Western formalism. This social emphasis is essential to effective institutions (economic and political) in the long term, and is the hall mark of any true civilization.

These themes are woven together to provide an unusual, original and scholarly text which I commend to the reader.

Senator Miriam Defensor-Santiago, Republic of the Philippines.
Chair, Committee on Foreign Relations; Professor of Law, University of the Philippines; PhD (Michigan).

ACKNOWLEDGEMENTS

Little in this book could have been done without the help and kindness of a great many people. Thanks is due: to Students at the University of Mindanao who made possible surveys of markets and businesses in Davao; to Fe Castañeda; and to officials at the Bureau of Customs (Davao and Manila), the Securities and Exchange Commission (Davao and Manila), the Department of Trade and Industry (Davao and Manila); the Business Bureau (Davao). Thanks also to Melito S. Salazar Jr. who, during my time in Manila, was a member of the Monetary Board of *Bangko Sentral ng Pilipinas*.

For their courtesy, generosity, candor, and patience, I am also very grateful to the Representatives of Congress (both Houses) and to their staff. I am especially indebted to: Ricky Castillo; Representatives Aquino, Ocampo, Valdez, and Zubiri; and to Senators Angara, Biazon, Defensor-Santiago, Enrile, Estrada (J.), Lim, Lapid, and Revilla. The patience of staff of the Senate Library and Senate Archives in the face of all my requests was extraordinary, and for this, too, I am most thankful. Gratitude is due also to Henry Sy (Filipino-Chinese Chamber of Commerce) and to the many businessmen and women in Davao, Manila, and Shanghai, who took the time to answer my questions so graciously. In China I was fortunate enough to have been aided by Professor Shen Yufang (沈玉芳) and students of the East China Normal University (华东师大长江流域发展研究院), Shanghai; by Professor Gao Jianguo (高鉴国), School of Philosophy and Sociology, Shandong University (山东大学哲学与社会发展学院); and by officials at the Industrial and Commercial and Administration Bureau (Shanghai) (上海市工商管理局), and at the Bureaux of Customs (上海海关综合统计处) and Statistics 上海市统计局 (2002).

vi

Special thanks are owed to An ka-pi (安姹悲); and to the 'Three Ladies' –
Consuela Tanebro, Teresita Gonzalez, and Obeth. They organised my days in the
Philippines and in China, and, through the very long hours, grumbled not once.
Finally, my thanks to the Economic and Social Research Council in the United
Kingdom for their financial support of my fieldwork through grant RA000223785.

Some those whom I interviewed have asked that I not use their names; and this
request for anonymity I have applied as best I can to all those working in
companies and in the bureaucracies. The politicians made no such requests: they
are used to all this; but I alone am responsible for the material that follows.

Introduction

The immediate purpose of this book is to examine business organisation, the practice of trade, and the political support of these activities in the Philippines and China. Particular, but not exclusive, interest is paid to those businesses trading between the two countries. The study begins with a consideration of the overseas Chinese who, it is commonly said, dominate the Philippines' domestic trade and its direct trade with China. However, it soon becomes clear that the apparent certainty of this knowledge does not fit with the highly complex circumstances on the ground. The people whom we study have a far more dimensional view of self and others, of their relationships and practices, and of their representations of the world. The reasons for this and, as a consequence, for the diminution of ethnicity and kinship in business organisation and trade within (and between) the Philippines and China, may be understood as part of the broader question of the transformation of these two countries' political economies from a condition of informality to one of relative formality.

This question is of interest to many branches of the social sciences, and to the people of whom the social scientist writes. In this book it is argued that transformation (informal-formal, and formal-informal) is an expression of shifts both in attitude towards social relationships and, consequently, in the quality of thought. It is the movement from a personalistic (or instrumental) state of mind to an affective state of mind – to a state of mind in which social relationships and, therefore, our ideas about the world are treated *as if* important in themselves, and from which our formalised institutions and procedures emerge.

From this attitudinal perspective, it is apparent that the staples of social science thought - the denizens of the formalised societies of western Europe and America – are only *possible* interpretative devices; and that in these devices – such as those of culture and structure - and in the details of the interpretations they cast, the influence of a writer's own attitudes and relationships is strongly felt. We also begin to see the political significance of our ideas about the world. When held with too much certainty, or treated with too much expediency, the social sciences' analyses may work contrary to informal-formal transformation. More particularly, cultural and structural explanations of the overseas Chinese, presented almost as absolutes, have inflated the economic significance of the Chinese, encouraged hostility towards them, and obscured the dimensionality and commonality of practices and organisations across ethnic and political boundaries. These scholarly representations of the Chinese, together with the social sciences' explanations of the informal quality and weakness of the Philippines' polity, have - in concert with similarly negative street representations of the political establishment - helped to erode the confidence of Filipinos in themselves and in those who govern them.

Our attitudinal perspective also suggests that there is emerging in 'the West' an excessive formalism rooted in a denial of our personalistic qualities. This Puritanism, it is argued here, starves us of a true appreciation of the affective; and may yet lead us into bouts of instability. The problems facing the informal-formal transition of 'developing' societies, then, include the very practice of analysing those societies, and the Puritanism out of which that practice emerges.

Although the immediate concern of this book is the Philippines and China, it has other interests. One is the political importance that the dialectic between street and scholarly representations confers upon social science thought. Another is to move towards an understanding of the general principles of the play of relationships, attitudes, and representations* which, it is argued, form the substance of our social world. It is with this end in mind that this present study attempts to untangle the play of *particular* relationships, attitudes, and representations, among politicians, civil servants, merchants, and scholars. It is from this emphasis on the particular but with the general in mind – for the general, I argue, is a mental device to help us organize the particular (our true lives) - that arise further representations of the Chinese overseas, of business organisation, of political institutions, and of transformation. These representations are not the end to which we are working, nor are they intended to be definitive or objective. They, too, must be drawn into subsequent rounds of similar analyses and made the subject of scrutiny and revision. Yet, because they arise partly and directly from the minds of the people in whom we are interested, they may provide some indication of those people's future actions and behaviour and, therefore, of possible change†.

A third matter is the question of how we think. Here I refer not to a discussion of the merits or demerits of positivist, humanist, structuralist, behaviouralist or cultural approaches, but to the problem of the nature of thought itself. How and why, as we have implied, do our relationships and attitudes influence our thought?

---

* This is an idea that takes us in many directions at once. See, in particular, Collingwood, R.G. (1946); Dilthey, W. (1976); Fodor, J. (1987); Frege (see Geach, P. and Black, M. eds. [1960]); Brentano, F. (1976). See also Baum, E. (2004); Moscovici, S. (1981); and Mauss, M. (1969).

† Around 120 interviews in Manila, Davao, and Shanghai were held with businessmen and women, with politicians and their staff, and with civil servants. In the course of these interviews the representations of each interviewee were, if relevant, introduced into discussions with subsequent interviewees. For instance, in the case of this book's study of the Philippines' Legislature, the representations of politicians were contrasted each with the other, and considered alongside the accounts of congressional staff, civil servants, and businessmen and women. We must recognise that politicians in Congress may often express opinions in order to advance their interests as well as disparage, criticize and undermine opponents, and that observers (including academics) are all too easily caught up in political disputes and hubris. Yet one cannot afford either to be too suspicious or to allow oneself to believe that an interviewer (especially if an academic) is more important to the interviewee as a channel for seeding rumour and allegations deliberately than is probably the case: for otherwise it becomes impossible to see beyond one's own doubts, cynicism, and self-belief. Although we must do what we can to weigh up the interviewees' representations carefully, we must also consider the possibility that politician, merchant, and civil servant, are either telling the truth or, more likely, are recounting what they believe to be a true representation of their world.

4

Why and how do we form the thoughts that we do, and why and how do they come to possess the qualities that they do? Might the influence, political or otherwise, of our ideas (both scholarly and 'street') upon our lives derive in part from our lack of understanding of thought, of the ways in which our ideas are formed, and so of their true meaning? How can we understand their true significance without an understanding of thought itself? How then, might we take this absence of knowledge into account when analysing, interpreting and forming our ideas about the world?

Chapter 1

The Chinese, Trade, and Transformation:

finding perspective

1.0 Introduction

The overseas Chinese are held to dominate not only the Philippines' domestic business and its trade links with China, but also the local and national economies, and much of their overseas trade, of many of the countries of Southeast and East Asia. The figures quoted vary somewhat, but for the most part they point very strongly and confidently to the economic pre-eminence of the Chinese. It is said that the Chinese, though they constitute just 10% of the population of Thailand, hold an 80% share of the country's market capital. In Indonesia, where they constitute just 3.5% of the population, their share of market capital is around 75%. In Vietnam the Chinese comprise just 3% of the population but account for 50% of Ho Chi Minh's market activity, and dominate its light industry, foreign trade, shopping malls, and private banks. In Malaysia they constitute about one third of the population, but they hold a share of between 60% and 70% of the country's market capital. In the Philippines, the Chinese constitute just 1-2% of the population, but their share of market capital is between 50% and 55%. They control the Philippines' major supermarkets, department stores, fast-food chains, stock brokerage firms, and nearly all the main banks; and, it is said, they dominate the nation's wholesale distribution networks, its shipping, construction, textiles, real estate, manufacturing, pharmaceuticals, and press. In Laos the Chinese make up just 1% of the population but they account for almost the entire business community. The Chinese, it is said, also dominate the economies of Burma and Cambodia (though figures for these two countries seem less readily available). Taken together, the foreign reserves of those Chinese whose economic networks stretch among Thailand, Indonesia, Malaysia, the Philippines, and Singapore, amount to well over US$100 billion; and worldwide, as a group, their floating assets are believed to amount to around $2 trillion (see Peng 2000; Chua 2003; Hutchings 2001). The Chinese overseas, states Peng (*op.cit.*), constitute the world's largest overseas linguistic and cultural group, exhibit remarkable cultural cohesion, and possess great commercial power.

2.0 Culture and structure

Mackie (2000) is surely right when he points out that, in their explanations of overseas Chinese economic success, there has been a tendency at times for social scientists 'to put more stress on behavioural and cultural aspects, especially the values and family solidarity of the Chinese than on economic and structural issues...' (p.237). Yet even before the economic crisis of 1997 and during the spectacular rise of many of the economies of east and southeast Asia there was no school of writers - nor perhaps any single writer - who argued that only Chinese culture could explain why the overseas Chinese behave and organise themselves as they do or why some Chinese are so successful in business. Culture was certainly a large part of the explanation; but there were other things at work - structure, circumstance, history, and economics among others – which, for different writers and even for the same writer at different times, were more or less important. And there were always those writers who were more directly skeptical of the cultural explanation or at least of the emphasis given to it by some, and who have preferred to shift the burden of explanation on to structure.

To some, Chineseness is largely, though not entirely, a deliberate and semi-political fabrication produced in response to structural forces. Greenhalgh (1994), for instance, argues that Chinese culture and tradition had never been quite as wholesome and its influences as benign as is often thought and, under the pressure of global forces, were certainly manipulated for the good of some and at the expense of others. In Taiwan, the drive to keep costs down and so to remain competitive and successful in an uncertain global economy, a government suspicious of big business, and banks who denied credit to small companies, left entrepreneurs with little choice but to create firms out of their families. To this end they exploited traditional family hierarchies and cultural expectations about the roles of men and women. The use of culture by scholars to conceal this fact was understandable: Chinese and Chinese-American scholars were attempting to disrupt the European-American cultural legacy and to give their own culture a place in the sun. But in so doing they drew on older Orientalist constructions (such that these scholars were participating in a kind of inverse Orientalism) and inadvertently contributed to a conservative, anti-feminist, intellectual-cum-political agenda in the US which idealised strong familism, strong tradition, strong social and political discipline, intelligence and industriousness. In other words, Chinese and Chinese-American scholars chose to see in the Chinese what it was that the dominant conservatives thought best about America.

Dirlik (1997) took a similar position. 'Chineseness' - a construct in which lies the notion of Chinese capitalism and the cultural explanation - represents, at least in part, a response to globalisation. The strength and intensification of transnational sub-contracting practices renewed the significance of small businesses; and to this end Chineseness was reshaped, reorganised, and reinvented. Production was, in a word, 'ethnicised'. But in doing so certain realities were ignored. In particular, cultural practices of uncertain ethnic origins were appropriated. The values and practices commonly ascribed to Confucianism (such as a strong family, commitment to education, strong kinship or pseudo-kinship, social networks and their use for economic and other purposes), were hardly unique to the Chinese and were much more the product of particular social and historical circumstances. Indeed, weaving such practices and values into the cloak of Chineseness represented nothing less than an assimilation of Chinese traditions to the values of European capitalism or, to put it in another way, the 'Weberising' of Confucianism. And yet at the same time differences such as class, gender and even ethnicity

8

among the Chinese were suppressed. The reconfiguration of Chineseness, argued Dirlik, also justified authoritarianism while transforming socialism into a historical aberration which stood briefly against the natural tendency of the Chinese towards capitalism.

In common with Greenhalgh, Dirlik (1994, 1997) argues that this resinification or the rearrangement of Chineseness is not conditioned by globalisation alone. It must also be understood as an assertion against centuries of Euro-American cultural hegemony - an assertion which Dirlik describes as a kind of self-orientalism which may itself have become hegemonic. After all, the idea that there might be a 'Chinese' variant of capitalism arose not in any Chinese society but in the US where 'two conditions, both of global significance....gave birth to it: the retreat from socialism in China, and the apparent regression in Euro-American capitalisms against evidence of unprecedented growth in East and Southeast Asian societies' (1997, p.305).

It was arguments such as these, combined with the fact of the economic crisis in 1997, and a concern that an emphasis on culture might serve only to hone 'the Chinese' into a target for frustrations and disappointments in the wake of the crisis, which had a hand in lightening the explanatory burden that culture has had to bear in more recent years. Certainly the view that there is something else at work other than culture was made more explicit. Greater emphasis was given to 'situation', historical circumstance (Cribb, 2000), organisational context (Hamilton, 1999), structure and institution, the broader social and political context, and even, on occasions, to chance (Chirot and Reid, 1997). At the same time some writers were more careful to distance themselves more explicitly from the purer forms of cultural explanations which in recent years have been described variously as incredible, exaggerated, probably mischievous, serving chauvinist and nationalist agendas, peddling caricatures and colonial myths, essentialist, reductionist, fallacious, and deceitful (see, for instance, Wang, 2000; Chan, 2000; and Ruskola,

2000). So deeply rooted do culture and tradition appear to be that they had become virtual hereditary properties (Chirot and Reid, 1997, p.3), such that 'even the most elevated review of the historical record and of competing social scientific theories which try to elucidate some of the questions raised by the comparison of Jews and Chinese can lend itself to gross misrepresentation and abuse' (*ibid.* p.5). The problem of definition, too, was given more than just a passing nod. No longer could differences among Chinese be acknowledged yet subsequently ignored. That not all Chinese entrepreneurs are successful economically - a not uncommon observation before 1997 - now became a standard phrase. Even the individual took on a little more significance: individual overseas Chinese exhibit diverse responses because they operate differently and have different capacities and perceptions, just as the individual indigenes' responses and attitudes to Chinese people are also varied (Jomo, 1997). Having retreated from his 'scientific approach', which involved the identification of those attributes that made somebody Chinese, Wang (1999) strongly emphasised self-identity as one of the few reliable tests of 'Chineseness'. Even being seen as Chinese by other people was no criterion unless the individuals concerned also saw themselves as being Chinese. Chinese ethnicity, then, derived from cultural identity and was subjectively determined. Estimates of numbers of Chinese and of their economic strength were therefore recognised more explicitly as being intrinsically vague, unreliable, and inaccurate. Thus the figure of 25 million given for the number of overseas Chinese in Southeast Asia (excluding Taiwan and Hong Kong) assumed an accurate definition of who was and who was not Chinese (*ibid.*); while estimates of Chinese economic power in Malaysia, including the assertion that the Chinese owned more than twice as large a share of all corporate stocks than did the *Bumiputera*, even though the *Bumiputera* population is one-and-a-half times that of the Chinese, were problematic (Jomo, 1997).

With such doubts abroad, comparisons highlighting structural similarities became easier. There was, argued Hamilton (1999), no certainty that the overseas Chinese operate in ways that are peculiarly Chinese. This point was echoed by Amber, Styles and Wong (1999) who suggested that it was unwise to assume without hard knowledge that any aspect of marketing practices in China and the West were different or, indeed, the same. In their 'creative and vulnerable role as "outsiders at the centre" in the dynamic process of change' (Chirot and Reid, 1997, p.34) the Chinese could be compared with the Jews of Europe. But why, asked Hamilton, should we focus only on these two groups? Certainly *guanxi* is not unique to the Chinese: it exists to some degree in every human society (Standifird and Marshall, 2000); and its practice is to be explained in large part by transaction costs. Flexible networks of information, supplies, and finance, lower the costs associated with negotiating contracts and searching for partners, and reduce the likelihood of opportunism. Ruskola found still deeper and broader comparison. He challenged Fairbank's view that there was, in China, no idea of the corporation as a legal individual. Even in imperial China, argued Ruskola (2000), clan corporations were true corporate and legal entities which met most, if not all, of the conventional corporate criteria of Anglo-American law - qualities that were retained during the Republic and under communist rule.

Despite these concerns, the consequential shift in emphasis from culture to structure, and from difference to similarity, did not mark an attempt to move outside the cultural-structural accommodation. Indeed, for many writers the pendulum has swung too far away from culture, and balance needs to be restored. They are in no doubt that culture helps us to understand how attitudes and practices instilled in the homeland may affect behaviour among the overseas Chinese. While even Jomo is willing to concede that 'there do seem to be business networks based on specifically Chinese cultural resources, including language, education, and social organisations such as clan associations...trade guilds, chambers of commerce, school boards, temple committees, and local community associations. Such frequent interaction has undoubtedly generated considerable "cultural" or "social" capital, which is crucial for explaining business trust, risk sharing, informal contracts, and information as well as transaction cost reduction' (p.250). After all, the main weakness of the cultural explanation, in Mackie's view, is not the presumption that it could explain, but that no attempt had been made to formulate a more systematic hypothesis about how and why cultural factors work. Collectively the overseas Chinese today do, of course, share many similar values and customs which derive from a common Chinese culture several generations old; and many strong arguments and much fragmentary evidence could be given in support of the idea that economic success among the overseas Chinese owed much to entrepreneurial abilities and to the values, traditions, culture, personalism, familism and socio-economic institutions inherited from China. For Mackie, then, there is little doubt that this historical-cultural legacy gave the overseas Chinese a major advantage, at least in days gone by, though today the 'values of trade' and an indirect historical-cultural legacy provide the more significant influences.

Wang's view is similar: the expression of Chinese culture has changed and continues to do so; but for him 'culture' remains a more vital force. There were in the past, and still are today, many kinds of Chinese. There are the traditional and the modern, and many grades in between. There are the sojourners whose norms are those of the Chinese who stayed at home in imperial China. And there are the local-born Chinese of the twentieth century who resisted both assimilation and resinicization, and from whom developed a form of cultural expression which, though it remains Chinese, does not depend upon traditional values nor even upon the Chinese language and script. Wang seems to be less certain about the features of this new form of cultural expression, but it includes family and networks, being effective in business, and being multicultural. Chinese culture is vital, adapting, changing, and surviving, and remains different in its nature as well as in the degree to which it exerts an influence. Nor does structure and circumstance deny that difference. Quite the contrary: the circumstances in which the Chinese find themselves, their uniquely structured history, and the force of events, help form the singular conditions peculiar to them.

Others see Chineseness as being something still deeper, and see tradition as being still more resistant. Identity, argues Wong (1999), is not simply a matter of preference: one cannot simply choose to be, or not to be, Chinese. The family is a well of experience and strategies from which the entrepreneurial spirit and identity draws (p.137): it is always seeking to maximise autonomy and avoid its subjugation to the state, and always reproducing a special type of overseas Chinese capitalism. For Hamilton (*op.cit.*) 'deal-making' is the quintessential cultural characteristic of the overseas Chinese entrepreneur's habitual economic practice; and it is cultural traditions such as this which have a significant bearing on explanations for success: local conditions, local histories, or sociologies of minority capitalism, are by themselves inadequate.

Still other writers, who follow similar, though less nuanced lines of argument, sometimes convey the impression that there has never been any critical debate on this issue: it is beyond question that Chinese culture and the orientation of the Chinese mind is a crucial mediating variable determining the nature of small firms (Siu, 2001). *Guanxi* does have profound implications for the dynamics of Chinese society (Park and Luo, 2001), and this could not be otherwise: it is a classic cultural phenomenon (Dunfee and Warren, 2001); it is a characteristic deeply embedded in Chinese culture; it is an integral part of Chinese culture. And it is the five principles of Confucianism that generate strong solidarity among family members, transforming family networks into fixed, stable channels through which flow the information, markets, finance and capital so necessary to the establishment and survival of a business (Luo, 1997).

Not surprisingly, the use of comparison to highlight cultural difference and its importance in explaining economic success has continued. In a study of the Chinese and the European Jews, it is not assumed, states Reid (1997), that the two groups, each considered as a whole, can be considered usefully to have common characteristics, and still less that they should be compared with one another (p.34). Indeed, 'in cultural and religious terms... the Chinese experience is about as far from that of European Jews as is possible within the spectrum of entrepreneurial minorities' (p.39). That difference is, for Hamilton (*op.cit*), highlighted by comparison with the Japanese, while Hui and Graen (1997) look to comparisons with Americans. *Guanxi*, they argue, is not unfamiliar to 'cross-cultural workers, but it is different in that it is rooted in Confucianism, and in that it tends to be more deterministic than, say, the American "leader-member Exchange'. Hui and Graen go on to argue that there is, in view of all this difference, a need to identify points of commonality around which a 'third' culture may be built (with the help of trans-cultural negotiators). Wong and Chan (1999), too, whilst noting similarities between the West and China, present China as a high context culture; and when understood as such, obvious differences emerge. To the Chinese, being considerate implies adaptability and accommodation. The Chinese evaluate a partner through human qualities displayed in negotiation. And the Chinese believe that, aside from the goal of profit-making, people must have feelings before they can be trusted to share profit and benefits.

The Chinese overseas, then, can still be viewed to some extent as a bloc, for how else can such generalisations be made? The circulation of statistics therefore continues. And still 'history' and 'socialisation' serve as the link between the cultural traits by which the Chinese are defined and enumerated. Indeed, in some instances, it is not so much the traits themselves as the power of history and socialisation which defines 'Chineseness'. There are, observes Gambe (1999), differences among Chinese businesses: older people tend to adhere to tradition while the younger people do not; hard work, thrift and trust are not peculiar to the Chinese; and the Chinese are not the only people to build networks. But what *is* unique about Chinese merchants is that these traits have their roots in Imperial China: there *is* a distinctively overseas Chinese transnational economy; there *is* an invisible empire of conglomerates without borders.

3.0 Transformation

Clearly, explanations of Chinese economic success, though commonly favouring cultural factors, have also had to take into account structure. Given their remarkable contribution, 'the Chinese' could hardly be separated from analyses of national and international economies. Understanding Chinese success has also profited when set within an even broader question - how society might transform itself from a condition of personalism and unpredictable informality to one of regularised formality. Outsiders in an uncertain and often hostile world, the Chinese had little choice but to depend upon relationships gathered around kernels such as kinship, ethnicity, language, and place of origin if they were to survive and prosper.

In a discussion of this matter of informal-formal transformation, the Philippines is often viewed as a classic case study. So distorted by personal interests is it said to be, that government has been unable to fashion and implement coherent policies and legislation for the country's economic development. An understanding of its informal qualities, and so of the requirement for effective reform, are widely seen to lie with broader structural, and deeper cultural, elements, rather than with attempts to re-engineer political institutions (Bolongaita, 1995). Writing some forty years ago, Landé (1965) argued that the informal structures devised by Filipinos who operated the formal institutions undermined the solidarity of political parties, leaving national policy and legislation without a clear sense of direction. These informal structures comprised, in particular, vertically-aligned patron-client relationships, and local factions based on dyadic ties. Although these local factions could act as agents for national parties, they also had their own strong and independent *raison d'être*.

This emphasis on personalistic relationships has remained central to many studies of the Philippines' political economy. Of particular note is Hutchcroft's (1991, 1994, 1998, 2001) patrimonial analysis. Drawing on a number of writers, including Crouch, (1979, 1985), Evans, (1989, 1992) and Weber (1968, 1981), Hutchcroft provides a broad historical and structural explanation for patron-client relationships and for the more generally personalistic quality of the political economy. The Spanish failure to engage in state building provided room both for the emergence of strong British, American, and Chinese trading houses, and for the entrenchment of a Chinese-mestizo landed élite. This decentralisation of power was reinforced by the Philippines' American rulers, who concerned themselves mainly with the construction of representative institutions, while leaving outside those institutions oligarchs with their own strong economic and social bases. After independence, these oligarchs, either directly or through their proxies, moved in and out of those institutions at will and, as they did so, continued to maintain and build up their own external social and economic power bases. Any disquiet which may have been felt in the United States was easily salved by opening up the archipelago's military facilities to the Americans. Meanwhile, in the provinces, local patrons drew money, materials, and authority, towards themselves through their personal relationships with the centre. Family businesses, faced with hostile and unpredictable circumstances, established complex and aggressive networks of relationships through which they could influence the political economy to their own advantage and to the disadvantage of their enemies and competitors. Thanks in part to this competition, and in part to public education and examinations, the membership of the elite proved to be socially mobile. But the centre remained weak, and the state was left vulnerable to influence from powerful individuals and factionalised groups operating outside its institutions. Thus was the Philippines exposed to exploitation by competing oligarchies and cronies (*ibid.*).

In its personalistic, informal and irregular qualities, the Philippines' state lies some distance from a strong, regularized, formal, impartial, legal-rational economy and polity of the kind described by Weber as a bureaucratic administration. In particular, argues Hutchcroft, the Philippines lacks calculation in the administrative and legal sphere; and family and business are not clearly separated. The essential question facing the Philippines (and many other developing countries) is how it might transform itself from its present condition of patrimonialism into a regularized, legal-rational, and bureaucratic state? As Hutchcroft (1998) and Callaghy (1989) point out, no theory exists to account for transformation. But Hutchcroft, following Weber, suggests that change might come from two directions: from above, through selected reforms, particularly of the relationship between government and business; and from below, prompted by the gradual balancing out of interest groups as competition amongst them intensifies, and by the entirely pragmatic demands of private capital for the rule of law and greater predictability. In short, the liberalisation of the economy, and top-down reform, may bring about transformation in the Philippines. Yet such is the influence of rich and powerful families, that the prospect of transformation is, at best, uncertain.

The patron-client framework, and an emphasis on the personalistic nature of Philippine society, has not gone unquestioned. Kerkvliet (1995) argues that whilst the patron-client framework is deservedly influential, analyses should move beyond it and develop a more textured view of the Philippines' polity. In its broad historical and structural sweep, Hutchcroft's patrimonial analysis does meet this concern to some extent. But other more radical variants and alternatives have been suggested (Thompson, 1995; Wurfel, 1988). Putzel (1999), by marrying institutional analysis with the concept of social capital, attempts to uncover those underlying cultural features which may explain why the Philippines is a weak or shallow democracy. By shallow it is meant that the Philippines meets only to a minimal extent the defining qualities of democracy - free and regular elections, universal suffrage, freedom of expression, the flow of accurate information, associational autonomy, and the rule of law effected by an impartial judiciary. The 'depth', or shallowness, of democracy, depends upon what North (1990) calls the informal institutions, and what Putzel describes as the cultural features (such as customs, traditions, and codes of conduct), that partly govern behaviour in state, society and economy. These features - in combination with the social capital (the trust, norms and networks) which accrue from familial relationships - are held to explain shifting coalitions of clan power, the appearance of regionally-based language groups, the exchange of votes for favours, the granting of public contracts to cronies, and other problems with the Philippine polity. There are similarities between this interpretation and Landé's (1965); but whereas Landé saw little sign or hope of change, Putzel, by the end of the century, saw evidence of a deepening of democracy. And in this process, civic associations - whose members promote democratic norms and values, and are independent of the state - may have a vital role. These associations, as they gather around the existing democratic framework, may act as a vigorous stimulus for change. Landé (2001), too, though cautious, later appeared to see indications of change in a polity now groping to strike a balance 'among the rights of the citizenry, the rights of public officials, and the needs of public institutions' (p. 101).

The broadening of perspectives from cultural interpretations of the Chinese to encompass the structural features of national and international economies (and the question of political transformation) is of much value to the study of the overseas Chines. It might also bring much to a study of the Philippines' trade with China, most especially in view of what is thought to be Chinese dominance of this trade. Cultural sympathy between the Chinese overseas and the mainland Chinese, and the structural characteristics of the international economy, are surely central to any understanding we might reach. So, too, is the question of China's informal-formal transformation: for is it not the case that in China, as in the Philippines, informality creates the space and incentive for overseas Chinese businesses to operate there most successfully, and, to some extent, also shapes how they operate?

The debate on informal-formal transformation in China is less clearly defined in comparison with the discussion on the Philippines. This is partly because the literature which might be thought to comprise this debate is far larger in quantity and possesses its own vocabulary. It is also strongly influenced by, and often reflects the writers participation in, the construction within China of highly stylised, self-conscious, and politically-valuable images of China's difference and uniqueness. There may be some agreement that China, in common with the Philippines, has some way to go before it could be described as a modern and legal-rational state; but there is far more uncertainty about what China's present qualities are, and about whether it should attempt to move towards that universal ideal. Thus the suggestion that *guanxi* is withering away (Guthrie, 1999; see also King, 1991; Chen, A.H.Y. 1999) in the face of capitalism and its impersonal legal-rational system has elicited strong counter-arguments in defense of the resilience of these relationships (Yang 2002; Wang, 1999; Smart and Smart, 1998); and it is widely argued that if a legal-rational system is emerging in China, then it is of a species different to any found in the West (Chen, 1999; Wang, 1995). Similarly there is little agreement on whether informal factional politics in China - at the heart of which lies *guanxi*, or so many writers would argue - is best explained by culture or structure; nor is there consensus on the extent to which factional politics is being formalised (Dittmer 1995; Pye, 1995; Nathan and Tsai, 1995).

Uncertainty also surrounds the nature of industrial organisation in China. The stated purpose of industrial reform - to create a commercially integrated economy (Yang Chengxun, 1984; Hu Bing, 1987) - undoubtedly carried with it a sense of impersonal market-driven rationality. Enterprises were to be allowed to establish their own connexions with one another; and they were allowed to do so according to market principles and, therefore, irrespective of bureaucratic divisions and hierarchies, both areal and functional. Through these linkages among freely associating entities, cities were to become points of commercial integration uniting the economy into a national whole (White, III, 1989). The pattern which emerged in practice, however, appeared to be somewhat different. Although more authority was ceded to provincial and sub-provincial levels, and to economic units which could now act with greater freedom, there was no clear separation of party, bureaucracy and enterprise. Now set against each other and permitted more autonomy, bureaucrats, party officials, and enterprise managers scrambled to form relationships commonly regarded as being strongly particularistic or personalistic. The most obvious *point d'appui* around which these extensive connexions were formed were existing, if decaying, bureaucratic, economic, institutions, reinforced by still more basic kernels of place of origin and language (see, for example, Keister, 2000; Nee, 1996; Nee and Su, 1998; Gore, 1998; Walder 1986).

It was hardly surprising that the art of social relationships (as Yang, *op. cit.* has described it) should have moved so easily and more openly to the centre of political and economic life. The personalistic quality of these relationships was peculiar neither to the reform period nor indeed to Chinese society, whether on the Mainland or overseas; and there was now more freedom to practice an art that attracted less censure. Nor was there anything new in the forms of expression that bureaucrats, party officials, and managers, brought to this art. Both before and after 1949 (with the exception of those periods after the revolution when a high degree of self-sufficiency in agricultural and industrial goods was expected), enterprise managers in Shanghai had used their personal relationships (including those formed around kinship and locality) to secure the money, markets, and materials they needed. Even during the early 1980s – when Shanghainese factories operating in other parts of China sold as much produce as six of the Municipality's counties - managers continued to make use of relationships that pre-dated revolutionary China (White, *op.cit.*). The political machinations required to form and sustain these linkages, however, had made supplies and outlets unreliable at best: enterprises and their officials had therefore already begun to look overseas.

In this atmosphere of loosening controls over economic matters, and of increasing openness in the establishment of personalistic relationships, the heads of government, party, bureaucracy and enterprise could never hope to exercise formal control over, and direct every detail and nuance of, bureaucratic, political and economic life. But material things and favours were still understood to follow

20

relationships. Some measure of order could be realised if those who formed these relationships adhered to the conventions of this art (Smart and Smart, *op. cit*; Yang, *op cit*; Bakken, 2000) and shared the same intentions. Securing money, markets, technology, contacts, and experience - most especially from overseas – came to be valued not so much as an economic achievement than as a new symbol and means of social-cum-political acumen and success. For instance, the reputation of brokerages and their opportunities for advancement in Shanghai was dependent not so much upon a healthy bottom line as upon relationships (almost tributary in their quality) with state officials (Hertz, 1998). Indeed, it is not too much to suggest that a dexterity in the management of relationships was often regarded as an expression of machismo (see, for example, XJJ [新经济], 2002).

By virtue of this art, and these common ambitions, combines of relationships were brought together (though often more by happenstance, by a kind of serendipity, than by any detail of design) such that the bureaucracy and industry worked. Even as efforts were made to create a leaner, more efficient, and competent administration, displaced officials frequently reappeared in other appointments* as bureaucrats acted to protect their family and friends as well as their own personal interests (Brødsgaard, 2002; see also Wu Hanfei). Thus, more through messy compromise than through the sound implementation of clear policy, a measure of improvement in administration was achieved without requiring too great a sacrifice from, and without creating too much dissatisfaction among, the rest of government and the Party. Within industrial enterprises, too, sets of personalistic relationships vital to their working created unpredictable and unplanned problems and advantages. So closely integrated through these relationships were enterprises, that ownership categories melded with one another. The assets and profits of state firms were often transfigured into new companies and alliances, and profits redistributed, blurring forms of ownership still further (Nolan, 1996; Lo and Chan, 1998; Ding,

---

* In many parts of the country the bureaucracy (party and government) actually proliferated (Brødsgaard, 2002).

2002; Huang, Y, Woo, W.T., Duncan, 1999; Ash and He, 1998). The majority of non-state companies often resembled in significant measure state-owned enterprises; or were, to all intents and purposes, expressions of state interests (Ding, *op.cit.*). Meanwhile, loans were either hidden or disguised or issued contrary to economic common sense.

As Cheng and Lo (2002) argue, these relationships and practices made it difficult to establish which enterprises were performing badly, or well, and also the reasons for this performance. Poor financial performance, they suggest, cannot be explained wholly by ownership or competition: and non-state enterprises did just as badly, and just as well, as state-owned enterprises. Indeed, such is the uncertainty created by the complexity and closeness of their integration, that state-owned enterprises, and the banks who finance them, may not be facing a crisis anything like as severe as many commentators believe. After all, relational capitalism, as it is sometimes called, is often looked upon favourably; and its advantages (such as lower transaction costs) are described in the literature on overseas Chinese business, on East Asian economies more generally, and on China (Keister, 2000; Wang, 2000; Chen, 1999). *In* China, too, the need for a clear legal and institutional framework is often regarded as a sign of weakness which plagues most especially those foreign businesses who complain the loudest about the opaqueness of China's 'systems' (XJJ, *op.cit.*).

4.0 Finding perspective

On the face of it, and in fairly broad terms, *how* we might study the question of trade and business in the Philippines and China, and *what* we are studying, would seem to be obvious. Our interest is with the cultural and structural features of the Chinese overseas; with those structural and cultural features which comprise the wider international context; and with the circumstances of the Chinese overseas within political economies that are in the midst of informal-formal transformation. And yet, even from the very limited account given above, it is equally obvious that interpretations are varied and multiplying. The debate on the overseas Chinese and their economic success has broadened in recent years. The opening out of the debate on the Philippines' transformation from its concentration on the patron-client framework, through to patrimonial analyses and beyond, has been still more marked and, as we noted above, seems to reflect the development of increasingly dimensional understandings of the Philippines political economy. Of events in China, too, we see a proliferation of views and conceptual devices as attempts are made to determine whether, and to what extent, informal-formal transformation is underway. If the Philippines seems unable to move towards a condition of greater formality, China probably has no need. Nor do we find in the literature on the overseas Chinese - a literature that has also felt the influence of, and participated in, the dialectic between writers outside China and the construction within China of confident images of itself - a sense that 'modern' necessarily equates with the formalised Weberian ideal. Interpretation, it would seem, expresses something of the relative economic and political standing, and confidence, of the people who are the subject of that interpretation.

We may argue that although there remains no generally accepted theory to account either for the economic success of the overseas Chinese, or for transformation, it is no bad thing to be faced with a plethora of contending explanations. Any framework which claimed an ability to account for the success of the Chinese *en masse*, or for transformation, would have to capture and explain the essence of entire societies. The consequences of any framework making such claims, or of attempts to put one together, might only be totalizing and prescriptive. A more productive use of time and energy - at least as far as the Philippines is concerned - would be to examine the political economy carefully 'while bearing in mind all or as many available interpretations and approaches as possible and remaining open to being surprised by findings that do not fit any of them' (Kerkvliet, 1995, p.419). It may be that, in the end, each of us will have to be content to exercise our own judgment: this perhaps is the best we can hope for.

But whilst a plethora of explanations may be desirable, the very richness of debate also illustrates that we have moved away from a position of apparent certainty, and towards one of greater uncertainty. What *is* the meaning of 'Chineseness'? Can we be sure who 'the Chinese' are? And if we cannot be sure of this, then how can we be sure of our estimates, let alone any explanations, of their economic power? The debates outlined above also show uncertainty about the meaning of culture and structure. Where does the one end and the other begin? Can we be sure that transformation is not so much a distinct process as it is the sum of various, perhaps unconnected, tendencies which come together in developing societies in a way that we happen to interpret as a single process? In assuming that we are faced with a specific problem - that of transformation - are we not in danger of abstracting certain features from the world around us such that those features are now made incomprehensible? Moreover, in confining ourselves to an interest in transformation in developing societies, might we not also run the risk of ignoring what may be learnt from the possible reversion of society now described as formal (and developed) to a condition of informality? Could transformation describe something (or many things) common, not just to a class of societies at a particular time, but to all human societies and at all times? If transformation is to be understood, then perhaps a range of conceptual frameworks is required? Then again, if we are not sure of what transformation is, or who the Chinese are, how can we be sure that what we are studying, and our conclusions, have not already been shaped in advance by our methods and theories and their underlying assumptions? How do we *know* that what we are looking at is what we believe it to be? How can we be sure, when we apply this or that method or theory in order to know, that we are not making assumptions about what we know? Will this not predetermine what has yet to be revealed and its interpretation? The problem we face is not merely *how* to analyse the overseas Chinese or informal-formal transformation; it is also to determine *what* it is that we believe we are studying. Indeed, we are prompted to ask a still more fundamental question: just what *do* our ideas represent?

4.1 The problem of thought

These questions seem to be leading us towards the view that without criteria (which are not forthcoming) to distinguish between reality and appearance we can never be sure that we know reality. This view is an old one; but one that is specious and sterile. We fashion our thoughts about the world through experience, and re-affirm them through our communion with each other. If I look at a busy road in front of me and envisage myself walking on to the road where I am hit by a car, I do not assume that I cannot comprehend reality or that I may be delusional. I know that my thoughts, or what I hold to be thoughts, are real; and that, whilst sometimes mistaken, they are grounded in reality and provide a serviceable description of that reality.

But there remains in the questions we have asked a problem of a rather different order. Experience and mutual affirmation tell us that our thoughts are workable descriptions of reality. Yet the fact is that we do not know what thought is, nor how we think. We do not know its limitations, nor whether we are restricted only to the first-person perspective. It is as if we are allowed to view only pictures of the world. Experience may tell us that the pictures we have in our heads are good enough to allow our passage through life; but we cannot be sure if we are in possession of a functional or faithful understanding of the world. Nor do we know whether those understandings, if functional, are functional in all circumstances. And though experience might tell us that these understandings inform our behaviour in such a way as to allow us to fit into that world, we cannot be sure that we fit into the world as we intend or believe. Moreover, if my experience is lacking then I cannot be sure that I possess a more or less workable hold on reality; nor, if those around me also lack that experience, can I know whether or not we are all mistaken.

Without a knowledge of what thought is, its limitations, and how it is that we put thoughts together, we cannot be certain of how that idea came into being, how and why it was constructed, nor of its true significance. Is a thought a thing? If so, how is it read or interpreted without other thoughts? If it is not, then what is it? How can one thought lead to another? How is it possible to think about the future and plan? When I think to myself 'I will go to the beach next weekend if the weather is fine', how do I get from one thought to the next, from 'nice weather' to 'going to the beach' (if indeed these are separate thoughts); and how and why did I arrive at the initial thought (say, fine weather) in the first instance? We may have the *sense* that some theories, methods and interpretations of the social and natural world around us are better than others, and some kind of consensus may emerge. But this sense is rarely permanent or complete; and distinguishing absolute knowledge from mere orthodoxy is no easy task. Whatever the subject of our interest, and whatever our method and approach, our study rests upon the assumption that we can be certain about something that we do not in fact yet understand - the nature of thought *itself.* Until we understand thought, uncertainty will always surround our attempts at explanation and interpretation.

It is not hard to appreciate why social science should have avoided tackling the problem of thought directly. Safer waters are offered by culture and structure, and by other approaches that we might loosely categorise as positivistic or humanistic. There is no question that the social sciences are ready to draw on, or to take part more fully, in philosophical debates on being, perception, appearance, reality, mind, consciousness and knowledge. There has also been a willingness, as in Brown's (1994) writing on ethnicity in southeast Asia, to draw from the field of psychology, or, as the notion of deep structures reveals, from the work of linguists. But the question of thought itself - any understanding of which still eludes us - should surely be left to only the most committed philosopher or natural scientist? Nor, then, is it hard to see why our analyses of the social world and our debates over how it might be studied should, in effect, substitute for discussions on thought itself. Since we understand neither thought nor, therefore, our imaginings, hopes, desires, actions, and behaviour, then we cannot but look for something

26

either outside or within ourselves (but other than thought) - whether, say, culture, structure, elements of consciousness and universal knowledge, genetics, or evolution - that are held to generate thought, shape how we think, and thus mould what we are and what we do. For is not the alternative simply to throw up our hands and say we know nothing with any certainty?

4.2 Representation, attitude, and relationships

Nevertheless, we cannot simply wave aside doubts surrounding those concepts that we accept so easily as the foundation of our studies and interpretations. Nor is there adequate defense in the argument that, as a starting point for our studies, recognition of an absence of an understanding of thought leaves us with only an empty and debilitating sense of hopelessness. Indeed, the contrary is true. If we must doubt what we think about the world (and even about the notion of 'I'), then we can at least be certain in our doubts about the world, about what 'I' am, and about 'I's place in the social world. We can, therefore, be certain that, however inaccurate they may be, we form representations of the social world and of 'I'. We can also be certain of social relationships and their importance. Whether we think that language is to some extent an ability 'hard-wired' into our brains or believe it to be a necessary expression of communion, and whether we believe it to be a medium for the communication of thought or the precursor to thought, we can at least be sure that without relationships we would not have possession of this common language with which to express our doubts. And while we cannot doubt the central importance of our relationships, we can doubt the meaning we attach to them. We are certain, therefore, that we strike differing attitudes to our relationships. Furthermore, since we doubt what it is that does, or does not, shape or govern our behaviour (whether we think this to be God, culture, structure, or natural selection and our genetic material), we can at least be sure that our representations, to the extent that they inform the practice of our relationships, have an influence upon the social world. And since we must doubt the accuracy of our representations – which therefore cannot be uniform - then we can infer that what exists *in fact* 'out there' is not a pattern in itself set apart from each or any one of us, but a fuzzy composite of relationships and ever-changing dimensional events. Such coherence and order as we bring to, or experience in, our own lives is thus a function, not of what is 'out there', but of what is in each of us. That is, in our practical everyday lives we adjust our constructs and the place we each imagine ourselves to have within the whole, such that we can in practice achieve some kind of *modus vivendi*. These common sense understandings of the world, formulated through experience and our communion with others, may be more trustworthy precisely because it is these, rather than our more sophisticated intellectualised accounts, that inform the practice of relationships from which the social world we study is fashioned.

We are then, in the absence of an understanding of thought and thinking, presented with a few certainties: our relationships, attitudes, and representations. Our attempts to understand the social world follow from the nature of these attributes.

(i) Since we are certain that we form representations, and that we can be certain of little else, we must therefore set out an initial or original representation of what we believe the play of attributes might be. This representation of the play begins with that quality which we cannot deny - our immediate knowledge. By this I mean a knowledge of our own sensations and emotions and states of mind which, no matter how much we might think of as illusory, are nevertheless keenly felt. In the light of this intense knowledge it is understandable that we should each take a personal view and, as best we can, manipulate and translate our relationships to advantage. Yet it is also reasonable, given our dependence upon relationships and our possession of this common language, that we should have the sense that we have emerged from our relationships: that we are not only in a community but *of* a community. In short, the distinction made between the individual and community implies a false antithesis. 'Self' and 'community' are two constructions of a single notion of being.

It follows that if we each deny our own individual sense of self and view it as no more than an illusion, then nothing matters; other people are transformed into material to be manipulated for our own illusory purposes; and we may behave as we wish. Community falls away, and the non-existence of self is reinforced. By the same token, if I deny community, then all is open to manipulation, and I have already begun to undermine that innate sense of all that I am.

So, too, if I make 'I' an absolute, fixed in me alone, I am alienated, and I am driven by my sense of alienation to seek affirmation of the absolute quality of my 'self' through the only way I can – the manipulation of other people for my own purpose. If, on the other hand, we make of community an absolute, we are compelled to deny self. Each of us must subject our 'self' to others with ambition; and as our sense of alienation takes hold, we too begin to manipulate those around us.

If we are to admit both aspects of our notion of being, we must treat 'I' and 'community' *as if* absolute. By this I mean that while we treat 'I', 'you', 'us' and our relationships *as if* important, valuable, valued and proper in their own right, we nevertheless admit to ourselves that this is not the case – that they are not in fact absolute. Seen through this more affective attitude, the value of 'I', 'you' and 'we', and of our relationships, is made dependent upon each of us. In this implied compact we find, and bring to our lives, true strength, predictability, reliability and equality.

Two points arise from this line of argument. First, shifts in attitudes are, to some extent, innate or spontaneous. If we deny or make an absolute of self or community, we move back towards a world that is personalististic and takes a form that is either loose and factionalised or, as an attempt is made to bring order and direction, strongly authoritarian. Yet the more we manipulate others, the more we deny our construct of being, and the more alienated we feel, then the more we desire a return to the affect. Second, the personal and the affective are not dichotomous. Rarely, if ever, we will be faced with people who are in their attitude purely affective or personal. Both attitudes are always present within each of us and among us all.

The influence of these attitudes upon the practice of our relationships are profound. But how might this influence express itself? The suggestion here is that it must do so through our representations of the world. Since the personal and the affective are not dichotomous, then they must colour representations and the practice of social relationships with constantly changing degrees of intensity. However, let us assume, for the purpose of description, that our representations and relationships are coloured by attitudes in their purest and ideal form. We might then imagine that viewed through the personal, my ends are everything. Empathy and anticipation are limited, for I am interested in what others think, feel, and do, only in so far as they impinge upon, or are of use, to me. And since I can, in practice, achieve my ends only through my relationships and through those relationships within and beyond my immediate experience, then relationships are all that I wish to see. My social representations are those of my networks of relationships, of alliances - monitoring, blocking, and manoeuvering. I place myself at the centre of a world undifferentiated. It is undifferentiated because I need make no distinction between different aspects of my life. Institutions, values, beliefs, practices, laws, and conventions - and even the notion that a particular activity is economic, social, political, artistic, or scientific - are construed as mere images resting upon the substance of our relationships. Beyond the centre of my immediate relationships exist distant combines of networks. As I contemplate the expansion of my will across these combines, I envisage the lowering of unyielding, unquestionable, and authoritarian certainties, subordinate only to me.

Drawn upon to inform practice, these representations lead us into coalitions that are suspicious, tense, rivalrous, and unstable. In this world, image is everything: even authoritarian certainties are subject to manipulation. Institutions, matted with intrigue, are made porous; laws and conventions, practices and procedures, are circumvented or dismissed at will. Monitoring, policing, and hierarchy, must now be strengthened; combines are made still more complex; the possibility of instability increases; and the need for authoritarianism is reinforced. As a consequence, our sense of alienation and nihilism continues to deepen.

Viewed through the affective, other people and my relationships with them are important in themselves. Empathy and anticipation are released, for what other people think, do, and feel, are of interest to me in their own right. And because this is so, then here, in my social representations, I am no longer the centre of the world. Other people and our relationships are, for their own sake, to be insulated from manipulation. Our relationships must differentiate, the functional distanced from the social, such that the different spheres of our lives are clearly demarcated. To that end, and in order to achieve stability, we must agree that whilst institutions, values, beliefs, practices, procedures, laws, conventions, and our differentiated spheres of life, are subject to debate and change, we will treat them at any one moment *as if* absolute, and to which all, including 'self' are subordinate. In our mind's eye we come together as networks of relationships and combines of networks that are less exclusive, more open, and which take on forms more sharply defined. Institutions, practices, procedures, conventions, laws, and the spheres of activity, come to be seen as discrete and differentiated, but flexible rather than rigid; and we are interested in their intrinsic qualities rather than in their appearance. There is less need for monitoring, policing and hierarchy. Institutions, now less tangled and less porous, are more focussed, flatter, and sleeker; and the capacity for ever-larger scales of combines is much increased.

(ii) We have argued that there is no distinguishable or explanatory pattern 'out there' beyond the particular except other particular instances. These particular instances are able to function in themselves, and collectively on a wider scale, because the practice of relationships is informed by representations of the immediate and wider world which, though not accurate, enable particular instances to achieve a working fit. We must therefore concentrate on attempts to understand the particular sets of relationships we come up against or participate in. It is these particular instances, and the wider representations that inform those instances, that we view through our original representation of the play.

(iii) Since the social world is fuzzy, dimensional, ever-changing, and coloured with attitudes of changing intensity, then we must expect that the influence of the particular relationships we come up against or participate in, will be uncertain and unpredictable, still more so given that how we deal with, and interpret, those relationships are coloured by our prior attitudes and representations. Nor can we separate our original representation of the play from our own attitudes and the practice of our own relationships. It is in an attempt to compensate for the extent to which attitudes and relationships colour our representations that we enter a constant cycle of dis-aggregation and reformulation. As we begin the cycle, we are guided by our original representation. With this we begin to tease out the attitudes, social relationships, and representations, that comprise particular instances. Our aim in this is to understand the play of these attributes in particular instances. As we attempt to do so, and as we attempt to communicate our understandings, we cannot but re-formulate our representations at different levels. For instance, there are: representations of the play of attributes that comprise particular instances (such as the company or legislature); representations of the world beyond our immediate experience (such as the Philippine political economy); representations that are of a more abstract form (such as informal-formal transformation); and there are still more abstract representations of the principles of the play of attributes. These representations, however, are not the end to which we are working. They are frozen expressions of what our understandings *were*; and because they are profoundly coloured by our own attitudes and relationships, we must serve them up as material for subsequent cycles. Our representations, then, are not intended to provide an accurate explanation and description of the social world beyond our immediate experience. They are simply the medium through which we continuously develop our understandings of the particular. And the more occasion we have to understand *a* particular, the closer we may be able to move towards an understanding of *any* particular. Without a knowledge of thought we will never manage to grasp the principles of the play. But with each cycle, as we come to appreciate the dimensionality of particular instances, we might begin to form a sense of the simple commonalities that underlie the surface complexities and differences of the social world; and therein glimpse something of the principles of the play.

(iv) It follows that when faced with particular instances - such as a Filipino family or a Chinese company – our intention is to elicit the attitudes, representations, and a sense of the meaning and practice of the relationships of those who comprise those instances. At the heart of this - no matter how many people we talk to, and no matter how many different point of views of the same event we are able to garner – lies empathy. In our everyday relationships, even in the most transitory interactions, we have little choice but to attempt to establish a sense of what others are doing and thinking. Indeed, if a specific definition of relationships is emerging from these pages, it is that they are abstractions - constructs of what you and I think and feel about each other, about us, and about the world. Empathy is also strongly implicit in our language -in what we write and say to each other. It is, therefore, essential in our studies, and this is so whichever approach we adopt. If I believe that you are shaped by cultural or global structures, then (whether or not you also believe it) I am assuming that I have a sense of your experience of the world. If I say that you are authoritarian in the way you run your company because you have been inculcated with Confucian ideals, or if you tell me this is the case and I say that I understand, then I am implying that I have a sense both of how you see and think about the world, and of your motivations, desires, and emotions. If I argue that, driven by global capitalism, you have centred your company on the family in order to keep costs low, I am again implying that I can see into your mind and through your eyes.

The question is not whether we are empathetic, but whether in our studies that empathy is hidden or open. To downgrade or deny empathy is to say that you and I are separate and can be understood only by reference to a knowledge of the working of what it is - perhaps culture, structure, history, or evolutionary psychology - that shapes or conditions. It is to reify my representations, to claim that you can be understood only with reference to my representations, and to give my thoughts a status they do not deserve. Should we on the other hand admit empathy, then it may be that we can enter with immediacy an understanding of each other. With the central importance of empathy acknowledged we can now begin to reach more deeply into ourselves in order to understand one another. The representations we create are still only representations. They are not a claim to truth. What we are doing, and what we must allow ourselves to recognise, is taking part in a collective enterprise. The representations that each of us form, if incorporated into another's thought, may, for a short time, become part of their understanding of the social world and its truths. Whether the ideas, interpretations, and stories we create will ever amount to more than this, is the concern of hubris.

5.0 Conclusions

In this chapter we have, in essence, argued for a preparedness to consider a rather different 'take' on the social world. It is not reductionist: it attempts to understand the rich 'ontology' – from the more elaborate to the more reductionist views – that inform the practice of social relationships. It eschews methodological individualism and holism, for it treats 'individual' and 'community' as two constructs of a single notion of being. Our interest is no longer centred on 'society or individual', nor 'culture or structure', nor even with their interaction: these are - as are all our thoughts of self and the world - representational categories. They take their qualities from our attitudes to social relationships, and they have an influence to the extent that they inform the practice of relationships. Our thinking is no longer confined within one or other representation. We can now step outside culture, structure, individual, and community, within whose parameters we often tend to think, and view these ideas as representations. This is not to dismiss such ideas. It is to suggest that their relevance may alter with attitude and from one particular instance to the next. For example, it is difficult to appreciate how culture or structure (in the sense of widespread, interconnected patterns of institutions and conventions) can be thought to shape behaviour in a regularized and predictable manner, until a critical mass of attitudinal shifts and formalisation has been attained, and such representations have begun to inform practice. Only then might structural and cultural explanations - that is, representations of cultural and structural features that are brought into, and inform, practice - come into their own.

Our attitudinal perspective moves the emphasis of our studies in a number of other ways. First, our interest moves from general representations of the world beyond our immediate experience, to the particular and the non-conformist. The particular instance of social relationships, and deviations from what is expected, now become highly significant. The particular is no longer treated only as material with which to build up or confirm our vision of the general; nor do we treat deviations as being of marginal or occasional interest, either to be ignored or taken as a signal to adjust the general. Indeed, the particular and deviant *are* the social world; while the general - because it is but a representation that informs practice - has now become a means to help us understand the particular and deviant.

Secondly, emphasis moves to the street. So intimately are our ideas bound up with what we study, that we must attempt not only to dis-aggregate the world, but to do so in the field. It is only when faced with the complexity of the flesh, that we are likely to appreciate just how deeply and in what ways practice, representation, and attitudes, permeate each other. Only then may we begin to see just how far our representations, attitudes, and relationships, have led us to misread those in whom we are interested, and to remain blind to so many of their dimensions. As we move from the pages we read and into the street, possibilities and dimensions more complex than we could imagine now appear. Always we find departures from what we expected. And while we talk, listen, read, and act, and as we come up against the relationships in which we are interested, we find that what we study changes us, and that, in some small way, we change what we study. Thus we are compelled to revise our representations; thus are we brought to the beginning of a new cycle.

Thirdly, emphasis now moves towards more improvisatory thought. For now that we are less confined by our representational categories, now that emphasis has shifted to the street and the particular, and now that empathy and the intimacy between our study and what we study are admitted, we can be even less sure of the direction in which our thinking will take us. We should, therefore, be prepared to experiment with lines of thought, with styles and mediums of expression, even if these may at first sight seem a little out of place or even contrary to the ideals of social science. We must reach across not only discipline and geography, but many aspects of human interests and expression - art and literature, music and religion, philosophy and natural science. In other words, we may wish to consider broadening very dramatically our understanding of the legitimate subject matter of social science, and of the ways in which we communicate our ideas. Thus emphasis moves from a determination to set the channel and the tradition within which a study will be conducted, to a willingness to allow the unplanned emergence of understanding.

Finally, our interest moves from the frozen page to what is alive in the mind. Because we do not understand thought, and so cannot be certain of our representations (including those which might emerge from our attitudinal perspective), we must pass through this cycle again and again. Our aim in this is not to construct such representations as we are able in order to freeze them on paper and present them completed and with a claim of accuracy. Rather, it is to excite in the mind of author and reader still more complex, fluid, and dimensional, representations of the play of attributes. It is in this - in what is alive in the mind - that the greater truth might be found.

Chapter 2
Thought

1.0 Introduction

The following discussion is necessarily experimental, and it is in this light that it should be read. It should not be taken as the foundation of our attitudinal perspective. Indeed, should they wish to, readers may leave this chapter now and move directly to chapter 3's study of Chinese merchants in the Philippines. Nevertheless, the discussion has a particular value and importance, for it appears to illustrate something of the influence of attitude upon representation. Seen through our attitudinal perspective, our discussion may be read as an expression of *a priori* thought, offering escape from the *a posteriori* – from the empirical, the certain, and the absolute. We dream and imagine, or so it seems, to rediscover the uncertainty that leads us back to an affective state of mind in which ideas are of interest in themselves. By the same token, when we find that we have begun to live our lives only in our dreams and to make these absolute, we look to the *a posteriori* to return uncertainty to our mind once again.

2.0 The need for representations

In the previous chapter (section 4.0), we argued that although what we believe to be our thoughts are real and provide a more-or-less workable description of reality, the fact remains that we do not yet know how we think. We cannot, therefore, be certain of how or why our ideas come into being, nor what their true significance might be. Our studies are based always on the assumption that we can be certain of something about which we know very little. The play of social relationships, attitudes and representations - which we have described as our attitudinal perspective, and through which we will consider particular instances of trade and business in the Philippines and China - is merely an attempt to take this absence of complete knowledge into account when forming our understandings of the world. It asks us to consider what is often held to be the foundation of analysis (such as culture and structure) and the prisms through which we interpret, as representations to be placed alongside many other everyday 'street' representations. And it suggests that the dialectic between attitudes, relationships, and representations - that is, the extent to which each colours the other - is intimate and intense. For these reasons, our representations (including the attitudinal perspective itself, as well as those representations which emerge from our view of the world through our attitudinal perspective) are made part of the subject matter. Although they constitute temporary and functional understandings of the world, they *explain* and influence the world only in so far as they are already present in, or are subsequently bound into, the thought of those whom we are studying, and are drawn upon by them to inform their practice.

This perspective opens up a great many questions. How do we arrive at our constructions, and sense of, 'I' and community? How do we form our attitudes and our representations of the world 'out there'? How do we explain the influence which attitudes, representations, and practice, have upon each other? And what explains the profound commonality in our representations and behaviour which this perspective implies? Given these questions, and our argument that social science should at least begin to consider the nature of thought, it would seem only fair that we attempt here some kind of understanding of thought.

Earlier, in chapter 1, we also raised the proposition that we must doubt our representations of the social world (including, not least, those thrown up by, and embodied in, our debate on appearance, reality, perception, and illusion). And we suggested that, to some extent, these representations compensate for our lack of understanding of the nature of thought. But might we view our representations of the social world as being more than this? Because we do not understand thought, we are compelled to look for its explanation outside our minds, to the social or natural worlds. Thus we have, through the ages, looked to God and our souls, to culture and civilization, as well as to our biology and psychology. Our drive to understand the social world is, fundamentally, a proxy for our desire to understand thought.

In today's world, an analogy (or what is for some perhaps more than an analogy) with computers and computer programming supplies the most obvious material from which to fashion possible explanations of thought. The brain is the hardware; the software are the rules and meta-rules governing the processing of information. Both the hardware and the software are encoded in our DNA; and both are the product of evolution and natural selection. As a consequence of random mutations, blind chance, and blind circumstance, only those living things which happen to be best suited to environment and to competition with other living things, survive and perpetuate their line. Of this process all living things are the product.

The task, then, if we are to understand thought, is to unravel the brain's DNA code; to understand its relationship with evolutionary strategies; to trace the workings of the hardware and software; and to determine the extent to which the form, structure, and mechanisms of that hardware and software are prefigured in our DNA. This does not rule out plasticity and room for adaptation even within an individual's lifetime. A retreat from an entirely pre-programmed existence would provide flexibility in varying and changing circumstances; and this, we might imagine, would constitute a very sensible evolutionary strategy for any living organism. We might also imagine, however, that the scope for plasticity is limited either by the genetic make up or by a high degree of contact and interaction among groups: otherwise pronounced differences would have emerged, making it impossible for different groups to comprehend one another. Alternatively, we might suggest that a marked retreat from programmed thought allows both flexibility and mutual comprehension. Commonality in thought and behaviour, we might conclude, are crucial to the survival of social beings.

Or is it that an understanding of our capacity to think can be found in language? Do our thoughts come to us through the language we learn from others? Language conveys not merely ideas and knowledge, but the fundamental ways in which we think and come to know the world. Perhaps even our sensations and sense of self we owe to language. Language, then, is not a means of communication; it is, as Collingwood put it, an activity prior to knowledge, and without which knowledge could not come into existence. In other words, language holds profound meanings about the connexion between the individual and the world - meanings that are understood through the rules governing language. These rules may be written into us. Or they may be conveyed by custom and practice: the meaning we learn is the meaning which communities have come to understand as the meaning of those rules. To understand language and thought we must take an anthropological view of the world.

Perhaps, then, we should look for an understanding of our capacity to reason in the cultures and structures of the social world? Geertz (1965) believed that our neurological systems were shaped by culture. This is a view that now seems to find sympathy with what appears to be a plasticity in physical structures which a brain exhibits during its lifetime in response to particular stimuli. It is a view which also finds succour in the argument that it is now through society, rather than the natural world, that natural selection works to secure what some believe is likely to have been the brain's accelerated evolution. Indeed, although we do not necessarily intend to convey the suggestion that culture leaves a physical imprint upon our neurological systems, we often speak of 'society', 'culture', 'institution' and 'structure', as compelling, conditioning, causing, affecting, and of being affected, as if they were discrete phenomena which, though created by us, now exist apart from us. This way of speaking and writing is sometimes no more than a simplification or compaction of meaning. But often it is intended to carry the sense that culture and structure are indeed real phenomena which do in some way - even if not biologically, or biologically only - shape us. For others, whether or not culture and structure exist as real and discrete phenomena is neither here nor there. What is important is that they are indicative of processes of some kind that are capable of moulding us. It is as if we, the analysts, stand outside ourselves and the social world, look down upon ourselves and, with reference to these proxies, attempt to explain. Thus, for some writers, Confucianism exists as a kind of force or spirit; to others, it describes ideas, beliefs, and mental patterns burnt into the psyche through upbringing and countless generations of socialisation. Either way, Confucianism creates among the Chinese strong hierarchical families in which authority is vested in the father; and it is on this account that Chinese companies are family affairs, hierarchical, and patriarchal.

The grandest set of cultural and structural forces or principles (which, some believe, Confucianism brightly illustrates) is carried in the word 'civilization'. When Gibbon wrote of Rome's empire in the second century AD that the union of the provinces had been cemented by the gentle but powerful influence of laws and manners, while their peaceful inhabitants enjoyed and abused the advantages of wealth and luxury, he provided what is perhaps its most simple and essential definitions. Certainly the word 'civilization' has today come to mean all that is good and much that is bad about humanity. It describes our escape from what was an even shorter existence dominated by an unequal struggle against base instinct and fear, the vicissitudes of the earth and its climate, and our own fragile bodies. It describes the accretion of technical knowledge and science, and the emergence of the civility, politeness, manners, customs and conventions that regulate our relationships with one another. It is the pre-eminence of communal life; it is justice, morality, order and cleanliness; it is a love for art, music, philosophy, literature, architecture and beauty; and it is a faith and confidence in the importance of these qualities and attributes. The ways in which this escape from barbarism were made added to its virtues. Although the paths differed, each was traveled against the odds: it was a triumph of intelligence, industriousness, belief, imagination, and luck, over base nature. And each civilization, some believed, would lead eventually to a united humanity. For Toynbee (1949) the boundary of each civilization described the smallest geographical or historical unit which for practical purposes made intelligible a particular country or group. Try to understand the US and one would have to look to Western Europe and to other overseas settlements of the Europeans; China or Japan could not be understood without a knowledge of the Far Eastern world; nor could Bengal be understood without a study of the Hindu world. But each was a synthesis, and each formed a stretch of the path leading to a synthesis of syntheses – to a single great civilization. Western civilization had had a remarkable impact on the others over the last five hundred years, and would continue to do so, bringing about, in Toynbee's words, a clash of civilization, most notably with Islam. But as the counter-radiation of influences from Islam, Hinduism, and the Far East altered it beyond recognition, the West would itself be subsumed as each civilization melted into the other. Being part of this single great society will, in that future world, be seen as a fundamental condition of human life.

It is in these same qualities that others see much that is bad, even hateful. The very word 'civilization' elevates a self-selecting few over the rest of humanity; by order of narrow criteria it separates the best from the worst; it is a shibboleth; it defines superiority. It represents values, modes of behaviour, methods of organisation, laws, government, conventions, and customs, that are unjust, restrictive, frustrating, and suffocating. And it implies a universality of process, development, history and explanation. It is hardly surprising, then, that those who see good in civilization should believe that this cynicism (this weakening of confidence and faith) has found expression in a retreat from civility, convention, and common humanity; in contempt for a literate culture, careful thought,   and clear communication; in a happy acceptance of easy images, popularity, the immediate satiation of desires and rights; in a disdain for art, music, learning, and science, as interests to be pursued for their own sake; in the erosion of trust; and in the strengthening of monitoring, policing, auditing, and propaganda. All this amounts to nothing less than a slow decent into barbarism. It has meant slaughter on the battlefields of Europe, and a willingness to look away as genocide is practiced. Perhaps that retreat from humanity has also found expression in the strange and disturbing transfer of interest and sympathy to the environment and to animals, such that the suffering of other people beyond our own immediate circle of relationships attracts little more than vague stirrings of the sentimentalists' pity. Nor is it surprising that those who look upon civilization with suspicion should view concerns over its apparent deterioration as little more than the thrashings of aging Jeremiahs who, imprisoned by the structure of values and beliefs of their own 'western' societies, think themselves better than the rest of humanity. After all, as Fernádez-Armesto (2001) asserts, cultures do not develop or progress. In some measurable respects they may get better or worse, according to different criteria, at different times. But they conform to no model, work towards no telos: they cannot decline; they simply change (p.4).

The apparent necessity for some thing or process (biological, social or psychological) which, from one generation to the next, transmits thought, practices, values, beliefs, and institutions, seems overwhelming. Freud (1995) put the case, perhaps, when he wrote:

'Without the assumption of the collective mind, which makes it possible to neglect the interruption of mental acts caused by the extinction of the individual, social psychology in general cannot exist. Unless psychical processes were continued from one generation to another, if each generation were obliged to acquire its attitudes to life anew, there would be no progress in this field and next to no development. This gives rise to two further questions: how much can we attribute to psychical continuity in the sequence of generations? and what are the ways and means employed by one generation in order to hand on its mental states to the next one?'

44

Direct communication and tradition were part of the explanation, believed Freud, but they were not in themselves sufficient. There was therefore something else at work:

> 'everyone possesses in his unconscious mental activity an apparatus which enables him to interpret other peoples reactions, that is, to undo the distortion which other people have imposed on the expression of their feelings. An unconscious understanding such as this of all the customs, ceremonies and dogmas left behind by the original relation to the father may have made it possible for later generation to take over their heritage of emotion.' (p.511-512).

Yet there is perhaps another way at looking at the question of the nature and origins of our thought. And that is to suggest that we feel the need for a cast or mould precisely because it is impossible for us to think about the nature and origin of our thoughts: to do so requires us to move our minds to a point before the moment at which our thoughts emerge and, as it were, think before, or behind, our thoughts. We look outside ourselves and attempt to understand the social and natural world not merely because we do not understand thought: we do so because of the very nature of thought. We are compelled to look for a cast of some kind that generates and channels thought. Whereas once we looked to God and to our souls (the thinker behind the thoughts), to explain that cast, now, as physicalists, we look to some combination of the structures, hard-wiring, soft programming, and underlying genetic coding, of our brain (and body); to evolution and natural selection; and to language, grammar, culture, society and civilization. It is understandable, then, why thoughts should be viewed commonly not as discrete and tangible things, but as processes which constitute our brain's interpretation of the world, and are to be explained by the brain's cast. It would seem to follow that 'I' is indeed merely a construct, a kind of organizing principle, a point of reference for our mind's interpretation of, and our movement and survival within, the world around us. The sense of 'I' (the sense that 'I' am thinking) is an illusion - a *post hoc* rationalization of those processes.

45

But if these constructs are functions of our inability to see behind our thoughts, then until we know more about how we think, and what thought is, we can hardly assume that our approach, our representations, and our debates, should be fixed within parameters of any one of those proposed casts. Even though we are led by our inability to see behind our thoughts to the conclusion that there is a need for some kind of cast to explain thought, should we not also consider the possibility that no cast in fact exists? That is, our reasoning - the path that our thought follows - is not peculiar to, nor the product of, the human body and its brain. Rather our brain and our reason are expressions of, and form around, what we might call natural reason.

3.0 Natural and functional reasoning

By natural reason I mean a quality that is unknowing and without intent (and therefore not God) but which enables the emergence of order, complexity, organisms, and consciousness. It does not describe the foundation of what, during the German Enlightenment, was held to be a natural morality. Rather it describes a quality that is independent of human faculties. It is what is left when we have divided matter again and again, distilled all forces, provided all explanations (physical and philosophical) for our actions, and then ask why? and what preceded this? Each movement, each interaction, occurs because it is ultimately in itself, and on no other account, reasonable: B not because of A, but because it is reasonable in the light of A and on no other account. And because each interaction is in itself reasonable, order and complexity are possible.*

With complexity comes greater possibility. The more complex A, then not only B, but C and D may also be reasonable in the light of A. Thus, complexity provides

---

* Prigogine's great contribution was to demonstrate that elements moved not towards chaos and disintegration, but towards order and complexity. His ideas, or variations of them, have been applied both to the natural and social worlds. In their application to a consideration of evolution, they have led to fundamental criticisms of natural selection. (See, for example, Laszlo, 1991; Khalil and Boulding, 1996).

the foundation for still greater complexity. And as the range of possibilities accompanying that ever-growing complexity increases, groups of complex organisation with the capability to replicate with variation must necessarily emerge, for otherwise complexity would break down under its own weight. Organisms, then, are an extension of growing complexity of the inanimate. They replicate with variation because their initial complexity provides for many possible trajectories, each of which is reasonable given its particular state and circumstances.

It is now only reasonable in a world of increasing possibility that these organisms should begin to choose (without any sense of awareness) in the light of their physical nature and circumstances. The very act of choice creates still more complex circumstances for themselves and other organisms, broadening possibility, and allowing for yet more complex choice. It is here, in the connexions made by the organism as it chooses, that the beginnings of consciousness may lie.

The connexions being made by the organism, and the 'choices' they take, are thoughts - physical manifestations of its perceptions of the events around it and of its own nature - perceptions that may or may not subsequently produce some kind of physiological or behavioural response. These thoughts just are. Existence is, for the organism, two-dimensional. But as complexity and possibility builds, as choice necessarily become less restrained and structured, a third dimension begins to emerge. If, or when, this event or action occurs in the world around the organism - of which the most important may be its relationships with other organisms - then there must be an association between what is being perceived and the fact of that perception: 'I' must be. It is a fragile, flickering thought. But it is a thought, a conclusion, that is being constantly generated with each association. The thought must strengthen. For if there is an 'I' associated with 'this' set of events, and with 'that' set of events, then must there not be an association between the two sets of 'I': must there not be a second-level 'I'? And if there is a second-level 'I' associated with this sets of events and a second-level 'I' associated with 'that' set of events, then there must be a third level and a fourth level, each linked into the growing breadth of connexions and possibilities from which it arose.

What we imagine here, however, is not a two-dimensional pyramid of 'I's - for this would lead us to a supreme 'I', a thought that thinks - but a three-dimensional arrangement: a circle comprising 'I's, each connected to the other. Each pair of these 'I's would generate a second-level 'I', such that the same number of second-level 'I's as first-level 'I's is created; and each second-level pair produces a third-level 'I' such that again there are as many third-level as second-level 'I's. Thus we might imagine ripples of 'I' constantly emerging, to form a layered, three-dimensional tube. Each 'I' in each of the subsequent layers of this tube is linked into a growing number of previous layers. As the layers accumulate, and the links deepen and broaden, and as their interconnections and possibilities multiply, the constructions of 'I' become more complex. To this, still more complexity is added as new events, new associations, and new 'I's' at the lower level emerge, setting off new ripples.

'I', then, is manifold; and each 'I' is the conclusion of prior thought. They are delicate and transitory. 'I' cannot think or observe thought, for this would be to ascribe to thought the power to think. But these 'I's, interconnected with each other and with the thoughts from which they emerge, are bound into subsequent thought from which still more complex and multidimensional constructions of 'I' are created. In this way ever-more complex 'I's are built into thought and subsequent action such that it is *as if* there are 'I's that think and observe.

The question, however, is why these thoughts - these constructions of 'I' - should not exist without any sense of being? Why should these 'I's be reconciled? Why does it seem, from the inside, that *I* am here? Let us leave these questions to one side for the moment (we shall return to them in section 3.1 below) and concentrate on the qualities that awareness brings. Just as organic life represents another level of complexity without which the tendency to complexity and the working of natural reason would breakdown under its own weight, so awareness introduces another order of complexity. With awareness comes the sense of being separate from thought. Unquestionably there is now an 'I' that is utterly in control of body and mind, yet apart from them. It is now *as if* there is an 'I' that thinks, wants, feels, desires, does and is done to; and this 'I' is now bound into thought. The cycle of thought from which 'I' emerges, and into which 'I' is infused, becomes evermore complex. Moreover, we are aware that others are aware and have their own thoughts, wishes, and desires; that just as we are interested in them, they are interested in us; and that our thoughts – yours and mine - are bound into each other. But now that we are aware of our thoughts and actions, we are also aware of an inability to see behind our thoughts. It is now that we must begin to create representations of ourselves and the world. All of this cannot but cloud our subsequent thought about the world and self. Thought can no longer follow only natural reason. We can no longer say B because it is reasonable in the light of A; we must say B because 'I' believe or think A.

Our thought is now more functional than faithful: it is mimetic. That is, whilst our thoughts are arrived at because, in the context of other thoughts, it is reasonable that they should do so (and on no other account), our thoughts about the world, are not accurate or free of doubt. We see only that which is necessary for us to exist given our sense of self and our awareness of others, such that whilst what we think we know seems to work, we do not see the truth. Even when our ideas work for us, and even though they appear to describe, predict, and explain accurately what is happening to the extent that we are prepared to trust our lives to those ideas (as we do when we get on an aeroplane), our ideas may not constitute a complete and faithful understanding of the world. They may work here and now; but they may not hold at all times and in all places.

3.1 Paradox and awareness

We have argued that our reasoning is mimetic and, therefore, that we find it difficult to know for certain the functional from the faithful. Can there be no way, then, of distinguishing the one from the other? And is there any possibility of being able to appreciate natural reason as anything more than an esoteric and intellectual concept that seems to stand outside our everyday lives and our material reality? The answer, perhaps, is that we might be able to catch a glimpse of, or even sense, natural reason in paradox and emotion. We shall consider paradox first, and in so doing return to the question of awareness.

The most famous paradox is the Liar. It comes in many forms, but here is one:

(a) the sentence written below is false
(b) the sentence written above is true.

What is of interest here is not possible solutions (for there may be no solutions within the terms of the paradox), but why there is paradox. The Liar leaves us with the statement true = false. If (a) is true, then (b) is false; and if (b) is false, then (a) cannot be true; thus (b) must be true; in which case (a) is true, and (b) is false, and so on *ad infinitum*. But false cannot in itself be true. 'False', like 'nothing', merely describes what is not; and if it is not, then it is not. Might 'false', and 'nothing', be functional ideas that we use help us define what we believe *is*? Rather like a sculptor, we draw a three-dimensional image in the block of stone in front of us by blanking out within our minds the material we are about to chip away. When we write '(a) the statement written below is false' we are simply applying a functional idea. We are describing what is not; but we do not say what *is*. When we write '(b) the statement written above is true', we are (with the caveat that we find it difficult to distinguish between the functional and the faithful) being truthful. The Liar attempts to do what cannot be done: to describe one world in the terms of the other.

Paradox, in other words, reveals the boundary at which two different worlds - the functional and the faithful - meet.

We can say something similar of other paradox. Take, for instance, the presence of infinity between the numbers 1 and 2. Add a half to one, then a quarter, then an eighth and a sixteenth, and so on *ad infinitum*. With each addition we get a little closer to 2, but we will never reach 2. Of objects and distance, too, though we have the sense that an object or a unit of distance has a beginning and an end, each can be divided again and again, in which case are they not infinitely large? And whilst we can think of time stretching infinitely into the future, we can, it seems, measure time up to this point, here and now, in which case surely time is not infinite? With regard to this first instance of paradox - that of numbers - might we not argue that 'number' is a functional idea? What, after all, *is* a number? To what does 1 or 2 refer? Do they refer to things or to sets of things, and to which particular things or sets? Or are they 'shadows cast by our activity', artifices within our minds, projected upon existence to help us pick out, define, and differentiate the movement and interaction of matter around which we, too, must move? Might not the *limits* of time and distance, then, be no more than functional ideas? If 'nothing' is a functional idea, and if there is to be order, then time must be sempiternal, space must be boundless, and both must be real. What exists must exist in time and space. It follows that matter must be infinitely divisible*. The units we give to time, space, and scale, whilst of functional value, are not faithful descriptions of our universe.

But what of death? If consciousness is dependent upon our body, as we seem to have argued, if it is a conclusion of the physical workings of our mind, then when our bodies die, 'I' can no longer be. From my point of view there is nothing. Nothing is not, from my point of view, functional, but faithful. And we might

---

* Physicists call this 'bootstrap' theory.

suggest that there is no difficulty in comprehending nothingness. My state, or rather my absence of state, before I was born will be my absence of state after I am dead. It might be argued that there is no inconsistency here: there is nothingness *only* from my point of view. The extinction of the individual mind and its thought does not mark the end of the continuing tendency towards complexity, and thus the end of all matter, space, and time. Even so, there are two question that arise. First, how is it possible to conceive of nothingness without first having a knowledge of being? If nothingness is indeed a functional idea that helps us to define what it is to *be*, then our certainty in nothingness after death (and before life) may be no less a belief - and, for some people, one that is even more comforting - than the belief in paradise. Secondly, in our consideration of the survival or extinction of individual thought, there is a danger that we overlook the possibility that thought and awareness are not one and the same, and that neither is the creation of the other. We have already argued that thought cannot think. It follows, therefore, that awareness cannot be thought. When I say that 'I am thinking' - and from my point of view I know this to be true - it can only mean that there is an awareness of the *thought* that thought can think.

This brings us back to a problem that we put to one side earlier in this discussion: how is awareness achieved, and what is awareness? We have already argued that with awareness another order of complexity is introduced. Let us suggest that as preconscious thought (infused with constructs of 'I') winds itself into an increasingly dense complex, it must enter a state of awareness if the tendency to complexity is to continue. This it does because it is reasonable that it should do so, and on no other account. With awareness of thought comes the question 'what is aware?' Since thought cannot think, the answer is to treat 'I' *as if* it were separate from thought such that it is now *as if* 'I' is the thinker behind thought. A paradox is realised (that of the *thought* that thought can think); and the many 'I's can be reconciled.

The problem however, is this: if there is to be this question 'what is aware?', if there is the sense of an 'I' who surveys thought, then thought must be aware of itself and of other thoughts. But how can thought be aware: to what does it report its awareness? The answer may be: either that thought can exist in two states at once - a state of body and a state of awareness - and retain ties between those states; or that thought is able to jump back and forth between these two states instantaneously*. In either case, thought in body comes to know of itself through its other self in a state of awareness.

Awareness, then, is achieved through the simultaneous connexions between thought in mind, and thought in a state of awareness. This awareness is experienced *as if* from the point of view of mind and body, though *in fact* that awareness is present outside mind and body. Thus it is *as if* thought comes to know itself; and, just as an association between observed events leads to the conclusion and construct of 'I', so the awareness of thought leads to the conclusion that there must be a thinker behind the thought. The thoughts do not think, but the *thought* that thought can think is bound into subsequent thought such that it is *as if* there is an 'I' who thinks.

So what *is* awareness? The answer we are left with is that, in common with time and space, awareness is a state which is the concomitant of natural reason, and that it is independent of the body. In common with time and space, it is boundless and omnipresent. It is revealed by the mind rather than created or generated by mind. Awareness is not thought: it is simply the sense of the existence of all things, of the working of natural reason, of time and space, and of thought. Awareness is not a God who thinks and intervenes; but being an awareness of all things, it is *as if* there is a supreme intelligence.

---

* Certainly many now believe that quantum mechanics plays some part in consciousness (see, for example: Chalmers, 1996; Jahn, 2001). An alternative, though similar, view is that consciousness is a self-referencing loop which forms between the brain and the electromagnetic field that the brain generates around itself. (See, for example, McFadden, 2001).

And what of death? Various possibilities follow from this line of argument. One is that thought remains in a state of awareness even after death. Another is that thought might undergo some kind of development: indeed, for some writers the evolution of consciousness into 'floating' or 'hyper-spatial' forms is entirely credible (Baofu, 2004). Or we might suggest that whilst constructs of 'I' and our other thoughts may end with the body, our sense of existence - not being of the body, and being rooted in a state of complete awareness - continues. With the end of body, and having been released from our constructions of self, we are now *of* that complete awareness. The awareness we experience in life, here and now, forms but a small chink through which we glimpse what we have always been, and always will be, part of - total awareness. With death, complexity continues, not through forms of floating consciousness, but in the social world: in the development of our thoughts about ourselves and each other; or, in other words, in our sense of morality.

3.2 Emotion: the heart of mind?

We have argued that our bodies (and brains) form around natural reason; and that our thought, infused with constructs and sense of 'I', is made functional. Implicit in this discussion is the suggestion that natural reason remains at the core of our thought. In other words, the line established between thoughts is that which is reasonable given the context of thought infused with our constructs and sense of 'I', such that the overall quality of our thought is functional. We have also argued, explicitly, that paradox may begin to lead us towards the boundaries of functional and natural reasoning. But if we are to really *know* natural reason - that is, to know it vividly - then clearly we need to look elsewhere; and that place might be emotion.

We are apt to think of our minds and hearts as distinct qualities. The former describes intellect and rationality; the latter describes passion and emotion. A more severe, Gradgrind, view would be that emotion is a physiological response crafted by eons of natural selection, and subsequently rationalized by our *post-hoc* rationalised self. Another view would be to admit of the possibility that emotion is a quality dependent upon thought and belief - that it is a thought experienced as pleasure or pain, and which, if schooled, may guide the intellect and charge it with creativity. In the reversal of this proposition, however, we might find pre-thought. Emotion, in other words, is the line established between one thought and another because it is in itself reasonable that there should be this line given the context. In this view, the distinction between what we feel and think, between heart and intellect, is erased; and it is emotion that leads to our physiological responses.

I am standing in a forest. I am bathed in weak moonlight filtered through the clouds and leaves. I hear deep and rasping breath; I see the glint of moonlight in teeth and coal-black eyes; and I am afraid. Why is this so? I am afraid not because I believe that the beast will attack me, cause me pain, and end my life (though I may have this belief); nor are my feelings a side-effect of my body's instinctive response - its release of chemicals and electrical impulses to quicken my heartbeat and breathing, to re-direct my blood flow, and to sharpen my actions (though all of this may be happening). At that moment standing there, I see only reason: I see that the line established to the thought that the beast will attack, that I should be afraid, and that my body should gear itself for response; and I see that this line is established because (and only because) it is reasonable that it should be established. In other words, when all other explanations of the qualities of the beast and my own being, and of the events which brought us face to face, have been razed, I see that (given our qualities and circumstances) the line established is that which is entirely reasonable, and that it is established on no other account. This line is emotion, and is generic in its quality. It is the clarity of my awareness of this line that gives depth to my experience of this line (to my sense of emotion). But being pre-thought we can describe it only in terms of the thought to which it leads. Thus, I believe that I can specify that my experience of the line (as fear), its cause (a belief in the attack), and the physical sensations of my body (as being fearful). I say that my belief in the attack makes me fearful, or that my physiology and instinctive responses explain my fear and action. But I am mistaken. In fact, as we have said, in my mind natural reason leads from the circumstances in which I find myself, to the thoughts with which I subsequently interpret my experience of that line. Natural reason is the kernel of my fear; and fear is the route to knowing reason

I escape the beast. I am now facing a woman who loves me and whom I love. I love her, not because I find her qualities endearing (though I may find them so); nor because this is a ritual honed by evolution and natural selection to ensure coupling, procreation, and the protection and rearing of young. I love because as I stand there looking at her there is only reason. When all explanations have been razed, when the qualities I once found endearing are commonplace, when sexual desire is gone, there is only acceptance of all that she is, has done, and has been. I love because it is only reasonable that I should do so. Natural reason is the kernel of my love; love is the route to knowing reason.

I turn around and see that the beast has followed me. I am filled with hatred, and I determine to kill the beast. I hate not because it will kill the woman I love; nor because I am honed by natural selection to protect the vehicle for the continuation of my genetic material. I hate because in that moment I see only reason. When all the qualities of the woman I love, and those of the beast, and my own, are explained and removed, I am left with the knowledge that I can feel nothing for the beast except hatred. In that moment, natural reason is glimpsed; and in that recognition is the intensity of my hatred. Reason is the kernel of my emotion; my unqualified desire to kill is the route to knowing reason.

We have, in effect, argued that to experience emotion *is* to understand natural reason; it is, therefore, to understand a truth about the world. Is it, then, only at those moments when faced with the immediacy of action and circumstance, and when it seems as if we are consumed by emotion, that we know reason so keenly? And how is it possible get across our experience, our understanding, of this truth about the natural and social worlds? It cannot be through the communication of ready-made thought. Since we can explain the line of pre-thought only in terms of the thoughts to which it leads, our explanations are by definition inadequate. If I say that 'I am afraid because of the beast', or that 'I see that this line is established because (and only because) it reasonable that it should be established', then you might know something of my meaning: from your own similar experience you may have some appreciation my 'fear'. However, you do not know the precise truth that I knew; you are not aware of the precise line that I was aware of when I faced the beast.

If we are not barred from reaching into, let alone communicating, pre-thought and its truth, and if we cannot rely on a statement of our state of mind, then how do we touch and transmit that truth? The answer must be to open up the line of pre-thought (the line to thought). We must, through the arrangement of forms of thought and representations in our own minds and in the minds of others, take ourselves to a point before thought: to a point which suggests a particular direction, such that each of us might then open up lines to thought, and in doing so experience a truth for ourselves. But how might this be done?

Let us consider the doubts we raised earlier in this chapter about the argument that language is a precondition for thought, knowledge, and consciousness. We have implied that this argument may derive from our inability to think before our thoughts, and from our modern suspicion with self as anything more than a simulation of the brain. It might also, perhaps, derive from a belief that those whose facility with language, most especially with speech, are by definition less capable as thinkers. This is a belief useful to those who wish to establish exclusive sets of relationships. But if we see language as a means of communicating thought, then it is not difficult to appreciate that we understand the meaning of a sentence because it corresponds to our own very similar, though dimensional, lines of thought. Accordingly, speech does not have to precise in order for it to be understood; and, by the same token, even when our speech is very precise, it may be given different interpretations. Nor is it difficult - given the understanding of thought that we have set out - to appreciate that whilst we may think in words, we may also think in, say, sounds, pictures, numbers, and actions. Indeed, we might imagine either that one thought can, in effect, morph into very different thoughts such that there may be very profound connexions between what might otherwise appear to be very different thoughts on different matters; or that the same thought can take on different forms (such as words, pictures, or sounds).

Might we not suppose, then, that forms of thought less burdened by the detail of representation, or thoughts arranged in a way that they merely hint at other possible thoughts, may open up particular, and focussed, lines of pre-thought? I have in mind, in particular, music. Take most simply the equal temperament scale. In that scale, each successive note vibrates at a ratio of 1.059 to the preceding note. And each note is a product of the other. Thus, (3rd) x (5th)= (7th), and (3rd) = (7th)/(5th), and (5th = (7th)/(3rd). The 3rd and 5th of the scale together with the tonic provide us with the major chord. The third is, as a ratio to the tonic, close to 1.25, and the fifth is at a ratio of 1.5. The divisions are not perfect mathematically, for if they were we would hear only discord. Yet what we hear is in harmony. (Perhaps numbers are indeed only shadows cast by our activity). We have a sense of completeness. But as I drop the third to a second, or raise it to a fourth, there is a need for resolution. Or, as I remove the third and strike the tonic or fifth, we are left with a sense of stark emptiness. Or, as I flatten the third, the sixth, and seventh, and then sharpen the seventh when it is the leading note, we create the minor. This is of – and yet it is seemingly apart from - the completeness. It lies parallel, and is connected, to the completeness, yet separated from it by a veil. Now set upon the major a melody of rising thirds and falling sevenths (I have in mind Elgar's *Nimrod* variation): we find ourselves repeatedly seeking, and repeatedly being denied, resolution; and as we float ambiguously between the major and the minor it is seems as if we are unable to throw off the veil. Only with the final resolution is the struggle lifted from our souls. Now bring in a melody resting upon the minor and centred upon an extended, hesitating, repetition of the fifth that moves briefly to the sixth, fourth, second, and tonic, and then back to the fifth. (I have in mind here Vaughan Williams' variation on Tallis's third tune for Archbishop Parker accompanying the verse 'Why fum'th in fight the Gentiles spite'). Layered with harmony, tempo, volume, rhythm, and the timbre of instruments, it is as if we are held behind the veil and filled with longing, pleading, and questioning. It is as if music does not merely express emotion but, as Budd (1985) puts it, reaches into emotion itself. And this I believe is so. The sense of a need for resolution, of stark emptiness, of yearning, is - given the nature of the scale, the physical qualities of the sounds, the physical qualities of my ear, and the contexts of thoughts in my mind - entirely reasonable in itself and on no other account.

Music, we may argue, is best suited to reaching into emotion because it is at once tangible (we can literally feel the sounds in the air), and yet seems to inhabit a dimension inaccessible to us: the notes of a theme fade away from the world; but, once played again, the theme reappears as alive and as real as when it was first heard. Music is, in other words, entirely abstract. It carries no message. It is uniquely unsuited to the transmission of detailed representations; and it is least effective when it is intended that it should represent and symbolize. It takes us back to the point before we begin to create the representations through which we otherwise think about the world. And in moving us so directly to the point before thought, and being free of representation, there is both clarity in our awareness of the lines of pre-thought that flow from music, and, therefore, intensity in our experience of truth. Music does not communicate thought to the listener. Rather, it sets up conditions in the listener's mind that hint at lines to thought. It is as we open up and follow those lines of pre-thought that we begin to experience the world for ourselves.

By the same token, words and images - since they are capable of carrying detailed representations - are the more difficult material through which we might reach into emotion. They are at their best when they are used to suggest. By this I mean that it is only when we move beyond the need to demonstrate intellect and to communicate 'my' thoughts, when we begin to shave away our representations, and when we concern ourselves with the sequence of particular ideas, that we can begin to set up conditions in our minds such that the reader may open up lines of pre-thought for themselves.

* * * * *

We have argued that emotion is the line of natural reason (what we have also described as pre-thought) which leads from one thought to another; that it is the clarity of our awareness of this line that gives depth to our sense of emotion; and that this line is necessarily interpreted in the light of the thoughts to which it leads. Thus, natural reason leads from the circumstances of myself and the beast to a belief that it will attack, that I should be afraid, and that my body should respond. The clarity of my awareness of the line to those thoughts is the intensity of my emotion. But this line I interpret in the light of the thought to which natural reason has led: and so I consider (mistakenly) that I am afraid because I believe the beast will attack, or I say that my belief and my fear are the product of my physiology. So, too, is it with music. I hear the rising thirds and falling sevenths, and the timbre of the instrument, and I sense the tempo; natural reason is the line that leads to my thought of the soul's struggle and final resolution. When I say that the music carries thoughts and emotions and communicates them to me, or makes me feel as I do, I am mistaken. Music has opened in my mind lines to thought, and in this I experience natural reason: I have come to know emotion, to experience for myself a truth. Writers face the harder task. For they deal in the detail of representation, and their tools are the tools for the construction of representations. They must, through the manufacture of representations, shape the space of what is left unsaid;

and in this way guide, such that in the mind of the reader lines will be opened up to the thoughts intended by the writer. Thus readers come to experience the line, to know emotion, to know a truth in the world, *for themselves*. Were thought merely to be stated, we would have succeeded only in communicating dull and lifeless representations that are but a means to an end.

The conclusion we are moving to is that thought can bring us closest to natural reason (and so to the truth of instances of the social and natural worlds) only when we find a form (such as music or action or words) and an arrangement which takes us to the point before thought, and begin to open up focussed and particular lines to thought. A piece of music does not communicate the thoughts of its composer. In the mind of listener it open up lines to thought such that they experience for themselves a truth in the world. The task facing the writer is more difficult. But the best of literature shapes representations leaving unspoken channels to guide the mind. If well done, it is - when we read, or when we listen to music, or watch the movements of others, or gaze at painting or sculpture - as if we are beginning to think in emotion. It is as if we are beginning to know reason and truth intimately. On the whole, academic writing does this poorly, for we think ourselves to be constrained by the need to demonstrate intellect and precision. Our writing is weighed down by our belief that its function is to create accurate representations. It is precisely because of this desire to look directly at the world, and to report it faithfully, that we find it difficult, perhaps impossible, to understand what we most want to understand. What is committed to the page must now lag still further behind what is alive in the mind.

4.0 Thinking thoughts

What then is 'I'? What is thought? And how do we get from one thought to another without there being a thinker behind the thought? The answer to the first question is that 'I' is my mind's conclusion: I am just a thought. To the second question, the answer (we have implied) is that thought is material and that it might take forms which symbolize things and events in the natural and social worlds around us. As the conclusion 'I' emerges, as representations of 'I' deepen, and as thought and the context of thought become more complex, thoughts emerge from that context itself - thoughts more abstract in nature and taking more complex symbolic forms. But even these more complex thoughts, even our more complex and deepening representations of 'I', and even the thought of the thinker behind the thought that emerges with awareness, are dependent ultimately upon constant stimulation by our observation of things and events in the world around us. It is easy to imagine that should this stimulus to the basic thoughts and constructs of 'I' be severely limited or removed, then the more complex representations of 'I', the thinker, will begin to disintegrate, and that more sophisticated lines of thought will fragment into incoherence. We might also imagine that if the natural and social worlds around us should alter suddenly, then our constructs and sense of 'I', and our thinking, will in some measure become disoriented and disjointed. Here, perhaps, lies the origin of our sense of the alien and unfamiliar.

The suggestion that thought may take material and symbolic form is anathema to many philosophers today, partly because it seems to require another mind to decipher and interpret. However, in pre-conscious thought there is no need for deciphering or interpretation: the thoughts just are. Nor do the symbols need to be constant over time. They need only remain constant in relation to the context of thought. Nor in conscious thought is there a need either for deciphering or for consistency over time. For we have argued that as thought enters a state of awareness, it comes to know itself. Indeed, because thought knows itself, then there is no need for consistency even within context. For with awareness, the morphology of thought can be traced. Thus thought can retain its original meaning, yet take on many unconnected forms. And while the same language may be used to communicate thought (whatever its material and symbolic form) there is no need for a single or fixed language. Nor is there a need for a single form of communication: we may think and communicate thought as well in pictures, images, symbols, sounds, and feelings, as we do in words.

To the question how do we get from one thought to another without there being a thinker behind the thought? - how and why do I decide what to do if the weather does indeed turn out to be fine at the weekend? - the answer may be emotion. Emotion we have described as the essence of our lines of thought. The line established is that which is established because it is reasonable and on no other account. (We might imagine it, perhaps, as a trace laid out by natural reason in advance of thought). However, our thought is so complicated by constructions of what 'I' is, wants, does, thinks, and needs, that whilst each line in itself follows natural reason, the nature of thinking in its overall context is mimetic. In other words, the decision to take my mother-in-law to tea is a line established through natural reason (and on no other account) in the context of this 'I' at this time. The line of thought 'I' settle on, say, going to the beach or taking my mother-in-law to tea, is simply that which is reasonable in the context of all that I am and my representations of the moment, as might be the decision merely to stare into space and allow whatever associations as may come into mind, such as turning into a blue triangle or pink elephant, or moving my little finger randomly. 'I' does not make the decision: the thinking and the decision-making simply describes an awareness of the lines of thought into which the conclusions of prior thought ('I') are bound, and out of which further representations of 'I' will arise. But so intimately bound into these lines of thought, and so acute the sense of awareness, that it is *as if* 'I' makes the decision.

Thought, then, is an extension of that tendency to complexity which leads from the inorganic, to our own bodies and brains, to our conscious thoughts about the natural world and our own nature, and to the world we form through our relationships with each other. To say I think is to say that I am aware of the lines of thought from which I emerged. When we 'think', we 'think' backwards.

5.0 Attitude and debate

In chapter 1 we argued that our attitudes to our relationships work their influence upon the social world through our representations of self and community; and that they do so only to the extent that our representations inform the practice of social relationships. This we described as the play of relationships, attitudes, and representations. We also left hanging a number questions: how do we arrive at the constructions, and sense, of 'I' and community that are the root of our attitudes? how do we create our broader and more detailed representations of the world out there? how and why do these representations come to inform the practice of social relationships? how and why does the practice of social relationships influence our attitudes and representations? And how do we explain the profound commonality implied in all of this? We have said that our present discussion on thought should not be taken as the foundation of our attitudinal perspective. However, it does seem to offer a few experimental answers to some of those questions.

We have argued that our interactions with, and observations of, the natural world and other people during the early part of our lives, stimulates the emergence of countless 'I's each possessing many dimensions. These are set within other constructs of the natural and social worlds. The subsequent practice of relationships, and our observations, are influenced by, and also have an influence upon, our representations of self and worlds, deepening and expanding those representations still further. With this intense layering of 'I', thought enters a state of awareness. With awareness comes a *sense* of 'I' and community; and from this emerge more coherent representations of 'I' and of 'I's place in the world. Views about how 'I' do, or should, treat and practice social relationships - or, in other words, my attitudes to social relationships - are now formed. At the same time my awareness of my inability to see behind my thoughts leads me into more complex and dimensional representations of this coherent 'I', and into more complex and dimensional representations of the world, infused with my attitudes. These increasingly sophisticated representations of self and worlds have a bearing upon the subsequent practice of relationships and, in turn, upon subsequent representations. Practice also works constantly, and still more deeply, to generate and reinforce my sense of 'I' and community, and to stimulate the emergence of representations in the very young. The commonality in this play, and in the social world 'out there', derives from our bodies, from the quality and experience of awareness, and, most fundamentally, from what we have termed natural reason. Natural reason, we suggested, is the heart of mind, and may be appreciated most intimately through emotion.

This view of thought also complements much of the earlier discussion in chapter 1 on the ways in which that perspective moves the emphasis of study. Our view of thought suggests, in particular, that ideas cannot be separated from our sense of self and community, from our attitudes, or from our relationships. Our soul permeates our ideas. The attitudes we hold, then, do not merely colour our representations of the social world occasionally: they are inherent in those representations. As I have attempted to illustrate elsewhere (Hodder, 2002), this finds clear expression in a debate which reaches back into core philosophical and religious texts, and to which most other debates in the social sciences eventually return: that of the relative influence of, and relationship between, the individual and the whole (by which I mean notion of a larger social presence carried by terms such as society, culture, structure, and civilization).

Our attitudes might also find expression through our explanations of the natural world. I have in mind here the idea of natural selection - an idea central to most present day explanations of the form and development of organic life; and one which has also been applied increasingly to explanations of human behaviour and social organisation. Natural selection, outlined simply, describes how the form and quality of living things is shaped by random mutation and the winnowing of all but those forms and qualities best suited to the survival and perpetuation of an organism and its kind. That this is so, we could add, is strengthened by two questions which might at first sight appear to imply criticism of natural selection. First, if what exists is best suited to that existence, then what conceivable advantage has the animate over the inanimate? (This is a question which presumes that we are not prepared to accept that the existence of living things is somehow different from the existence of the inanimate, and, therefore, that natural selection only applies to living things.') Secondly, if what lives is best suited to living, then what advantage does the complex organism have over the simple? In answer to both questions, and possibly in response to any obstacle that we might wish to set up to natural selection, we need only look at the fact of our existence. The complexity and dominance of the human brain, and its manipulation of the material world, amply demonstrate that complex living things are the best (though not perfect) evolutionary strategy. Unlikely though it may seem that life in all its extraordinary complexity could be the result of a random, blind, and unknowing process, the very fact of complex life with all its imperfections declares the extraordinary power of that process.

But now let us ask if there is not something teleological in all this? Natural selection (and here we are forming an argument not against evolution, but against natural selection) presents us with an open declaration of insentience; yet it also carries with it a sense of purpose. Organisms, however blindly and unknowingly, are understood to have been moving toward their present form - a form best suited to the environment and circumstances.

The teleological quality of this argument carries with it a number of problems. If organisms are by definition a part of the process of natural selection, then presumably they cannot exist outside that process. The question which then arises is this - do we explain the organisms' ancestors in the light of the organism as it is today, or as it will be in the future? We might, for instance, peer into a lake and see

---

* Popper and Eccles (1977), however, have suggested that the idea of natural selection might be applied to unstable elements.

there slim, blue, and fast-swimming fish that share the water with slow, but well camouflaged, fish-eating turtles. And we might say that the fish's qualities of speed, slimness, and colour, emerged by degrees because they were qualities that best suited the survival of the fish. We are explaining the existence (and survival) of the fish, here and now, and the success of their ancestors through the generations, by the quality of the fish as they have become. Yet the fish are still subject to natural selection. This being so, then surely the survival of the fish, here and now, and the survival of their ancestors in the past, can be explained only be what the fish have yet to become? So how do we explain the fish - by what they are now, or by what they will become?

We can object to this criticism, and reply that the fish as they will become are certain to be explained by coming changes in the environment, in circumstances, and in their genetic make up. And we can argue that this was so in the past. The ancestors of the fish were big, slow, and red. After the appearance of turtles the fish kept their red colour but, by degrees, became slim and fast; and then, in this blue-watered lake, changed their colour to blue.

Now, however, another problem appears. Had we been alive at the time when the fish were big, red, and slow, we would have had to explain the existence of the fish in the light of those qualities - by what the fish had, up to that point, become. But the fish and their ancestors (who were in the process of becoming big, slow, and red) were still part of natural selection and, as it turned out, were becoming small, fast, and blue. Unless the response of the fish to changes in their environment and circumstances was instantaneous, then there were many generations of ancestors who were not best suited to the environment. So how did they survive? Similarly, since the fish we see today are still subject to natural selection, and if changes in their form are not instantaneous, then how do we know whether the fish we see here today are best suited to their environment?

We are now left with no choice but to argue that changes in the quality and form of organisms take place *before* changes in environment and circumstance. These changes are blind; and they may, or may not, equip the organism for subsequent changes in environment. Either their survival will be helped, or at least not hindered, by changes in their form and quality; or they will die. Step by step, with each set of changes in both themselves and their environment, organisms move towards their eventual form and particular qualities. Thus, we may argue, organisms moved towards what we see today through a series of changes that, at any point in time, happened by chance to best suit the environment of the day.

But now another problem emerges. If changes in organisms are limited in number and occur uniformly across their kind prior to environmental change, then with every subsequent change in the environment, the chance that genetic changes will allow these organisms to survive will gradually diminish. If their chances are to improve, then it would seem to follow that there must be increases both in the numbers of organisms and in variations across their kind. If the increases in number and variations are sufficient, then survival, rather than extinction, will become more likely. At the same time, however, continual changes in these organisms - if they prove to be harmful or less than optimal - will also be shaved away by natural selection * even prior to subsequent environmental change. Assuming that periods of environmental stability are long enough, these organisms will necessarily settle into a particular niche, and fall into stasis. This renders them less suitable for subsequent environmental change especially if those changes occur at a rate faster than the rate of biological change. Indeed, the likelihood is that subsequent environmental changes, or changes in circumstance, will lead to extinction. Thus we are led to the conclusion that natural selection leads, eventually, to extinction. The only question is whether or not it does so after a long

---

* *c.f.* Csanyi and Kampis (1991) who, in their critique of natural selection, point out that neutral and harmful traits may be found in species that are not removed by natural selection.

period of stasis. It is, in other words, extinction that explains the forms and qualities of life we see today.

That extinction should lead first to the evolution of life of any kind (let alone its most complex forms) merely in order that life should then be erased, seems much more like the functional, if not perverse, reasoning of the human mind than a true account of the natural world. Would it not be more simple to raze any promise of life altogether? Again we are drawn back to the doubts raised earlier: what conceivable advantage under the terms of natural selection does the animate and complex have over the inanimate? It is certainly curious that we should attempt to explain what *is* by what is *not*; and it may hint at the essential difficulty with natural selection. Viewed from the outside - as if we were looking down on the natural world - the argument is wholly believable: the removal of what is not suitable will leave only that which is suitable to continue the line; and the continual scraping away of superfluous forms through the ages will craft the organism into the shape we see here today. But let us imagine life in world with a stable environment and in which there are no extinctions. Given that biological changes are random and occur prior to environmental change, then presumably a huge variety of organisms of all kinds would soon appear on this environmental *tabula rasa*. Now let us re-introduce events and environmental change which erase a third or a half or four-fifths of all kinds, and which also begin to remove particular organisms within the surviving kinds. It is as if large patches of darkness have fallen upon the natural world, blotting out expanses of a far greater complexity. We are now aware that we have only an incomplete picture, and an incomplete understanding, of that complexity. The vast swathes of darkness - the non-existence of some kinds and individuals - cannot explain the form, qualities, and complexities, of those organisms that remain. Nor can we say whether those organisms are either the better or best, for we have nothing with which they might be compared. We can say only of those that were, that they do not exist. And we can say of those that remain only that they are, by definition of their very presence, suited to life. It is possible, therefore, to interpret any form or qualities which they might possess as being suitable and adaptive. But we can never know if other forms and qualities would have been equally viable; nor can we be sure whether or not the organism has either moved to find an environment better suited to its qualities, or adapted the environment to itself.

As we look between the pools of darkness, and contemplate the fragments of the greater complexity that once existed, we may begin to interpret at will. These fragments we once saw as the work of a higher intelligence. Today the more popular story into which we draw these fragments is that of fitness, suitability, and adaptation. And in writing this story we call upon the darkness, upon what is not, to interpret what *is*. Whereas once we believed intelligence brought form and light to the darkness, now we believe that darkness shapes intelligence.

In both these stories there is much of ourselves. Both these stories, those of God and Natural Selection, are intensely personalistic accounts of the world and of our place within it. Once we believed we were the creation of, and of interest to, a Supreme Being. Now we believe that evolution, through the process of natural selection, tends blindly, randomly, unknowingly, towards the best (though not to perfection). The human brain, by virtue of its complexity and dominance, is the best. It was therefore towards the human brain that things have been moving, and the existence of the brain may be taken as confirmation of this. The human brain is first, not in time, but in the order of things. To understand living things we must understand them in the light of the existence of that which now contemplates them. All interpretations of the qualities of other organisms, living or extinct, are now shaped into an explanation which, naturally enough, places what it is (the mind) that understands them at the centre of that understanding.

It is not surprising, then, that Natural Selection should set itself against any sense of communitarianism beyond that which is necessary under its terms to the survival of individual and kind. Nor is it surprising that it should present us with stark choices: either God or natural selection, either science or superstition. Yet these are choices which succeed only in diverting us from what may be a more important question: why and how do we create such representations (religious, scientific and social) and what is their bearing upon the practice of social relationships? Answering these questions may, in the end, provide us with the knowledge to understand both the natural and social worlds accurately enough to dissolve the distinction between them.

6.0 Conclusions

We have suggested that we create representations of forces and substances apart from us that we believe shape our thought and behaviour. This we do because we are unable to think behind our thoughts. We have also suggested that natural reason finds expression through our bodies and thought, and that it is the root of our commonality; but that with the emergence of consciousness we find it difficult to distinguish between functional and natural reason. In the previous section we went on to suggest that our discussion on thought, whilst it should not be taken as the foundation of our attitudinal perspective, does appear to fit in with many of the arguments running through that perspective. It is consistent both with argument that our ideas – whether they concern the social or natural worlds - cannot be separated either from our attitudes or from the practice of social relationships; and with the implied assumption that we possess a fundamental commonality. We can take this last point a little further and suggest that we are released from conformity precisely because the commonalities which bind us are extraordinarily profound. In other words, difference may be understood as a state of mind. It describes our disorientation as we move beyond those relationships from which our constructs of self and community emerged, and as our very sense of what we are weakens. It also describes our response to disorientation. We anchor ourselves in a world unfamiliar either by making the people around us alien, or by making an alien of self among ordinary people. To do this self must establish conformity either among the alien or the ordinary. In doing so, a self that is predisposed to manipulate is centred in a world of black and white. An appeal to conformity, then, is an appeal to difference, just as an appeal to difference is an appeal to conformity. Not until we are inured to the relationships around us, not until our sense and constructs of self and community have been re-constituted, are we open to the affective. Only then does the world, despite its coating of variation, seem familiar once again.

Our account of thought would also seems to fit in with our suggestion (in section 5 of chapter 1) that our thinking should be less deliberately intellectual, and more visceral. We might, in particular, consider the possibility that empathy and our emotional responses – that immediate sense of what the problem or answer might be, or of the nature of what we see in front of us - provide us with a more faithful understanding of the social world. Moreover, because we admit empathy and emotion, and because we are no longer restrained by the parameters of existing representations, we can no longer be sure of the direction in which our thought will lead.

Nor, then, can we be sure any longer of whether our categories of thought (such as scientific, social, artistic, intellectual, emotional), or our mediums of thought (such words, pictures, shapes, music or numbers), are distinct. Might we not also consider the possibility that complex images and sounds may communicate and convey ideas better than the written word? Indeed, our arguments leads us to the suggestion that the social world comprises a layering of thought, an understanding of which may ultimately depend upon the marriage of social and scientific spheres of knowledge, enquiry, and communication.

*   *   *   *   *

This account of thought is no more than a representation. At its heart lies the suggestion that reason is not peculiar to the human mind, nor is it shaped by a cultural or biological cast of some kind. It is an extension of what we have termed natural reason. We conceive of reasoning and awareness not as states of mind, nor as things or phenomena, but, rather like time or space, as qualities or dimensions of existence. As such, reason and awareness have a presence not in us or outside us but through us. They find expression, but they have no substance, in the material world.

Is this a representation that we should take seriously? Kant believed that reason tells us what to do – primarily that we should not treat others as our own personal instruments – and in this sense is real. Yet it was, for him, apart from, and could not be reconciled with, the natural world. Perhaps we have in these pages given reason a dimension that it does not possess? This question is left with the reader. However, natural reason is a thought which leads us to other ideas that are interesting in themselves. Still more important, in the context of this book, is that just as we can see something of our attitudes reflected in our discussions on the social and natural worlds, so we can see reflected in our discussions on thought something of our attitudes towards social relationships. It is an illustration of our need to imagine, to dream, and to reach beyond a reality grounded in experience. A world devoid of imaginings and dominated by empiricism and convention will, in pinning our minds to absolutes, lead us towards the personal just as surely as a world dominated by dreams and faith alone.

Our discussion of thought, then, is merely one instance of our many parables of uncertainty. It does not lead us to the conclusion that we cannot know the world, natural or social, within our immediate experience. Nor does it force us to reject what might seem to be more sensible and rational explanations of thought. It does not demand that we put aside the immediate physical mechanisms of the brain nor even the culture as possible explanations of thought and behaviour. But it does suggest that whilst experience and the affirmation of our representations by other people may sometimes provide us with the line between fantasy and reality, they might also only confirm us in our functional understanding of the world. Our discussion on thought, then, merely asks us to leave our minds open, and to treat all our representations *as if* absolute.

Chapter 3
The Overseas Chinese

1. Introduction

In chapters 1 and 2 we suggested that for as long as we remain ignorant of the nature of thought, we cannot but doubt our understandings of the social and natural worlds. Consequently we are left to search for ways of understanding which, though they may not be able to overcome this essential weakness, may at least be able to take that weakness into account. One way is to centre attention upon what are held to be the few certainties in our knowledge of the social world: our social relationships, our attitudes to our relationships, and our representations of the social and natural worlds. If we are to understand the social world, then we must first understand the play of these attributes.

This bring us face to face with what is, until we understand the nature of thought, an insoluble problem. We may be certain about the fact of our relationships, attitudes, and representations; but any statement of the play of these attributes, and any interpretations of the social world that follow, must remain uncertain. To accommodate this problem, we must attempt to understand the attributes of the social world within our immediate experience through a constant cycle of dis-aggregation and re-formulation.

The first step in this is to present an account of what we think the play of those attributes might be. We argued in chapter 1 that attitudes shape representations; that representations inform the practice of social relationships; and that the practice of our relationships has an influence upon attitudes and representations. Whilst our representations of the world within and beyond our immediate experience allow us to manage the particular sets of relationships which we come up against and participate in, and so enable us to function collectively on a much wider scale, we cannot assume that our representations depict the social world faithfully. Indeed the nature of our representations, and their play with attitudes and relationships, strongly suggest that the social world which exists 'out there' is a fuzzy, dimensional, and ever-changing complex, that does not lend itself to being described and elucidated accurately by such representations as the human mind is capable of imagining and communicating.

The second step is to tease out the play of relationships, attitudes, and representations, of those who comprise particular instances on the street. As we do so we must bear in mind that those who write about the street, and their writings, are no less part of the world they study; and, therefore, that there exists a dialectic between street and scholarship.

Thirdly, as we attempt to formulate and communicate our understanding, we cannot but re-fashion our representations of the particular and the world beyond. These representations are not an end in themselves. They are bound into the particular and, together with the particular, constitute the starting point of a subsequent cycle during which they may be altered. Yet the more often we repeat this cycling and come to understand *a* particular, the more likely is it that we will be able understand *any* particular. Our intention, then, is to move towards an understanding of the general principles of that play of attributes. We know that until we have a complete understanding of thought, we will never fully comprehend those principles. But we might yet catch a glimpse of the simple commonalties that underlie the surface complexity, fluidity, and difference, of the social world.

This chapter continues the cycle begun in chapter 1. It attempts to draw out and examine the play of relationships, attitudes, and representations, which comprise particular instances of trade and business in the Philippines and of that country's trade with China. It is argued that the attitudes infusing scholarly representations have aided both the inflation of Chinese economic success in the Philippines, and the passage of these representations onto the street. Here they have been absorbed into practice, encouraging hostile treatment of Chinese, undermining the confidence of Filipinos in themselves and in the Philippines' political economy. Chapter 4 goes on to argue that these representations have also worked to obscure the complex dimensionality of particular instances of trade and business in the Philippines and China.

2.0 Attitude and representation

We noted in chapter 1 that the economic pre-eminence of the overseas Chinese has today come to form part of a basic knowledge of Southeast Asia; and that explanations of their pre-eminence have emphasised the work of Confucianism, *guanxi*, and other cultural influences. We also noted that, following the economic crisis of 1997 and a deepening interest in the all-encompassing idea globalisation, attention has shifted in more recent years towards the role of structure in the emergence of modern or hybridized forms of Chinese behaviour and organisation. It is doubtful, we argued, whether this discernible (if marginal) shift in emphasis from cultural to structural (or institutional) explanations of the overseas Chinese and their economic organisations and practices in Southeast Asia, marks any fundamental movement in the debate. There is in the work of writers such as Jomo and Ruskola some admission of the individual; and some doubts, too, are expressed not only about the relative importance of structure, but even about its very meaning. But for the most part, the criticisms levelled against the cultural explanation only strengthen a more explicit recognition of what the culturalists already recognise - that structure shares the explanatory burden with culture; and when analysis finds itself leaning to heavily towards structure, it appears to have no alternative other than to right itself first, and then lean towards culture. Across the disciplines the study of the Chinese overseas has settled within the parameters

78

of cultural and structural analyses. So entrenched are these parameters that there appears to be no question of looking outside them. Those who minimize or dismiss factors of culture, states Wang (1999), 'invariably attribute all significant developments to the forces of modernisation' (p.11). Chirot and Reid (1997, p.3), in setting the question for their study, also present the reader with a limited choice. Are there cultural traits that determine groups' prospects in modern economies? Or is the success of any particular ethnic group situationally determined and explainable in terms of recent, almost chance, political and economic configurations? It is, therefore, rather difficult to share the confidence with which Wang (2000) asserts that there has, for at least fifty years, been a major disagreement about 'whether Chinese are like all other migrants when they leave their country or whether they are quite different' (p.39). Whether the Chinese were different and whether culture and structure explained this difference has never seriously been in question: the only doubt has been the extent to which the Chinese were different and precisely where the burden of explanation lay. A kind of accommodation has emerged between the structural and the cultural, the former embedded in the latter, and each mediated through the other producing some degree of change, and together providing some level of explanation.

Might scholars' attitudes towards relationships account for the resilience of these cultural-structural representations? To the scholar imbued with the affect - with the attitude that relationships, and our constructs of 'you', 'I', and 'us', should be treated as important and proper in their own right - these representations seem to remove the stain of instrumentalism from those who are being studied. Yao (2002), for instance, may now[*] make more explicit arguments that 'the political and material condition in which [culture] operates must be brought into focus' (p. xi); that analyses of the Chinese may have been influenced by romanticized images of them; and that behaviour motivated by calculation and ethical beliefs is practiced

---

[*] Compare this 2002 work with Yao's earlier 1984 work.

by each one of us. Yet the desire of the merchant to extract social pleasure from the practice of social relationships, Yao argues, is strong. And in this desire there is, for Yao, something peculiarly and culturally Chinese. This must be so - for if we do not recognise the saliency of culture, then we are led into a crude and clumsy world of super-rational materialists and political-ideological manipulation. If we are to understand why people think and behave as they do, then we have no choice but to begin and end our analyses with the play of culture and structure. The alternative, Yao believes, is to admit into debate explanations that are intellectually and morally wanting.

At the same time, in their appeal to phenomena capable of shaping thought and behaviour, the scholars' representations have taken on an absolute quality - a quality much strengthened by precedent. As we argued in chapter 2 (section 5), the language may have changed, but the debate over the relative importance of the individual and the collective is an ancient one: ancient because it is rooted in our sense, and in our most basic constructs, of self and community; ancient because, in an absence of an understanding of thought, we are bound to look for a substitute – for that 'something' that shapes our thought and behaviour. More recently, over the last half century and more, writers have often described society as the hierarchy within which individuals are positioned, and culture as the standardized patterns of behaviour, socially acquired; to others, society was the totality of social relationships (or, more specifically, the 'structure' or networks of relationships among and within systems of groups) and culture the content of those relationships. And just as culture might influence the society, so might society influence the culture, though as to where the balance of power lay every writer had their own view. As for the significance of the individual, there was less uncertainty about this matter. For many, the individual was incidental and individual freedom an illusion; for once culture had come into existence the individual then became permanently subject to this irresistible force. For many more, culture and society were the context, the precedence, the ready-made solutions, the limitations on a possible range of actions and responses, by which individuals were constrained but within which they might vary their actions. The individual might reflect the culture but not exactly so. Small variations in the behaviour and relationships of some individuals would bring about changes in the behaviour of others; these changes would build up, alter the broader circumstances, and make inevitable further discoveries and changes in practices. In this way, through a kind of convection or conduction or drift, even the basic patterns of culture and society might change.

Even when the word culture was hardly mentioned, and the attention was on society, a force of some kind was ever-present. For Elias (1994) it was the unintended actions of individuals. Under the pressure of competition, social functions became more and more differentiated. As they did so, people became more interdependent and therefore had to attune their conduct more strictly; they had to behave correctly, though the sum of their actions and plans gave rise to changes and patterns in the web of social relationships that no individual had planned. Thus did the patterns blindly formed from social interaction blindly produce changes in human mentality that were imprinted upon individuals from early childhood. Thus arose an order more compelling and stronger than the will and reason of any individual

We can, then, make the case that the resilience of the scholars' cultural-structural representations derives from an ambiguity of attitude. Infused with the affect, these representations saved the overseas Chinese from the stigma of 'being manipulative'; while their treatment as absolute, which had much precedent, brought to those representations an impression of certainty, permanence, and authority. This ambiguity of attitude, and the qualities which this lent to the scholars' representations, may also have aided the inflation of Chinese economic significance.

3.0 The inflation of Chinese economic success

In chapter 1 we noted that more restrained estimates of the Chinese have emerged in recent years as the purer forms of cultural explanation of Chinese economic success have come to be viewed more critically, as more fluid conceptions of 'the Chinese' and Chineseness' have gathered favour, and as concerns about the abuse of even the most elevated cultural structural explanations deepened. But aside from these kinds of concerns there are few studies that attempt specifically to consider just how unreliable more recent and current estimates may be, and why this might be so. It is very likely, as various studies have shown (see, for example, Brown, R.A., 2000; and Hutchcroft, 1998), that the economic significance of Chinese business in certain activities - such as textiles, banking, retailing and wholesaling - and at certain times and places, has indeed been very marked, and remains so today. Yet as these more nuanced studies make plain, the position of the Chinese is so complex and fluid that it is probably unsafe to use vocabulary which conveys anything more than a general sense of what their importance might be.

This is evident from the very first problem confronting any attempt to arrive at estimates - that of identifying those who are Chinese. One of the few attempts (Postan, Mao, and Yu, 1994) made to provide an open and comprehensive assessment of the number of Chinese in every country throughout the world appears to indicate than even where national censuses provide figures for the numbers of Chinese, the reliability of this data is far from certain. Estimates provided for any particular country (with the possible exception of the United States) appear to vary considerably (commonly by hundreds of thousands or even millions) from one source to the next (compare, for example, Postan *et al* [*op.cit*] with Pan [1999]). In most cases, and this is not said critically, the bases of figures given for the numbers of Chinese are neither clear nor perhaps even known. This is hardly surprising as there are, in the view of some commentators, many degrees of Chineseness; and, as Brown, R.A. (2000) points out, the degree of assimilation in many southeast Asian countries is such that it makes little sense to put a figure on the percentage of population that is Chinese. Arriving at some kind of working definition is therefore not easy. Indeed, the more capable of capturing something of the complexity on the ground any definition may be, the more awkward are its categorizations likely to become, such that categorization may serve only demonstrate that we should have profound reservations about the purpose and meanings of such exercises.

With these comments in mind it is suggested that the simplest, most direct, and possibly most inclusive criteria are those of name and, because Chinese may adopt Filipino names, an assessment of whether or not those who are identified as Chinese see themselves, and are seen by others as such. This, at least, is the definition of 'Chinese' used here; and it is one that *includes* Chinese who do not hold Filipino citizenship * . 'Chinese' with foreign citizenship are therefore excluded from the definition of 'Internationals' – a term used here to refer to individuals who are foreign citizens. Thus 'Filipino' refers to individuals with Philippines' citizenship and who are neither 'Chinese' nor 'Internationals'. 'Filipino' may therefore exclude a small number of individuals who originally held Filipino citizenship (but who are not 'Chinese') and who have taken on foreign nationality; and include a small number of individuals who were originally foreign (but not 'Chinese') and who have taken on Filipino citizenship. 'International' therefore also includes small numbers of former citizens of the Philippines who are not 'Chinese'.

The question of definition is complicated further by a need for a working definition of the ethnicity of corporations. Ownership of, and interests in, corporations are most often complex, dynamic, and diverse, so much so that from the vantage point of the Central Bank, one is bound to wonder about the purpose of attempts to

---

* Where this is the case I specify in the text and in figures 1-3 the country from which those 'Chinese' originate and their citizenship.

define and measure the potency of any specific group*. And again, increasingly cumbersome definitions and categories soon begin to emerge. Companies owned[†] solely by 'Chinese' or by 'Filipinos' or by 'Internationals' are describe here as 'pure', as are companies dominated by one of these groups and in which the interests of one or both of the other two groups is 'nominal'[‡]. Exclusive' is used to describe companies: that are owed solely by 'Chinese, or by 'Filipinos', or by 'Internationals'; and in which neither of the other two groups has interests, nominal or otherwise. The term 'cosmopolitan' is used here to encompass companies that comprise: either pure Internationals with nominal Chinese or, in the majority of cases, nominal Filipino interests; or some combination of Chinese, Filipinos, or Internationals, each of whose interests in the company are more than nominal. These rather ungainly categories into which the problem of identity seem to lead us, are but a taste of the complex and fluid patterns of economic activity within which we must attempt to set the position of the Chinese.

3.1 Local figures: Davao

With these apparently simple criteria in mind, we turn first to the city of Davao on the Island of Mindanao in the southern Philippines. The city is large enough to trade directly with Greater China (China, Hong Kong and Taiwan) through its own

---

* Interview with Melito S. Salazar Jr., Monetary Board Member, *Bangko Sentral ng Pilipinas* (August 2004).

† Information on ownership provided is derived from updated records (as of 2002/3) held at the Securities and Exchange Commission in Manila and in Davao. These are supplemented in some cases either by personal communication with major shareholders or by records held at the Business Bureau and other local government departments in Davao, Makati, and Manila. The records held at SEC provide details on the value of shares of companies (public and private) held either by individuals or by other companies. They also provide details on the nationality and addresses of named individuals and companies and, where relevant, on the official position of those individuals within the company. The records held by the local government departments provide details on company sales, names and addresses of owners (in the case of sole proprietorships), and local tax to be paid. These records are compiled by local governments in order to give them a handle on local tax revenues due.

‡ 'Nominal' is defined here as an ownership stake of less that 10% in the company. In most instances that stake is in fact less than 1% and is usually attached to board membership.

port, and yet modest enough for the smaller (and what some writers may regard as the more traditional) companies to stand out. Here, we find that exports to Greater China are dominated by seven companies which together account for some 90% of exports (by value) (table 1). One of these companies is owned solely by Chinese. In a second Chinese company, Filipino interests are nominal; and in a further two companies Chinese interests are dominant. These four companies, largely Chinese-owned, account for some 60% of exports. Among the remaining nineteen companies, Chinese interests are less strong, though only marginally so. Five are pure Chinese. Another four are dominated by Chinese interests. Of the remaining ten companies, seven are pure Filipino and three are pure Internationals.

Companies with strong Chinese interests are also responsible for the lion's share of imports (by value) from Greater China. Of the ranking twelve companies (which together account for just under 75% of imports), three are owned solely by Chinese; and in another two Chinese companies, Filipino interests are only nominal (see table 2). Together these five companies account for just over 52% of imports. If we include those companies ranked ninth and tenth, then the share of imports accounted for by those companies in which Chinese interests dominate, or in which Chinese interests equal Filipino interests, rises to 56%. Among the thirty-five remaining companies Chinese interests are also strong: eight are owned solely by Chinese; in another four Chinese-owned companies Filipino interests are nominal; and in yet another four companies, Chinese hold majority ownership.

If we consider direct trade with mainland China only (and exclude trade with Hong Kong and Taiwan), the pre-eminence of Chinese-owned companies is even more pronounced. Some 60% of exports rest with just two companies that are predominantly Chinese (ranked 1 and 3 in table 1); and again some 60% of imports rest with two, predominantly Chinese, companies (ranked 1 and 9 in table 2).

More generally in Davao, the strength of the Chinese within the city's economy, whilst notable, is not quite so marked. Around a sixth of sole proprietorships, and a quarter of partnerships and corporations with sales under fifty million pesos (but over one quarter of a million pesos), are exclusively or largely Chinese. The presence of the Chinese among the very strongest companies must be considered as part of the national view; and to this we shall return shortly.

The picture which emerges so far is one that might have been expected given our knowledge of the Chinese in southeast Asia and the statistics which accompany that knowledge. Nevertheless, there are several observations that are worth noting. First, it is clear that Filipino interests are substantial. Companies which are purely 'Filipino', or in which Filipino interests dominate, account for just over a third of exports to, and for just under a third of imports from, Greater China. Filipinos maintain a strong interest of 20% or more in two of the Chinese firms (ranked 1 and 3 in table 1) leading exports, and in two of the Chinese companies ranked 9th and 10th among the importers (see table 2). Indeed, if Chinese firms with Filipino interests of 10% or more are excluded, then purely Chinese companies account for just under 20% of exports. And although the proportion of imports accounted for by pure Chinese companies remains high at 54%, this figure is dominated by a single company whose market for those imports is heavily dependent upon a leading Filipino exporter (ranked 2 in table 1).

Secondly, connections with southern and southeast China (excluding Hong Kong and Taiwan) are not as strong as one might expect. Looked at in the round, it would seem that those companies in Davao which look to China are more likely to be Chinese. Of those firms in table 1 whose prime (and direct) export market is mainland China, three are Chinese (ranked 1, 14 and 19), two are Filipino (7, and 9) and two are International (10, and 11). And of those companies listed in table 2 whose main source of imports is China, nine are Chinese, five are Filipino or International. But in all cases, whether Chinese, Filipino or International, the source of imports and the destination for exports (and these are direct trade connections) are predominantly in central-east and north-east China.

Thirdly, of those companies shown in tables 1 and 2, and which also exhibit a strong national presence (when measured and ranked by domestic sales), most are Filipino or International. Of the twelve Filipino or International companies and twelve Chinese companies with a strong national presence, only three Chinese companies and nine Filipino or International companies are ranked among the strongest two thousand nationally.

Fourthly, and most interestingly, among those companies shown in tables 1 and 2, only four (all of whom export to Hong Kong) rank among the Philippines' main exporters (through Manila) to mainland China. Two are solely Filipino companies, one is predominantly Filipino (with an international interests exceeding 10%), and one is International (with nominal Filipino and Chinese interests): none is Chinese.

3.2 National figures

This latter observation is neither too wayward nor surprising if taken as a rough indication of the relative national significance of Chinese, Filipino, and International companies' trade with China. When we take the national view, and even though we concentrate on the Philippines' trade axis with mainland China (along which we would expect the overseas Chinese to show a strong presence), the balance of interests - Chinese, Filipino and International - appears to be almost the exact reverse of that which is found in Davao. Only around 11% of those companies dominating exports to China are predominantly Chinese (and are primarily Taiwanese, Singaporean or American Chinese). Of these, only two are owned solely by Chinese; two others have significant International interests; and seven have nominal Filipino interests. Some 22% of exporters are predominantly Filipino; and two-thirds are International. Of these International companies, most (over half) have nominal interests that are Filipino only; just 5% have nominal interests that are Chinese only; a tenth are exclusively International; and about a quarter have nominal interests that are both Chinese and Filipino.

Figures 1-3 attempt to set these top exporters within their relationships of investment and board membership among the Philippines' strongest (as measured by gross domestic sales) 120 companies. These 120 companies account for around 55% of the domestic sales of the nation's top 7000 companies (SEC, 2004), and for more than 40% of the nation's gross domestic sales*. Among these 120 companies the proportions dominated by Chinese and Filipinos rises to 25% and 31% respectively, whilst the proportion of Internationals falls correspondingly to 42%. Moreover, whilst there is some fit between these companies and the strongest exporters, most exporters (including those which comprise part of the core indicated in figure 3) are not ranked among the strongest 120 companies, nor are they linked into those 120 companies networks of mutual investments and board memberships. If we consider the balance of interests among those companies that are purely Chinese, Filipino or International, then we find that, among the top exporters, the proportion of the balance of interests falls to 9% and 13% for Chinese and Filipinos respectively. The remaining exporters may be described broadly as cosmopolitan. The pure Internationals (most of which have nominal Filipino interests) account for nearly three-fifths of all exporters; and getting on for another one-fifth are exclusively International. Of the strongest 120 companies the proportion of companies which are purely Filipino drops marginally to 12%, while the Chinese share rises to 16%. Some 41% comprise some combination of Chinese, Filipino, or International interests. And the proportion of pure Internationals falls to 30%. Taken together, of all the companies shown in figures 1-3, 13% are pure Chinese, and 17% are Filipino. Of the remaining cosmopolitans the majority are predominantly Internationals.

---

* These estimates for the top companies share of domestic sales for 2001-2 are not much changed from, and were calculated in the same way as earlier figures for 1995-6. An explanation of how these estimates were reached are set out elsewhere (Hodder, 2002).

As in Davao, imports from China create a more complex picture. The share of imports is spread relatively more evenly over a larger number of companies (more than 1600 companies) and over many thousands of transactions. Nevertheless, there are sufficient concentrations to give rise to a discernible and interesting pattern. The top twenty-three importers account for just over half of all imports by value. Of these twenty-three companies, six are included in figures 1-3. Two of these six are predominantly Chinese as are another eight within the top twenty-three (but not shown in figures 1-3). But although they account for some 43% of the top twenty-three companies, they account for only a tenth of the top twenty-three companies' imports. There are indications that this characteristic - that of a low share of import value relative to the share of the numbers of companies - holds true among the remaining Chinese importers. Within most provinces or provincial-level cities across the Philippines the proportion of the total value of imports from China is a little higher (by about 5%) than the proportion of the total number of companies importing from China. Yet in Binondo - a part of Manila which loosely equates with the heart of the Philippines' Chinatown - the proportion of the number of companies is more than twice the proportion of the value of imports. This holds true when we expand our definition of Chinatown to include Tondo, and even when we include Manila. We also find similar proportions in Pasig where there is again a concentration of Chinese businesses, some of which are owned and managed by mainland Chinese. This comparison is made even more dramatic if set against Makati (where the share of the total number of companies and of the value of imports is ten and three times the national averages respectively). Here the city's share of the total value of imports is nearly four times its share of the number of companies.

If we exclude both our expanded definition of Chinatown and Makati from the calculations, then we find that nationally the share of the total number of companies importing from China is on average greater than the share of the total import value from China by about 15%. Whilst Binondo no longer appears so exceptional in that nationally the average share of companies is higher than the average share of the value of imports, the situation in Binondo remains marked. And if we remove only Chinatown from the estimates of the national averages, then we find the comparison is still more dramatic: whilst nationally the share of the value of imports is on average 24% greater than the share of number of companies, in Chinatown the share of the number of companies is more than double its share of the value of imports. In short, whilst there are in Chinatown more companies engaged in importing goods from China than in any other part of the Philippines, this is not matched proportionally by Chinatown's share of the value of imports.

A further observation concerns the origins of imports from China. These show a strong concentration in Shanghai (a little over 40%). The next highest concentration of originators are to be found in Guangdong (and Shenzhen), Zhejiang, Fujian, and Jiangsu, each with under 10% of the total. Viewed nationally, however, there is a clear concentration in central-eastern China, spreading out, in order of importance, north and west, and lastly southeast (with just 15% of the total). Yet it is from southeastern China that the majority of Chinese in the Philippines are said to originate.

Looked at in the round, the strength of Chinese companies would appear more evident in Davao where their scale of operation is relatively small. However, as the scale of operations increases and as we take a national view, it is Filipino and, even more so, the cosmopolitan firms that are of far greater economic significance. That Chinese companies are more likely to be exclusive may also be telling. Increasing cosmopolitanism with economic strength is also coincident with a kind of hierarchy. In Davao, as has been argued elsewhere (Hodder, 2002), whilst there are fairly complex, though fairly contained, networks of ownership (which again often exhibit varying degrees of ethnic exclusivity) among those businesses with a strong local presence (indications of which can be seen in tables 1 and 2), the very strongest companies in Davao lie outside those local networks. These companies also have a strong national presence, usually centred in the national capital region, and often form part of more complex and often less contained networks of ownership and board memberships. It is these webs that dominate the economy and into which international companies are entwined. Here again, though, some of the strongest companies in the capital, and certainly the strongest exporters, exist outside these combines, but form part of still more extensive and complex international relationships.

It is also worth noting that a broadly similar state of affairs seems to exist in Shanghai where the heart of Philippines' trade with China appears to lie. Here, in Shanghai, the organisation of industry takes on a sharper form and direction: investments cascade down from state organs or companies charged with the administration of state assets, into loose combines of companies, each combine being defined in part by the tendency of its members to invest in one another and by the operation of its members within the same or similar or closely related sector. As in the Philippines, however, whilst foreign companies in Shanghai are closely integrated into these combines, some of the strongest companies, and most especially the more important exporters, tend to lie outside, or exhibit only tenuous connexions with, those combines. And just as the international companies operating in the Philippines dominate the Philippines' trade with China, it is these foreign companies in Shanghai (some of which are branches of the same companies operating in the Philippines) that figure most strongly in Shanghai's trade with the Philippines.

3.3 Three strands

The explanation suggested here for the discrepancy between the more common estimates of Chinese economic strength in the Philippines and the more restrained estimates introduced above, comprises three strands of argument.

(i) Chinese economic strength appears to be greater than their share of the total population of the Philippines would lead us to expect, that strength is nevertheless modest, and falls far short of national or even local dominance. However, within a picture of economic activity dominated by Internationals and cosmopolitans, it would appear that there is in Binondo a concentration of Chinese interests in the trade of large volumes of low-value, everyday goods. This would suggest a strong interest in wholesaling. This is confirmed by a consideration of the patterns of activity in Davao City. Here we find that traders selling dry and manufactured goods (including clothing) in the marketplaces* are heavily dependent for their supplies upon wholesalers who are to be found in and around Uyanguren Street – a part of the city that is commonly, if very loosely, referred to as 'Chinese'. And indeed some 54% of all establishments (sole proprietorships and corporations) in this area are wholly Chinese; and around 11% are predominantly Chinese-owned. These wholesalers commonly obtain their goods either through their suppliers in Binondo or from marketplaces in Manila whose sellers in their turn buy goods from suppliers in Binondo. Moreover, although it would seem that only a small proportion of Davao's wholesalers' goods are brought in directly from Greater China through the port of Davao, it is clear from the material presented above in section 3.1 that, more generally, the city's direct trade with Greater China is dominated by Chinese companies. This observation – which is in itself already striking– takes on added significance when it is realised that a sizeable proportion of imports is accounted for by fertlizers and other chemicals that are of strategic importance to the city's agricultural economy.

We must also note that marketplaces have long been associated with the city's physical growth. The main foci of this growth were Trading (the original landing

---

* Close to 2000 traders in markets in and around Davao and Manila were interviewed (2002-3) The markets primary source of dry and manufactured goods were wholesalers in the city, Around 350 wholesalers were subsequently surveyed. Surveys of both markets and wholesalers focussed on - among other questions - ethnicity, language, family involvement, origins and source of goods, and frequency of attendance.

place of the Spanish) and its attached market at the junction of Bolton and Magallanes; the market sited at Recto and Uyanguren – the junction between the commercial heart of Davao and the wharf of Santa Ana; the market at Agdao where marine products were landed and where agricultural goods from the north and from the south (via Bankerohan) were brought for sale; the market at Bankerohan, the main point of entry into the city for agricultural goods and other foodstuffs and specialties from the hills, valleys and mountains to the south and west; and Toril – a junction between the coastal plains and the highlands to the west.

It is not difficult to appreciate why for anyone in the street in Davao - and most especially for those who rely on the marketplaces, the wholesalers, and the cheaper shops for everyday goods - 'the Chinese' should have become so much a part of their daily routine that economic success itself has become the prime marker of Chineseness. Viewed *from the street* - and that is the crucial point – there clearly *are* notable concentrations of Chinese interests in wholesaling in everyday goods in local and national economies; and it has been around these concentrations that the city has grown physically. The existence of prominent Chinese entrepreneurs on the national stage, and the strong presence of Chinese in certain activities nationally, reinforced street representations of the Chinese made it easier to extrapolate national dominance of all economic activities from local dominance of certain activities. It also made it easy for anyone on the street to point to this or that building or business and - regardless of complexities of share holdings, ownership, and background - say 'Chinese'. Thus emerged a kind of street representation - that of the Chinese middle-man, dominating the economy and much of daily life.

There are three further dimensions to this pattern which may help reinforce the sense of overwhelming Chinese economic power. The first is historical. To the American businessmen in the early 20th century, the Chinese immigrants were a crucial source of labour; to the civil administrators the immigrants - who were disposed to set up small businesses and thus find themselves in direct competition with the Filipino - were a source of tension. Given the proximity of the Filipino on the street and their presence in what was to the ordinary Filipino the more important area of the economy, it was only a matter of time before the Chinese would be accused of everything from impenetrable bookkeeping to sedition. How could it have been otherwise that their economic power should have been exaggerated? And so, even though it was the Americans, and before them the Spanish, who had by far the largest share of profits from the colony, it was the Chinese who were charged with owning three-quarters of the rice mills, dominating retail trade, and exerting undue influence upon the banking system (Callis, H.G. 1942). Even after the Second World War, and with independence, such was the frame of mind of people and politicians that figures showing the Chinese with, at best, a third of the import-export trade and a quarter of national assets and sales (*Manila Post,* March 11, 1947, cited in Purcell, 1965) were magnified into a Chinese monopoly, sufficient to warrant retail nationalization laws which unintentionally pushed Chinese merchants into wholesaling and manufacturing (Mendoza et al, 1999). One cannot but help wonder if the ripples of this part-colonial and part-nationalist image of the Chinese, and the actions taken under its influence, are still being felt today.

The second dimension is political. The reasons for, and ramifications of, the cynicism with which Philippine political institutions are viewed, are complex. But the influence of business interests on politicians is commonly seen, not only by academics, but also on the street, as being central to an understanding of the country's political weaknesses (Bolongaita, 1995; Hutchcroft, 1998 and 2001; Landé, 2001; Putzel, 1999; Rafael, 2003; Skene, 2003). It was entirely logical, given the economic power of the Chinese, that they should be closely allied with politicians who received a low salary and no state financial support to meet the costs of their election. The involvement of Chinese in banking, in particular, carried with it all kinds of connotations. And since there were indeed Chinese bound up with politicians, then surely, it was reasoned, most Chinese were exerting undue influence? There was a historical aspect to this too. Prior to the Second World War the Chinese in many parts of southeast Asia had been seen as revenue collectors, channeling money from the indigenous peoples through to their rulers; as competitors to local businesses; and, in the case of the Philippines, as raiders of the territory's coffers, drawing off - through piracy, money-lending, the silk trade and tax avoidance - the silver sent from Mexico to pay for the islands' administrative costs (Purcell, 1965; Wickberg, 1962). Finding themselves in such an invidious position, Chinese entrepreneurs had to cultivate relationships in many directions simultaneously. After 1945 the Chinese developed still closer relations with Japanese, American and European firms as well as with the political elites of southeast Asian states - relationships which would become closer still as China opened up. All of this could not but add grist to the mill, strengthening the street representations of the ubiquitous Chinese who, if they dominated economic life, must surely corrupt political life, and vice versa.

The third dimension is the apparent diminution of the Chinese among the larger and more important companies which dominate the Philippines' domestic economy and its trade with China. As we have already noted above, whilst Chinese were certainly present and sometimes influential in various sectors of the economy before and after World War II, they were by no means omnipresent, monopolistic or uniformly wealthy. Indeed, given Chinese involvement in the lower levels of the economy (a presence which had generated so much friction with Filipinos in the past), and the marked cosmopolitan quality of the upper levels of the economy today, we cannot rule out the possibility that the apparent diminution of Chinese may in fact indicate the relative strengthening of Chinese economic significance in a broader range of activities. In other words, Chinese entrepreneurs have managed in more recent times to break out from wholesaling and certain other sectors (and often from the lower levels), and move on outwards and upwards. This break out may have been helped by the creation of a fictitious and crude antitype (the traditional Chinese) against which the younger, more cosmopolitan, modern

Chinese could define themselves. Fashioned from the street representations floating around them, this antitype may have made it easier for those who were Chinese to establish greater empathy, and to highlight their similarities, with the non-Chinese. 'Traditional', then, may be something of a recent invention.

The power of the street representation of the Chinese, buttressed by these various dimensions, is illustrated by three observations. The first is that as we move down the economic hierarchy into the marketplaces, we find that the proportion of Chinese traders operating there is large, perhaps surprisingly so, at around 16%, though only 1% speak Chinese. Yet there is among marketplace traders no general sense of a Chinese presence in this area of the economy. And one can always find instances of individuals of families and individuals who, though they bear Chinese names, are not regarded as being Chinese. Nor is Chinatown easily defined. A closer look at the areas of 'Chinese' wholesalers reveals that less than a quarter of the two-thirds who are Chinese speak Chinese. A substantial proportion (more than two-fifths) are therefore either not Chinese or, even though they are identified as being Chinese, do not speak Chinese. This would suggest a much looser and more fluid sense of identity (Chu, 2002 a and b) and interactions in this 'Chinese' part of the economy in this Chinese part of town. And yet it is not unusual to find examples of establishments who, even though they are neither staffed, owned or managed by Chinese, are nevertheless regarded as Chinese by traders in the markets who buy their goods.

The second observation is that whilst traders selling dry and manufactured goods in the marketplaces are clearly dependent upon Chinatown, there is considerable variation in the level of dependency from one market to the next, and even within the same market during the day and over the seasons. This is so for the simple reason that the balance between dry and manufactured goods on the one hand, and wet or fresh agricultural goods on the other, is always changing. For instance, in Calinan – a small town to the north west of Davao City proper - agricultural goods are brought to the market there each morning from informal, *ad hoc*, bulking-up stations along the roadsides for miles around. But some forty per cent of all traders in that marketplace look to wholesalers in Davao's Chinatown for their supplies of dry and manufactured goods. The marketplace is a point of exchange between countryside and city. Meanwhile, in the large markets of Agdao and Bankerohan in city proper, and in Toril, the level of dependency of *all* traders on Chinatown falls to between twenty and twenty-five per cent; and in the smaller marketplaces – and these tend to feed off the larger ones for supplies of wet and fresh agricultural goods – the level of dependency is even less. An additional complication is that marketplaces (especially the larger ones) may feed off themselves to some extent: marketplace traders will occasionally buy in new stock from other stalls in the same market. There are also within the city small, specialised markets selling cheaper versions of the goods to be found in glossy supermarkets and department stores nearby. And there is in all markets a sizeable proportion of traders who bring in goods over long distances (though usually from within Mindanao).

A third observation, which also demonstrates the power of street representations of the Chinese, is the extent to which Japanese ethnicity may have been almost entirely subsumed by 'Chineseness'. Japanese from Kyushu, Okinawa, and western Honshu first came to the Philippines to help the Americans to construct roads. The Japanese also worked the plantations, and soon proved themselves adept at managing large estates and, despite legislation introduced in 1919 to limit their growing wealth, acquired land. More importantly, they came to dominate commerce and it was they, rather than the Chinese, who controlled retailing and industries such as hemp, fishing and lumber. After World War II, with the decline of the abaca and the apparent disappearance of the Japanese, commerce began to thrive more than ever as new merchants from the north moved in. Although this is explicitly denied by the few remaining Japanese associations in the city, there are in circulation anecdotes which suggest that some Japanese traders, and many more of their descendants, stayed after 1945, but frequently changed their names, adopting Chinese forms where necessary.

It would seem that although street representations of the Chinese and their economic dominance owe something to the details of everyday life and experience, those representations also work to blind us to the complexity of that experience.

(ii) The second strand of our explanation comprises the merchants' and scholars' transformation of these negative street representations into more positive versions. The rise of East and southeast Asia turned the 'Chinese' into one of the most important symbols of the belief that the non-western was just as good as, if not better than, the western at delivering prosperity and the good life. And this was so for good reasons: three of the economies of East and Southeast Asia (excluding mainland China) were populated mainly by Chinese; it was common knowledge that the two which had led the way (Japan and South Korea) had been heavily influenced by Confucianism; and, in most of the remainder, street representations of 'the Chinese' were already well-established. At the same time there were various problems facing entrepreneurs as they attempted to build up their companies part of the solution to which lay in the construction of cultural images (see Dirlik, *op.cit;* Greenhalgh, *op.cit*; Hodder, 1996).

That such images, picked up and elaborated upon by scholars, may also have found their way back to Chinese entrepreneurs, seems entirely likely; as does the possibility that merchants would have taken those scholarly representations, modified them slightly, and fed them back to the scholar. Thus it may have been that a dialectic between entrepreneur and scholar refashioned negative street representations, and re-presented the Chinese, traditional as well as modern, in a kinder light, and with pride.

98

In short, the rise of East and Southeast Asia constituted the context within which entrepreneurs and scholars married both the region's economic success, and the fact of a strong Chinese presence in particular activities in those southeast Asian states where they formed a minority, with the fiction of their general monopolization of domestic and regional economies, to produce a more positive image of the Chinese in which economic success was an enduring and inextricable quality.

(iii) A third strand of an explanation for the inflation of the Chinese economic significance may lie in the very attempt to abstract any group from the wider social context for enumeration, assessment and analysis. The suggestion here is that as we begin to abstract a group from its wider organic context, it becomes easier to conceive of the possibility that the group can be defined and distinguished in absolute terms. The strengthening tendency within the social sciences to treat representations as absolutes, has made such possibilities a matter of probable fact. Consequently there remains the implication that, however fluid and nuanced we might still believe the boundaries of identity to be (see Clifford, 1997), the group and its behaviour, and the behaviour of any one of its members, are to be explained at least in part by the attributes by which they are defined. Thus, as we abstract (from the context) and as we attribute (cultural and structural features), we may find, inexorably, that analysis itself begins to take an active part in the creation of 'the Chinese'.

Scholars appear to have felt comfortable in participating in this creation. Asia was in the ascendancy; and there was growing interest in 'Diaspora' – a term which, by the last quarter of the 20th century,[*] was being applied to every and any group. The fall of the Soviet Union and the metamorphosis of communism in China; the re-emergence of national boundaries almost medieval in their porosity; the re-

---

[*] During the 19th century and through the first half of the 20th century, the word was used to describe, most commonly, to the dispersal of Jewish and black communities

acknowledgment of the importance of the movement of people and things; the broadening range of stimuli to dispersal (while the significance of conflict as one of those stimuli has deepened); and the speed and ease of movement and communication: all this seemed to demand that the study of diasporas should attract far more attention. And out of the mass of publications on diaspora over the last twenty years has emerged the idea of a kind of third nation or community - a community that is neither of its home or destination, kept separate from both by nostalgia, harsh memories, and its own strengthening tradition of stories, literature, stories, arts rituals, practices, and institutions (see, for example, Duany, 2000; Bhatia, S. and Ram, 2001; Bhatia, 2002; Slobin, 2001; Toloyan, 1996; Naficy, 1993). Carried by their somewhat self-conscious *zeitgeist*, it was only natural that scholarship on the overseas Chinese (most especially if the authors themselves were Chinese overseas) should have become part of the literary tradition of a new 'third' community.

3.4 Explanation

There are, then, three strands to our explanation of the inflation of the economic success of the Chinese: long-established and very powerful street representations of the Chinese; the more positive representations of the Chinese which have been crafted by merchants and scholars; and abstraction and attribution.

Early street representations of the Chinese - that of the middleman (*auri sacra fames*) dominating the economy and daily life - constituted the basic knowledge upon which the very idea of turning the economic success of the Chinese into a matter for analysis was cast. Thus was attention and energy centred upon why the Chinese were pre-eminent and not whether this was so. The next step was to enumerate and assess and, therefore, to abstract. The more cleanly it was abstracted, and the more closely it was defined, the harder the concept of the Chinese became, such that it was possible to conclude that the Chinese could be explained at least partly by the criteria which defined them. With the rise Hong

Kong, Singapore, Taiwan, China, and much of the rest of East and Southeast Asia, merchant and scholar fashioned more positive images of 'the Chinese' in which an elemental and defining quality was economic success.

The cultural-structural representations which emerged in this way, were also strongly influenced (as we argued in section 2 above) by the scholars' own attitudes towards social relationships. Imbued with the affect, scholars desired to remove from their representations of the Chinese what they saw as the slur of manipulation: since the Chinese merchants' behaviour was shaped by culture and structure, instrumentalism added very little to explanations of their economic success. The details of these representations, bolstered by their treatment as absolute, merged with the hardening concept of 'the Chinese' that had arisen in the wake of attempts to enumerate, assess, and abstract. There was now little doubt: the Chinese *are* successful; they *are* shaped more by culture and structure than by calculation; they *are*, historically, culturally, and instinctively, adept at business. And the assumption that where successful businesses were to be found, there would be Chinese, and vice versa, was just a matter of course. Viewed through this glass, and now so keenly sensitized to the presence of the Chinese, it was not surprising that analysis began to lose sight of those who were not Chinese, and of the complexity and significance of interactions among Chinese and non-Chinese. Thus was the economic significance of the Chinese inflated.

This ambiguity of attitude might, perhaps, reflect a broader counter-shift in attitude within scholarship away from the affective. The treatment of scholarly representations of the Chinese as absolute has undoubtedly helped to transmute 'the Chinese' into politically useful material. Within academe, these cultural-structural representations are in danger of being twisted into a stifling orthodoxy. Meanwhile, on the street, they take on an importance that extends beyond the professional interests of academics in Europe, America, or Asia. The certainty that the pre-eminence of the Chinese within the domestic economy is to be explained in large part by their Chineseness, and by regional or global structures, is only likely to separate out for adulation or recrimination those who are seen, or who feel themselves, to be Chinese. Filipinos, meantime, are left to ponder the implication that their comparative lack of success is to be explained both by those traits (presumably their culture and their historical genesis) which define them as being Filipino and, consequently, by their inability to take full advantage of global and regional structures. It also follows quite logically that Chinese influence is likely to play some part in explaining the achievements of those Filipinos who are successful. The particular quality of the Filipino and Chinese cultures, some have argued, combined with complex historical events, have strengthened the economic power of the culturally pure Chinese, and brought about creolization of such a scale and intensity that mestizos (the offspring of Chinese and Filipino unions) 'were not really absorbed into indigenous society..(but)... merged with it to form modern Filipino society' (Skinner, 1996, p.90). Many better-off Filipinos are, despite their Filipino names, Chinese or of Chinese descent and, it has been suggested (*ibid.*), exhibit aspects of Chinese and mestizo culture even today.

It is true that we may look with more favour upon the political meaning of the scholars' cultural-structural representations. We may, perhaps, see there an attempt to manage what is believed to be the subsumation of the local, non-western, identities (read culture) by what are regarded to all intents and purposes as western or western-style institutions, practices, values, and behaviour (read international, global, economic, political and social structures). One message carried by the cultural-structural accommodation is that it is possible to retain one's local identity and, however slightly, to re-shape those western structures in one's own image. Another is that the inevitable transformation of local cultures into western-style liberal market democracies can be made a little less painful if conducted under the illusion that the integrity of local cultures can be preserved. Still another message is that both global-western structures and local cultures must adapt to, and adopt, something of the other such that both are transposed into rather different forms.

Yet whilst there may be those who feel that the cultural-structural accommodation constitutes a valuable rationalisation of a political project, we must ask ourselves whether the kinds of subtle qualifications and adjustments in emphasis which have appeared within the cultural-structural accommodation in response to practice (see chapter 1), will percolate out on to the street in the Philippines or elsewhere in southeast Asia? Can the cultural-structural accommodation effectively manage what it sees to be the tension between the local and global-western? Or will it only exacerbate or, by setting up this self-conscious dichotomy, even generate such tensions? Will, for instance, the suggestion that western economic and political structures helped to create today's Chinese culture only fuel a determination to prove that Chinese culture is very much more than a western creation? Is it not likely that attempts within and outside academe to strengthen Chineseness and to give vigorous expression to it, will only prompt similar movements by non-Chinese? Is it possible for such creations to avoid generating friction, however well intentioned and laced with qualification they may be? And is not the belief that such tensions may be defused by the transformation of local cultures into cosmopolitan and liberal market democracies, only likely to prompt a reaction against such transformations?

4.0 Conclusions

We have argued that estimates of Chinese economic significance in Southeast Asia have been inflated. So marked were these estimates, that it has often seemed as if economic success itself defined an individual as being Chinese. This inflation owes much to long-standing (and usually negative) street representations of the Chinese; to the more positive street and scholarly representations of the Chinese which emerged with the growth of the economies of East and Southeast Asia; and to the simple acts of defining the Chinese, and of calculating their numbers and material worth.

There are, it should be said, questions surrounding our more modest assessment of Chinese economic strength, and these need further consideration however brief. To begin with, doubts must attend the figures and information gathered on ownership and investments. The extent of smuggling and tax evasion is, almost by definition, unknown; and this, together with shortages of staff in government agencies in the Philippines, must cast doubt on the accuracy of data. And though we do have a few earlier studies to provide us with a longer view (see, for example, Palanca, 1997), investments and ownership change constantly. Furthermore we have, in this book, considered only domestic sales and merchandise trade with China, and we have done so over a short period. Nor has any direct attempt been made to estimate the scale of investment between the two countries.

It might also be suggested that the more modest estimates provided above indicate an absolute but recent decline in the wake of the 1997 crisis and increasing competition with foreign capital. It is in response to these considerations that Chinese entrepreneurs have been adopting more fluid, cosmopolitan identities. Or it might be that the apparent decline is only relative. After all, even with the figures provided here, there is little doubt that the economic significance of the Chinese in the Philippines is greater than the figure commonly given for the proportion of the Chinese in the population as a whole. And there is no doubt that the value and volume of China's trade with the outside world, the value of streams of investment in and out of China, and the number of countries participating in this trade, have been increasing very quickly and have done so particularly in the run-up to, and since, China's membership of the WTO. Relative to these increases, the interests of the overseas Chinese were bound to shrink. That this is so may be reflected in an apparent reversal in the balance of interests nationally among Chinese, Filipino, and Internationals, when compared with the balance found in Davao; and in what appear to be falls in the proportions of companies (among the strongest 100 nationally) that are exclusively Chinese or Filipino from around 5% and 13% respectively in the mid 1990s to less than 5% each today.

104

A more fundamental question is whether or not the definitions of Chinese and Filipino adopted in this book have taken into account the complexity and, perhaps, the peculiarity of circumstances in the Philippines? Could it that the Chinese have been assimilated to an unusual degree at least partly under pressure from Filipinization policies in the years after independence? Or should we look again at Skinner's (*op. cit.*) suggestion that modern Filipino society arose out of the fusion of mestizo and indigenous societies? Has creolization indeed been of such scale and intensity that many better-off Filipinos, despite their Filipino names, are of Chinese descent and, even though they may not be aware of this, exhibit aspects of Chinese and mestizo culture and behaviour? Might we not conclude, therefore, that Chinese economic influence is in fact even stronger than we think, but appears less so, precisely because of Filipino society's elemental Chineseness? Because it is everywhere, we see little of it. A reliance on name or indeed self-identity cannot but deflate the significance of the Chinese.

Another possible reason why the Chinese are less significant than might have been expected, is that traditional Chinese business operations and traditional Chineseness have given way to broader, even universal, techniques and practices. A variation on this theme is that Chineseness has merged with the practices of a homogenised and globalised world to create a new form of Chineseness whose qualities, in Wang Gungwu's view, include neither language nor traditional values (let alone name). If so, then again the criteria adopted in this book could not but deflate the economic significance of the Chinese.

Clearly, then, there is a need for a more detailed consideration of a greater range of data over a longer period and for more of the Philippines' trade partners. In particular, a detailed examination of records (as far back as they go) of imports, exports, and investments is necessary if we are to determine whether or not the role of the Chinese in the Philippines' trade with China was exaggerated (as still appears to be the case in Davao) by smaller and narrower trade flows and weaker economies in earlier years. If the true extent of the economic influence of Chinese is disguised by assimilation and new forms of Chineseness, then there is also a pressing need for detailed comparative analyses of changing perceptions of self and others among Chinese, non-Chinese immigrants and Filipinos, and for comparative analyses of the past and present institutions and practices of these and other groups (such as Japanese, Koreans, and Indians). And accompanying all of this, is the need to explore fundamental questions about the purpose and possibility of defining and assessing the economic power of specific groups.

Yet the problems referred to above may cut both ways. While forcing us to acknowledge the need for more extensive work, they also bolster the explanation outlined above (section 3.4) in a number of respects. With regard to the accuracy of data, we cannot but note that doubts attend all such data; and that, whilst the source of many of figures for the dominance of the Chinese is not always known, we have in this book relied mainly upon raw data. The fluidity of investments, ownership, and trade flows, must also prompt questions about the ease with which Chinese economic power is declared and figures are provided. Moreover, although we cannot rule out the possibility that the Chinese figure more strongly in trade with Hong Kong and Taiwan (the Philippines' more important trade partners) or with the US and Japan (the country's most important trade partners by far), we would expect nevertheless that the significance of Overseas Chinese in trade with the Chinese mainland would be marked and directed more towards south and southeast China. This is especially so given Pye's (1995) view that economic imperatives are subordinate to *guanxi* in the mind of the Chinese merchant.

The suggestion that there has been an absolute decline in the significance of Chinese business probably holds true for a very specific period immediately before and after 1997. But it would seem unlikely that Chinese businesses would have suffered more than any others; and if we take the longer view, and in the absence of a clear benchmark, it is impossible to be sure that the more modest figures presented above are part of any such decline. Furthermore, whilst it may indeed be a response to certain problems, growing cosmopolitanism is nevertheless difficult to dissociate from an expansion of opportunities and a strengthening of the economic significance of Chinese and other groups. The same point can be made in reply to the suggestion that our comparatively modest estimates indicate a relative decline. It should also be noted in response to this question of relative decline that, whilst the absolute value of trade with China has increased, there are indications that opportunities for relative changes have been limited. For instance, the absolute value of exports to China quadrupled and the value of imports from China have increased more than five-fold since the early 1990s; but exports to China as a share of the Philippines' total exports have remained below 3% (compared with the 16% share of the Philippines' exports absorbed by Japan); while imports from China as a share of the Philippines' total imports have remained at a little over 3% (compared with the figure of 21% for the value of imports from Japan as a share of the value of the Philippines' total imports). If it is assumed that Chinese businesses have an advantage in trade with China (or, at least, that they do not have a disadvantage), and given there has been no marked shift in trade away from China, then it would seem unlikely that Internationals and Filipinos would have increased their share relative to Chinese businesses.

The argument that the assimilation of the Chinese to an unusual degree may have led to an underestimation of their economic influence is certainly plausible. But if this is not an argument made to emphasise the very fair comment that there is indeed little meaning in attempts to identify, enumerate, and assess, then it is an argument that would appear to make all kinds of assumptions about the human condition, culture, biological inheritance, socialisation, and history. It implies, for example, that being Chinese is not a matter of preference (Wong, 1999), and that individuals are Chinese even if they do not think of themselves as such. These kinds of assumptions need to be made explicit and examined carefully, for they bring us face to face with the question of abstraction and attribution. Are we not also bound to ask why assimilation should occur in only one direction? If non-Chinese have borrowed much from the Chinese, then should they not also be classified as 'assimilated Chinese'?

Similarly the argument that the influence of the Chinese is disguised by fusion such that a new kind of Chinese has emerged from the global and traditional is no less plausible. Once again, however, if this is not a way of saying that Chinese in the Philippines, and in Southeast Asia more generally, have become more cosmopolitan, and that 'traditional' may have been a recent invention, then it leaves itself with a number of problems. The idea of melding seems merely to transpose traditional Chineseness. We are also left with the possibility that unless transposition is uniform and agreed upon (and it is clear from the different views of 'Chineseness' to be found on the street and among Chinese academics that this is not the case), then are we not saying that it is indeed impossible to realise any meaningful assessment of the economic significance of 'the Chinese'? On the other hand, if the 'traditional' is not being transposed, then, as suggested earlier, must not those non-Chinese who have assimilated certain 'Chinese' ways also be defined as the new kind of Chinese just as surely as those 'traditional Chinese' who have assimilated formerly non-Chinese practices, techniques, values, and patterns of behaviour? We can take this line of argument even further, and suggest that we are all, in one way or another, the product of hybridization. (For we must in our everyday lives, and generation by generation, accommodate and compromise if we are to live with each other). In this view, how is it possible to define 'the Chinese' and what is the purpose and value of doing so?

108

TABLE 1					

TABLE 1
Companies exporting from China through Davao, 2000-2002/3:
significance and ethnicity

I	II	III	IV	V			
1	28%	CF	China (Hebei)	1			
2	21%	F*i* 1554	HK	2 __F__ (F1533)			
3	15%	CF2888	Taiwan	3 = 32IMP			
			China (Tianjin)				
4	12%	Cf 3925	Taiwan	4 = 12IMP			
			HK				
			China (Sichuan)				
5	6%	F1965	HK	5			
6	5%	C5699	HK	6 = 24IMP			
7	3%	FC	China	7			
			(Shanghai, Hebei)				
8	>2%	C*F*	HK	8			
9	>2%	F	China (Liaoning)	9			
10	>1%	Ic	China ((Hebei)	10			
			Taiwan				
11	"	If	China (Shandong)	11 =29IMP			
12	"	F	HK	12			
13	"	F	HK	13			
14	"	C**F**	China	14 ___(FC)			
15	"	C2576	Taiwan	15			
16	"	C	Taiwan	16			
17	"	C*C*(T)*F*	Taiwan	17			
18	"	Ifc	HK	18 ____(If79, Set 2)			
19	"	C	China (Shandong)	19			
20	"	C	HK	20			
21	"	F	HK	21			
22	"	F	HK	22			
23	"	C5057	HK	23 =37IMP			
24	"	C*F*	HK	24			
25	"	F1532	HK	25 _4IMP	26IMP		45IMP
26	"	F192	HK	26			

Source: various files (raw data entries) Bureau of Customs, Davao City

TABLE 2

Companies importing from China through Davao, 2000-2002/3:
significance and ethnicity

I	II	III	IV	V
1	40%	C 1299	China (Tianjin)	1 C____C
2	7%	C 1867	HK	2 C4626
3	5%	F 387	Taiwan	3_ _F___F____F____F____F1659
4	5%	F 1079	HK/ Taiwan	4_F(26E)_F_ F__F__F_(CFI 34, Set 1)
5	3%	Cf 2920	Taiwan	5
6	3%	F	Taiwan	6
7	3%	F	HK	7
8	2.5%	Ifc 59	HK/Taiwan/ China	8- -(CFI 34, Set 1)
9	2%	FC	China	9
10	1.6%	F=C1392	Taiwan	10
11	1.3%	C	HK China (Zhejiang) Taiwan	11
12	1.2%	Cf 3925	HK/Taiwan	12 Cf
13	>1%	FIc 92	HK	13 (F 488, Set 1; FI 1146 & Ifc212, Set 2)
14	"	C	China (Shandong) Taiwan	14_ C____C
15	"	I 194	HK/China	15
16	"	C90	China	16_ (C 195, C 122, Cfi 93, Set 2)
17	"	C 4926	China (Shandong)	17
18	"	Cf	China	18
19	"	F	Taiwan/China	19
20	"	F 5983	China (Henan)	20
21	"	Cf	Taiwan	21
22	"	FI	HK	22_(Fc[Hh], F450. Set 2)
23	"	Cf	Taiwan	23

Source: various files (raw data entries) Bureau of Customs, Davao City

TABLE 2 (continued)
*Companies importing from China through Davao, 2000-2002/3:
significance and ethnicity*

24	"	C 5699	HK	24____CF (8E)			
25	"	CF	HK	25____C			
26	"	F1904	HK	26			
27	"	F	China (Shandong) HK	27____ F4637____F____F5155			
28	"	F	Taiwan	28			
29	"	If	China (Shandong)	29			
30	"	C 6066	Taiwan	30			
31	"	CF	China (Shandong)	31___ CF			
32	"	CF 2888	Taiwan	32 (also 3E)			
33	"	Cf	China (Shenzhen)	33__ _C			
34	"	C 4645	China (Jiangsu)	34			
35	"	C	Taiwan	35			
36	"	Fc	HK	36			
37	"	C 5057	Taiwan	37__ _C			
38	"	FC	China (Shanghai)	38			
39	"	F 179	HK China (Fujian)	39___ F 487…(Set 1)			
40	"	FC	Taiwan	40			
41	"	IF 1731	Taiwan	41			
42	"	F	HK	42			
43	"	FC	Taiwan	43___ _Fc			
44	"	CF	Taiwan	44__ C___C			
45	"	F 1532	HK	45			
46	"	Ifc	China (Tianjin)	46___ _Ic204 (Set 2)			
47	"	F 3587	Taiwan	47			

Source: various files (raw data entries) Bureau of Customs, Davao City

Key to Table 1	

Column I — Company ranking by export value through port of Davao (to Greater China 2000-2002/3)

2 — Company also ranked among top exporters nationally (see figures 1-3)

X
Y — Same individuals or individuals or companies with shares in both companies X and Y

Column II — Company's percentage share of total export value

Column III — Letters refer to ethnicity of owners (see key to figures 1-3). Numbers refer to national rankings (by domestic sales)

Column IV — Origin of goods

Column V — Other companies in which owners also have a significant stake (and are usually ranked among top 10 shareholders). 'Sets' refer to the sets shown in figures 1-3

6=24IMP — Company ranked 6 is also ranked 24 in table 2

41IMP — Company ranked 41 in table 2

Key to Table 2	
Column I	Company ranking by import value through port of Davao (from Greater China 2000-2002/3)
X ⎤ Y ⎦	Same individuals or individuals or companies with shares in both companies X and Y
Column II	Company's percentage share of total import value
Column III	Letters refer to ethnicity of owners (see key to figures 1-3). Numbers refer to national rankings by domestic sales)
Column IV	Origin of goods
Column V	Other companies in which owners also have a significant stake (and are usually ranked among 10 shareholders). 'Sets' refer to the sets shown in figures 1-3

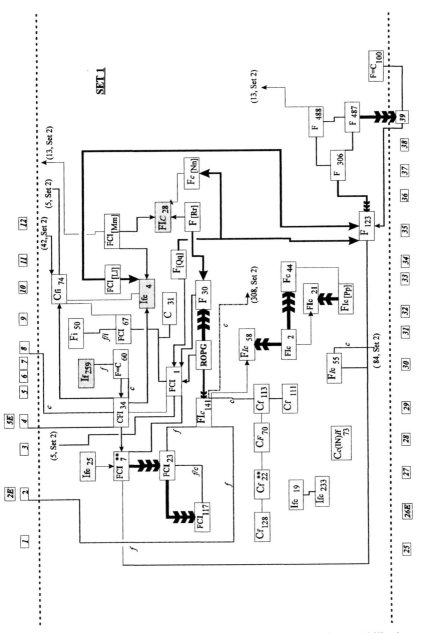

Figure 1. Networks of Investment among Selected Companies in the Philippines: Set 1. *Source: see keys to figures 1-3.*

114

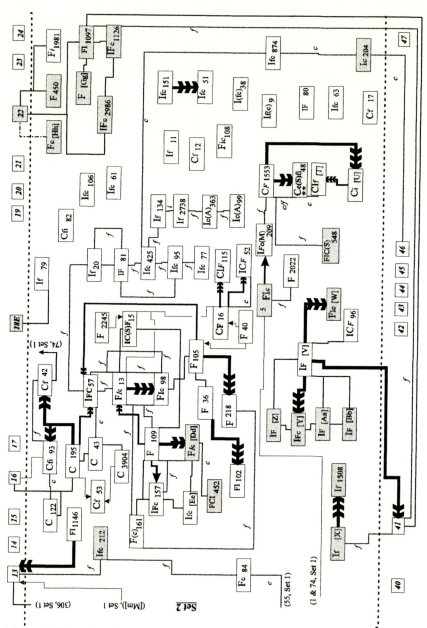

Figure 2. Networks of Investment among Selected Companies in the Philippines: Set 2. *Source: see keys to figures 1-3.*

115

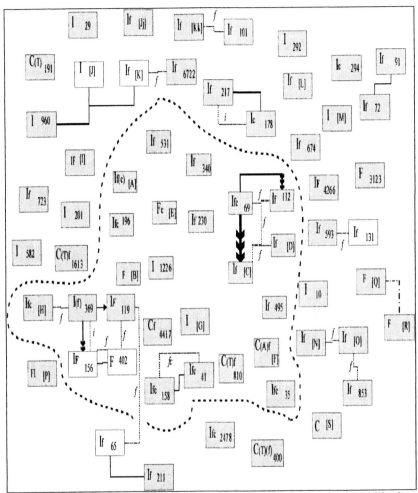

Figure 3. Networks of Investment among Selected Companies in the Philippines:
Set 3. *Source: see keys to figures 1-3.*

| 29 | Company's ranking among strongest 7000 national companies (as measured by domestic sales) |

| 29 | Company also ranked among top exporters (to China) |

29** Company also ranked among top 23 importers from China

| 29 | Company as ranked in Table 2 |

| 29E | Company as ranked in Table 1 |

| [Aa] | Company not ranked among top 7000. Companies outside top 120 are included if key exporter; or if linked to top 120 or key exporter through investments; or if same individual or individuals with kinship ties sit on boards of both companies. |

| X ——➤➤➤ Y | Company X with more than 80% share ownership of company Y |

——➤➤   with more than 63% ownership

———➤➤➤   with more than 33% share ownership

——➤➤   with more than 20% ownership

——➤   with less than 20% but more than 10%

——➤   with less than 10% but more than 1%

——➤   with less than 1%

———   Same individual or company holds shares in - and is usually ranked among top 20 shareholders in - both companies X and Y

———f———   Same individual or individuals (f[Filipino], c [Chinese], i [International]) holds directorships or board memberships in both companies)

-----------   Encloses the top 23 exporters who are not linked through investment or board membership to companies shown in Sets 1 and 2.

Key to Figures 1 - 3

I	'International'
C	'Chinese
F	'Filipino
I=F	Equal share ownership
IF	Latter party hold more than 33% of shares
IF	Latter party hold more than 20% shares
I*F*	Latter party holds more that 10% shares
If	Latter party's holdings are nominal (less than 10%, but in most instances less than a 1% stake associated with board membership)
I(f)	Latter party is company officer, but is not board members and holds no shares
FCI	Roughly equal shares, but largest holdings ranked left to right
FC*I*	Last party holds more than 10%, second party holds more than 20%
C[A]	Chinese (American nationality)
C[T]	Chinese (Taiwanese nationality)
C[S]	Chinese (Singaporean nationality)
C[IN]	Chinese (Indonesian nationality)
ROPG	Philippine government

Key to Figures 1 – 3 continued
Sources: Compiled from raw data from: Bureau of Customs (2000-2002/3), Davao and Manila; Department of Trade and Industry, Davao and Manila; Securities and Exchange Commission [SEC] (2002/3); Business Bureau, City Governments of Davao, Manila and Makati. Rankings provided in SEC (2003).

Chapter 4
Business Organisation

1.0 Introduction

In the previous chapter we began to tease out the play of relationships, attitudes, and representation, that comprise particular instances of trade and business in the Philippines. As we did so we also began to reformulate our representations of that play. We argued that scholarly analyses, treated as absolutes and fused with street representations, have been drawn into practice, stoking hostility towards the Chinese, and weakening the confidence of Filipinos in their own representations of self, society, and world.

Scholarships' cultural-structural representations have also had other more positive, if subtle, effects. The doubts we raised about the accuracy of estimates of Chinese economic significance are sympathetic to the more circumspect interpretations and estimates noted in chapter 1 (section 2), though it suggests that more than just a kind of pernicious mischievousness accounts for the inflation of Chinese economic power. It is also sympathetic to the more broad-brushed, institutional view of Chinese capitalism (the Chinese as 'go-between') in Southeast Asia to which we alluded in chapter 3. Indeed, if we accept our more restrained estimates of Chinese economic power and set the Chinese as more modest players within a complex of relationships and interactions between merchant and state, then we are left with an interesting possibility: that Chinese businesses have not so much dominated or driven economies, as acted as catalysts. In common with Japanese, Koreans, Indians and other groups, they at once helped to create a competitive and cosmopolitan atmosphere, and to show that one did not have to be western to run a business and to do it well. The inflation of Chinese economic power worked to enhance the catalytic effect of representations of the Chinese beyond their true economic importance.

However, perhaps the most important effect of the cultural-structural representations fashioned by scholarship, has been to obscure the more complex dimensions of particular instances of trade and business. These representations, when bound into analysis, have worked this effect in a number of ways.

(i) First, representations of the Chinese - at the heart of which now lies the quality of economic success - act to narrow interests. We noted earlier that some 16% of traders in the marketplaces and on the streets of Davao are Chinese - a proportion smaller than that found among wholesalers, but larger than that found within the upper echelons of the national economy. Yet there are few, if any, studies that focus on, and explain, the meaning of those Chinese who are either unsuccessful or less successful.

(ii) Second, representations of the Chinese have tended to colour, or prefigure, the interpretation of particular instances. Features which match or embroider our initial representations are selected from the particular, while very similar features present in the behaviour and organisation of those who are not Chinese are ignored. The product is an ideal or typical Chinese company. Deyo (1983), for example, argues that a Chinese company can be identified by virtue of certain managerial practices such as centralised decision-making, an emphasis on personal touches that enhance trust and control, and the importance attached to loyalty as a criterion in the selection, recruitment, and promotion of personnel. Lim (1983), too, presents a succinct description of those characteristics which are often taken to constitute the typical Chinese company: it is usually owned by a family and exhibits a mix of wage-labour and family-labour; its scale of operation is small and localised geographically; and it is in a commercial sector of the economy (such as money-lending, import-export, and rural-urban retailing) which is dominated by a particular ethnic (dialect) group. Even if the company grows into a large, modern, corporate enterprise and is transformed into a joint-stock company, control and ownership still tend to rest with a single family or group of families related by blood, marriage, clan, or dialect; and business activities remain concentrated in the traditional, primary, and tertiary sectors of the economy (Lim, 1983, p.245). Other characteristics may be added: networks extend outwards from the family, permeating the company and reaching beyond it; the level of specialisation is low, job specifications are not detailed, there are few specialised departments, and individuals are responsible for a wide range of different activities; the style of leadership is authoritarian; goals are decided upon in much secrecy; lines of business are diverse; and, because of family tensions and sibling rivalry, the typical Chinese company rarely lasts for more than three generations. Wong (1988 a, 1985) builds this last characteristic into a model of the Chinese company. Wong argues that the concept of familism has different layers or meanings: paternalism (in which case the family serves as a model for the administration of personnel within the company); nepotism; and ownership - the family enterprise. Three development phases are then identified: the emergent phase which is characterised by a partnership that is inherently unstable; a period of centralisation and vigorous growth during which the majority of shares come under the ownership of a single entrepreneur, and there is an intense urge to enlarge the family; and a segmented phase which describes the transfer of responsibility for the company to a younger leader who must now earn the respect that his new position demands if he is to be successful. As friction builds up among competing brothers, this third phase is followed by the disintegration of the company. Wong further suggests that in Hong Kong the Chinese company's distinguishing features - a fluid economic hierarchy, a centrifugal force encouraged by the desire of family and employees to set up on their own enterprise, and a tendency to make decisions centrally - all stem from 'entrepreneurial familism' (the term describes the family as an impetus, and a support, for innovation and the necessary risks associated with innovation) which, in turn, derives from China's bureaucratic past.

(iii) Cultural-structural representations of the Chinese also work to obscure the complex dimensions of particular instances by marginalising both the significance of deviations and the meaning of our apparently unrelenting need for categorisation, treating both as the mere by-products of academic practice. It was often acknowledged that there were in the field some departures from what our representation had led us to expect. Inevitably, the more limited our representations of the Chinese were in their dimensions, the more categories we would need to produce. But unless it was accepted that our representations - with their increasingly refined categories - did indeed reflect a general truth, then it would be impossible to achieve any kind of meaningful or practical analysis of the Chinese. As a consequence there has been a growing plethora of kinds of Chinese from 'traditional' to 'modern' and 'hybridized'. In chapter 1 we referred briefly to the various grades or types of Chinese identified by Wang, G.W (*op.cit.*). And there are many others. Lau (1978, 1982) argues that in Hong Kong the family has become increasingly utilitarian as it moves away from its traditional form. The traditional family is based upon a clear set of values, ethics, and ascriptive relationships, which clearly prescribe the roles, status, behaviour, and duties of individuals. It is an exclusive group with a corporate personality which is 'not artificially constructed to serve some limited purposes' (p.23). The traditional family reflects a philosophy of life which merges the individual with the family, and the family with society. The utilitarian family, on the other hand, is 'the normative order for the regulation of the operation of a group deliberately organised for some specific purposes' (p.34). A very similar line of thought has been pursued by Murphey (1977) and King (1987) who suggest that new kinds of Chinese, pragmatic and rational in their use of traditional Confucian values, have arisen in commercial and cosmopolitan Southeast Asia.

Mackie (1992), too, leans more towards the view that the characteristics which seem to explain the initial success of the Chinese 'do not necessarily fit so well in explanations of why some of them have been able to make the transition to much riskier levels of large-scale enterprise, although thousands more have not. In trying to explain these processes we need to treat them as quite distinct analytical issues' (p.59). Following Myers, Mackie suggests that '...the latter-day Chinese who are willing and able to operate large-scale enterprises along modern lines, relying less than previously on personal connections as a basis for trust in their business dealings, should be regarded as in many respects a *quite different kind of Chinese* from their predecessors. They are *more capable of transcending the constraints imposed by the traditional values and cultural predisposition* that made it difficult to trust strangers. In many cases, the impact of better education, exposure to the modern world and the processes of acculturation to Southeast Asian values, have eroded the influence of traditional Chinese values' (p.59, italics added). In a later article, Hicks and Mackie (1994) appear to increase the differences between the 'new' and the 'traditional' Chinese still further: today's Overseas Chinese, they observe, are more like the indigenes than Chinese.

(iv) Fourth, scholarly representations of the Chinese provided merchants with material that could be fed back to scholarship, masking the true complexity of particular instances. The expression of views and explanations by Chinese, Filipino, and other merchants - and by politicians and bureaucrats - kind enough to talk to this writer during the preparation of this book, often seemed to bear a strong resemblance to those commonly found in the academic and journalistic literature. And on more than one occasion, it was made quite explicit that literature had indeed been recycled. The motivation is endearing: politeness, and a desire by men and women who are very busy, to produce what they believe the academic will take to be thoughtful answers. That such dialectics have long been extant and vigorous is recognised implicitly in the work of various writers (Greenhalgh, *op.cit.;* Dirlik, *op.cit.*).

In this chapter it is argued that the dis-aggregation and reformulation of particular instances in the practice and organisation of trade and business in the Philippines and China, reveal striking complexities and deviations, regardless of kinship, ethnicity, and geography. This, it is suggested, reflects the play of our commonalities - our representations, and our attitudes towards, and practice of, social relationships. Terms such as 'traditional', 'modern, 'convergent', and 'hybrid', as well as those of 'ethnicity', 'culture', and 'structure', capture only limited and static dimensions of that play.

2.0 Distancing, authoritarianism, professionalisation, and the affect

The working of the company, the drive for profit, and the need to instill direction and discipline upon relatives, friends, and employees, will inevitably confront expectations associated with social relationships irrespective of whether our attitudes towards those relationships are strongly personal or affective. Distancing social relationships provides space for those who make up the company to behave, and to be treated, in ways that outside the company appear to be offensive. Thus may the company avoid, or at least mitigate, the tensions, the loss of focus, and the collapse of coordinated and predictable behaviour, that would otherwise occur.

2.1 Authoritarianism

The most obvious, if somewhat crude, expression of distancing is the exercise of authoritarianism and centralised control. The wishes of the leader - his own representations of the world - take on an absolute quality, such that relationships between superiors and subordinates appear to be set aside or obliterated. Authority is often vested in the older male; and it is he who makes the most important decisions, most especially those concerning supplies and markets, imports and exports. It is a quality characteristic of the smaller companies (whether corporations of sole-ownerships), especially in those where the leader has few relatives about him. Take the case of 11 If (table 1): the company - which exports semi-finished and finished goods to Japan, Europe, the US and, to a lesser extent,

China - is owned by a Korean.* He set up the business in the early 1980s, and he has lived in Davao for much of the time ever since. It is managed predominantly by Filipinos: their responsibilities are carefully defined and limited to technical matters (concerning the manufacture of goods), and they are expected, and they expect, to do what they are told. A similarly prescriptive approach is to be found in any number of wholesale companies. Thus in 31 CF (table 2), a hardware company, even the lowliest parts manager (a Filipino) must refer most decisions - including the order for replacement stock, and any substantial sales - to the owners. In 14 C (table 2), too, information on suppliers and markets, and decisions on purchases and sales, is strongly centred in the father of this family business.

But this degree of centralisation and authoritarianism is not peculiar to smaller organisations, nor to those thought to be soaked in the Confucian tradition. Rule by fiat is sometimes practiced in the larger companies. In 18 If (table 2) – many of whose managers in Davao are from Central America - there are times when matters of safety or money demand quick decisions. On these occasions, fast and instinctive decisions are needed far more than carefully weighed and formulated judgments.

Nor does authority lie exclusively in the hands of men. Audrey, a Filipina, started her first business in 1937 after marrying the suitor with the largest wage packet and thereby escaping an unhappy stepfamily. She bought an army-surplus jeep, renovated it and sold it in Manila for a profit which she then used to buy others. She continued with this circuit even during the war until she had built up her own fleet of sixty vehicles. After the war she diversified into gasoline stations. The profit margins from the transport business were small, but there were few competitors and her turnover was large. Always diversifying as competition intensified, and always maintaining a high turnover, she created a business empire

---

* He has a share of more than 90%

which eventually came to revolve around a real estate company. She and her husband had an equal part of the majority of shares in the company: the remainder were divided equally among their children. Yet she alone made all the decisions concerning this core asset. Her remaining gasoline station was handed to one of her son, James, and his wife Betilda, who together also owned and managed a construction company.

Audrey would always retain a strong influence over their affairs, and those of her other children and grandchildren. She had educated them, provided them with introductions into professional institutions at the start of their career, or set them up in their own private practices; she established extensive lines of credit (which she had underwritten) for those of her offspring who had ventured into business; she funded their political ambitions; and she integrated them into her business empire. And if her children and their families did not live in the houses she built for them one next to the other on strips of land which she owned, then they would live with their parents in a huge, chalet-style mansion.

The monopoly of power she had over her core assets, the dependency which she fostered, the networks of relationships she drew upon herself, and, through these networks, the influence she wielded over her family's various business, professional, and political interests, were deliberately engineered largely in order to limit family squabbles which might otherwise spill over into the core of the family's trading interests. There was, after all, much to play for. Audrey's lands and properties were abundant, she and her husband were old, and her children and grandchildren were many. On Sundays she would hold court, sitting on a large, heavy, ornate mahogany throne, her legs resting on a foot-stool; and as her grand-children and great-grand children gambled about her, she would dispense her favours, and shower them all with crisp bank-notes from a large bag hung over her wrist.

With the death of her husband, Audrey acted with prescience, judgment and a certain unselfishness, to ensure that her empire would not be the cause of her family's disintegration. She sold the smaller businesses, much of her land, and even her grand mansion. The money she divided evenly among her children and grandchildren. The core of the empire, the real estate company, would be left intact. Each of her children was given equal shares in it, and the presidency would be rotated among them. However, Maria, one of her daughters, was made the company's permanent treasurer, and no cheque could be spent without her agreement and her signature. A smaller, though still spacious, bungalow was bought into which she moved with Maria who ministered to her. Only then did she allow herself to lose her grip on the world. There would no more Sunday gatherings now, and few of her children would visit her. When Audrey died, Maria found herself both the controller and figurehead.

A similar concentration of authority in a woman is also to be found among the smaller companies. Returning once again to Davao's Chinatown, we find a store – registered as a corporation – whose manager and largest shareholder is Fe. She bought herself into the business with a low-interest loan from the owner (a Chinese woman) of another nearby store selling bicycles, and for whom she had worked for five years as a sales girl. Before that, she had worked as a trader on the streets and in the marketplaces. Fe is a Filipina; she is in complete command of the store; and as far as she knows, she has no Chinese ancestry. Her partner in the business, also a Filipina, stays in Manila where she scouts around for goods, buying mostly from wholesale and retail markets in Divisoria and Bacloran. Fe has also dispatched her brother to General Santos where he buys in supplies for the store, and sells its goods. In both Davao and General Santos the company sells to small traders from the local marketplaces, and to the larger supermarkets, department stores, and other retailers. Fe's nephew works as her driver, and her niece handles the company's accounts. The rest of her staff, who work as sales girls on the shop floor, were hired through an agency.

128

2.2 Rules and roles: professionalisation

The practice and organisation of trade and business organisation on the ground is made still more complex by the presence of more subtle forms of distancing that exist alongside, and temper, authoritarianism. These include more clearly defined roles within the company among owners, managers, and employees; and the emergence of clear rules, regulations, conventions, and procedures, which govern behaviour within the company and the company's external dealings. Put another way, shared representations of the company and its purpose, and the place of individual members within that whole, are substituted for centralised and authoritarian control. These shared representations constitute a framework for coordinated practice. An explanation for this shift in the form of distancing from authoritarianism to professionalism comes in three parts.

Practical advantage

Practical advantage accounts in part for the move towards the professional. Whilst authoritarianism may be the most obvious and immediately effective means of bringing direction, purpose, and coordination, it also makes the company fragile. This is so for a number of reasons.

(i) Authoritarianism is clearly unable to handle the demand for increasingly complex decisions. Take the instance of 1C (table 2) – a company owned by a first generation migrant from China (Fujian). In addition to a small, permanent staff (around twenty in number), three of the owner's relatives work in key positions: his nephew is comptroller; his brother (the company's vice-president) is in charge of port operations; and his wife, who administers both the permanent staff and the hundreds of piece-time workers and drivers, exercises considerable authority over pay-rolls, contracts, work allocation, welfare, disputes, and discipline. The company's logistics are complex: large quantities of agricultural chemicals are imported from Indonesia, Malaysia, Singapore, China, the US, and elsewhere; each shipment is administered and paid for separately; and supplies must be funneled to a myriad of small farmers throughout Mindanao, as well to many of the largest agricultural enterprises in Davao, including 18Ifc and 2Fi (table 1) and 8 I59 (table 2 and fig 2). Estimating, ordering, and delivering supplies of the right quality and at the rights times is no easy matter, even though the company keeps a large stock in reserve which it may draw on if shipments are late. So closely integrated is it, that decisions made in any one part of the company are likely to have an effect on its entire operations. Thus, whilst the owner focuses responsibility for overseas orders on himself, most decisions, including those concerning the type and timing of orders and shipments, are necessarily made in consultation and in the field: for it is only in the field, and in consultation, that the intricacies of the operation, and the ramifications of any decision, are made apparent. Formal meetings in the board room are therefore few and far between.

(ii) As the company grows, as its tasks multiply, and as its complexities intensify, there is a need to establish clear roles and areas of responsibility. This in itself creates interdependencies among the different activities. But other forms of interdependencies may also develop; and these, too, cannot be brushed aside easily. Another first-generation migrant (again from Fujian, China) owns a wholesale company – let us call it 'Welcome' - dealing in agricultural commodities in Davao's Chinatown. The company, which figures as a source of agricultural products for traders in the city's marketplaces, has begun to diversify from rice to cocoa, coffee, and corn; and, although the value of its shipments are too small for the company to appear in table 2, it now imports ceramic tiles directly and regularly from Fujian. The owner, Song, has lived in the Philippines for more than thirty years; but he speaks neither Tagalog, nor Visayan, nor English. He is therefore dependent upon his children and his wife, who work in the company with him, for translations. Both daughters are married, and their husbands' families have their own business interests: his eldest daughter's in-laws own an insurance firm; his other daughter's in-laws own a hardware company. Song and the fathers of both families were friends even before their children were born. All three

130

companies buy goods or services from the other, or will point customers in the other's direction. But risks will not be pooled: there are no cross-subsidies, no investments, and no loans.

Song believes that he has had little choice but to loosen his grip over his company and his family. This is so on two counts. First, although diversification in itself spreads risk, the various interests within the company must still be insulated (just as they are among all three companies) such that the mistakes or ill-fortune of the one do not bring down the other. Flour is kept separate from rice and corn; both these divisions are also separated from coffee and cocoa; and all three divisions are separated from tiles. His wife and his daughters are each assigned to one division, and the costs and income for each division are drawn up independently. At the end of the year, his wife and his children must provide him with a summary of accounts; and each will receive a modest proportion of the profits. This they may keep for themselves or reinvest in their division.

Second, he cannot simply rule by fiat over his children with their own cross-cutting loyalties, especially when he is so dependent upon them for communication and desires that they should continue the business when he is too old or no longer around. A degree of freedom, and opportunities to develop experience and confidence, have had to be devolved.

A similar division of responsibilities, and separation of interests, are to be found in a larger group of Filipino-owned companies (centred on 2 Fi [table 2] in Davao) which are spread throughout the Philippines. In this instance, too, it is the father who ultimately makes the broader strategic decisions for the group. Again the companies' accounts are monitored centrally: all books are kept in Davao; partly for tax purposes* and partly so that the eldest daughter can keep an eye on financial affairs of the group as a whole. She is her father's right hand, and it is she who exercises authority in his absence. Again, however, responsibilities are distributed among the children: the eldest daughter runs the core business in Davao; her sister runs operations in Mindoro; one brother holds the company in Pampanga; a second brother controls the business in Manila. Again each company is insulated from the other: each is run independently; there are no cross subsidies or loans; and profits and losses are accounted for separately. And again this arrangement is worked to spread the risks, and to provide each child with the opportunity to develop experience and exercise their ambition. Otherwise each might feel the need, as did their eldest brother, to set up their own companies entirely beyond the reach of father and daughter.

Masquerade

The second part of the explanation for a move in the form of distancing from authoritarianism and towards professionalism, is a shift in attitude towards the affect. Reasons for this attitudinal shift are suggested below.

(i) The distancing of relationships within the company is a denial of the nature and origins of our sense and representations of self and community (see chapter 1, section 3.1). This denial, and the consequential sense of alienation, is felt even more keenly under an authoritarian regime which, at its most extreme, appears to obliterate social relationships altogether. We are prompted therefore to seek refuge in the idealisation of our social relationships outside the company; and, as we do so, to define a clearly social sphere of life.

Creating this social sphere, and bringing to it sharper definition, requires the performance of what is, in effect, a masquerade. Within the social sphere we

---

* Local tax must be paid to the administrative jurisdiction in which the books are held. The tax rates are, for this group, more favourable in Davao.

behave towards 'I', 'you', 'we', and our relationships, as absolute (as important and interesting in their own right). This is *necessarily* paralleled by the treatment of the rules, regulations, procedures, and patterns of behaviour - the walls and frames of institutions (economic and political) - as absolute. This parallel behaviour is necessary; for otherwise, in admitting the social essence of our rules and roles, we would have to acknowledge that our social relationships are indeed instrumental in quality. In this case, we would have breached the social sphere.

However, at the same time that we treat our relationships - and, implicitly, our rules, roles, and institutions - as absolute, we must also admit to ourselves silently: that they are not *in fact* absolute nor *in fact* distant or separate from the company; that our relationships are also the material of the company and of all other aspects of life; and that our rules, roles, and institutions, are but expressions of the practice of social relationships.

This treatment of social relationships, and the social sphere, *as if* absolute, and thus the implicit admission of the social qualities of the professional sphere, is essential to the protection of the social sphere. If we do not make this admission then (as we argued in chapter 1, section 4.2) 'I' is made an absolute; and we create within our minds other rigid phenomena -' you', 'we', 'relationships', 'rules', 'roles', and 'institutions' – whose meaning, presence, and influence, are no longer dependent upon our common but implied compact to treat such representations *as if* important and proper in their own right. And it is to these pure absolutes - now set above us - that those in authority, and those with ambition, appeal in order to justify, explain, persuade, and demand. This elevation of our representations and relationships, their separation from us, and our appeals to these hollow absolutes, nurture a strengthening sense of alienation. Our reaction is to move towards instrumentalism. Now, as this breach of the social and professional spheres grows, we enter a downward spiral of deepening alienation and instrumentalism, until are propelled by our sense of alienation back towards the affect.

We have said that admission of the social essence of professional life must be made silently. Were it to be made openly, were we explicitly to regard the frames and walls of institutions as but an expression of relationships, then once again the instrumentalism of our social relationships would have been made plain; the mystique of rules, roles, and institutions, destroyed; and the social sphere breached. Social relationships, though they are the true material of the worlds outside the social sphere, must remain a shadow, their existence acknowledged but left unspoken.

Because it is left unspoken, we must find oblique reminders of this truth. We may, for instance, make quite explicit the distancing of social relationships through, say, the introduction of rules forbidding the employment of kin within the same division of a company; or through maxims - such as the need to 'keep private and professional life separate', to 'keep emotions out of business', to 'leave family matters outside the boardroom', and to 'leave problems at work' – that have become the creed of many family-owned businesses. Alternatively, ways might be found to remind ourselves symbolically of what we will not admit openly. For instance, within a company, or across different companies, or between a company and politicians and bureaucrats, ritualistic social ties may be established, not as a prelude to manipulation but, quite the contrary, in case we should otherwise forget that the true strength of our rules and roles lie in their unspoken social quality. Were we to lose sight of that truth, then the appeal to absolutes would soon reveal an essential instrumentalism, destroying the mystique of our rules and roles, and compromising the integrity of the social sphere.

(ii) Another possible stimulus for attitudinal change lies in the attempt to defend authoritarianism or, more specifically, to defend the absolute quality of the roles, rules, and procedures, from which authority is derived and through which it is exercised. As the company grows and becomes more intricate, some measure of devolution and decentralization is necessary such that, whilst a hierarchy is preserved, the leadership at all levels becomes more interdependent and collective. As those in authority struggle to cope with this increasing complexity, their own fallibility, weakness, and mistakes, become more evident. To admit such failings, however, is to weaken oneself fatally in the eyes of superiors and subordinates. It is better, therefore, to appeal in public to the absolute qualities of rules and roles while in private cultivating relationships with those who can help both to cover up faults and to give the impression that the aims declared publicly have been met. With the vulnerability and dependency of those in authority – and with the social quality of rules and roles - now made blatantly apparent in private, the mystique of institutions begins to dissolve. Concerned to hide their private world as best they can, those in authority publicly and loudly acknowledge the absolute quality of rules and roles, publicly demonstrate their adherence to them, and demand publicly that their subordinates do similarly. Meanwhile, in private, selective and narrow strands of personalistic relationships are thrown out and deals are done, circumventing and ignoring those same rules and roles. Thus a mutually reinforcing cycle is created. As the shell of orthopraxy hardens, and as its innards become softer and more personalistic, the demand for more elaborate monitoring and enforcement begins to escalate. The complexity of skeins of evasive personalistic relationships then intensifies. This is turn demands more effective countervailing webs. The company begins to seize up, or break apart, or is driven violently back towards authoritarian and centralised control.

It is in this light that we might view China's state industries*. In an attempt to control and direct the practice of relationships strongly imbued with the personal, the walls and frames of authoritarian institutions – political and economic – were

---

* These passages are based on interviews with serving members of state companies or former state companies, and with former members of state companies now working for private firms. The institutions they refer to include: G1(上海宝钢集团公司) (fig. 8), G11 (沪东中华造船集团有限公司) (fig 14), M29 (上海氯碱) (fig 11), G10 (上海申达集团有限公司) and G27 (上海化学纤维集团有限公司) (fig 12) , together with the Bank of China (中国银行) and now-privatised sections of the Shanghai Industrial and Commercial Administration Bureau (上海市工商管理局)。

lowered upon China. In these huge and complex institutions, authority was necessarily devolved to some degree, forming a leadership that was, in practice, necessarily interdependent, collective, and poorly defined. The further down the hierarchy its members found themselves, the more precise and circumscribed became their roles, to the extent that members were robbed of initiative and responsibility. Indeed, many desired firm instructions and limitations, and eschewed responsibility; for it was these bonds that protected them from unintentional transgression, and from the retribution they would suffer at the hands of superiors who, as we have said, could not afford to appear fallible. Nor, therefore, did subordinates, their roles tightly circumscribed, have either the desire or need to form representations of the broader organisation and their place within it. They were content to preserve their own small niche. In private, through their own personalistic relationships with superiors and subordinates, they would promise to help or hinder the flow of information and orders upwards and downwards in return for protection. Meanwhile, the guileless, who accepted the absolute quality of rules and roles, opened themselves up to easy manipulation. In this atmosphere, the harsh and ambitious were rewarded. For as the innards of the company softened, and as the need for public acknowledgement of the absolute quality of rules and roles strengthened, and as the need for monitoring, enforcement, and evasion grew, it was those who were most willing to take risks and circumvent, and, in their turn, to police most ruthlessly, who would survive and rise.

This was not so much a commercial organization with bureaucratic methods, as it was a bureaucratic organization that existed for itself. To sit at its apex was to sit atop a leviathan only part-formed within the mind and part-shrouded in haze. It could not respond quickly or easily to directions. Only by sending down hidden strands of personalistic relationships to the right people in the right places might it be steered. Meanwhile, those lower down found themselves within an organization that seemed extraordinarily small. To them, the world outside their unit was opaque. As far as they were aware very little, if any, direction or planning from the outside was channeled to them through their superiors; nor were they asked to form plans. The tasks given to subordinates by their superiors were small, precisely defined, repetitive, and often devoid of apparent meaning or purpose. At worst, tasks were conjured up merely to prevent subordinates from witnessing even the most fleeting sign of weakness in their superiors. If their superior wanted to leave work early for whatever reason, he would first send them out on a pointless errand rather than let them stare at his empty desk. Nor was there any room for creativity. Many found themselves the end of each day writing reports on what they had done that day. These were submitted to their superior who would confirm whether or not what they had done had indeed been done correctly. Nor were they aware of any explicit criteria for promotion. All that really mattered in the end, as far as one could judge, was to nurture good relationships with those who had your promotion within their gift.

As a consequence, such contact and dealings one unit might have with another within the company, let alone with another unit outside the company, were necessarily difficult. The representations which each had of the other were vague. Nor was there much willingness to develop - or to encourage others to cultivate – representations of the broader organization in which they worked, or to experiment with thought and ideas about how things might be improved. There was always constant fear of committing errors; mistakes were hidden; one could not admit that something could not be done; and such information and authority as they had, and their role as a link in the chain, were the stuff with which to defend their own small world. Information was therefore withheld and decisions were slow in coming as members considered what effect the smallest action or slip might have upon their own prospects and those of their unit. To get even the simplest thing done they would have to dance on egg-shells. No wonder the lines of communication seemed long and painful.

And yet, for all these faults, advantage could be found in these organisations. They contained much experience in the arrangement of relationships on a large scale. More importantly, between public declarations of the absolute quality of rules and roles, and private (but explicit) admissions of their social essence, there formed a matrix of suspicion in which each member supposed that the other might be participating in illicit and hidden personalistic relations to protect or advance their own cause. From this, something else emerged: an experience of rules, roles, and institutions, that were at once absolute and yet not absolute, at once apart from us and yet of our social relationships. Experience of this suspicion, though it may not have stimulated the affective, might have made those who worked within the company still more susceptible to the idea that rules, roles, and institutions, could be treated *as if* absolute.

Perhaps, then, we should not be surprised to find what appear to be patches of professionalisation and the affective even among older staff in the state companies or their surviving remnants. Take, for instance, a Chinese-German joint venture - which ranks among the top five exporters (by value) from Shanghai to the Philippines. The Chinese yard - let us call it '*The Patriotic Yard*'- receives all of its domestic investment from G11 (沪东中华造船集团有限公司) (figure 13)* from which it is now, managerially at least, entirely separate. Although the communist party and trade union cells remain in place, the party (whose secretary is also head of the trade union) are not involved in management. Their role is limited to negotiating contracts and furthering the interests of workers. The Board, weighted in favour of their German partners, makes the strategic decisions. The General Manager is Shanghainese: it is he who runs day to day operations; and, aside from a handful of German technicians, all his staff are also mainland Chinese. His departmental heads, who are provided with clear remits within which they exercise

---

* Its investment is routed indirectly through a subsidiary. Neither the subsidiary nor the joint venture are indicated on the figures 4-15. G11 (沪东中华造船集团有限公司) in turn receives the bulk of its investment from Ww (中国船舶工业集团公司).

much independence, turn to the General Manager only when solutions to the problems they face take them outside the scope of their authority. The General Manager, then, is a kind of lynch pin, integrating, and coordinating behaviour, and resolving problems. Most of the managers (a dozen in all), and the bulk of their subordinates, have known each other for many years or, in some cases, for decades. But there is very little social contact among them outside the company.

We find equal single-mindedness in a smaller joint venture between a Hong Kong textile company (into which Filipino-Chinese money* is routed) and what had been the technical and research division of a subsidiary of G10 (上海申达集团有限公司). Its four managers are again all mainland Chinese; they, too, have worked together for decades (more than thirty years); and their behaviour towards each other has the directness of warm familiarity. They are very clearly focussed on two goals: buying in the machinery from overseas that will enable them to compete internationally; and selecting younger personnel with the imagination and technical ability to design and manufacture high quality textiles. Nothing, it would seem, is allowed to intrude into their work or divert them from their work. Although it would be easy to attribute the atmosphere of professionalisation to their foreign partners, the lucidity with which the Chinese managers see the problems they face, the clarity of their aims, their determination, and their age (the youngest is in his 50s), suggest that would indeed be too easy an explanation.

Tolerance, creativity, empathy, adaptability, and leadership
We have argued so far that practical advantage may explain something of the move towards professionalisation. This move is firmed up through the deepening of the affect in the social sphere and the parallel behaviour this demands of us in the professional sphere. There is no suggestion here of any causal connexion between professionalisation and the deepening of the affect. However, there is a kind of

---

* The precise source of this investment was not known to the managers. Nor did the Industrial and Commercial Administration Bureau hold a record of the Hong Kong company's investors.

synchronicity or sympathy between them. As the burden of alienation grows heavier within the company, there is, in reaction, outside the company a strengthening of the treatment of relationships, and of 'I'. 'you' and 'we', *as if* absolute. This is necessarily paralleled by the treatment of rules and roles in professional life *as if* absolute. This parallel behaviour may have been primed to some extent by the matrix of suspicion already generated by attempts to defend authoritarianism.

A third part of the explanation for growing professionalism lies in the various other qualities which the masquerade brings to professional life. In the treatment of social relationships *as if* absolute there is an implied admission of the social quality of professional life: we admit, in effect, that rules and roles emanate from us. In this we acknowledge that they depend entirely upon the extent to which each of us is prepared to accept them and to shape our behaviour accordingly. We enter a compact in which we are equally responsible for, and equally subject to, those rules and roles. None of us stands above the other.

In this admission, acknowledgement, and compact, true strength lies. Treated *as if* absolute, rules and roles are, through common and open consent, alterable and capable of varied interpretation. Relieved of the brittleness of the absolute, and of an easy convenience that would be suggested by their constant violation, they are no longer regarded as instruments to be wielded or discarded for our own advantage. Nor do we need any longer to bear constant suspicion, monitoring, and enforcement. As a consequence, our energies are now more concentrated, our behaviour more coordinated, and greater predictability and reliability is brought to our lives. The treatment of social relationships, and of our rules and roles, *as if* absolute, and the emergence of more clearly defined spheres of life, bring other qualities, too, which happen to be of value to the professional sphere.

(i) The first of these is greater tolerance. Behaviour within the professional sphere, which might otherwise have been regarded as improper, unsocial, or anti-social, is now accepted because it is understood to be *of* the professional sphere. Song, the owner of 'Welcome' to which we referred to above, is undoubtedly authoritarian. And he takes 90% of the profit earned by his daughters. They argue with him over this and other matters. May, his eldest daughter, feels that her younger sister (who joined the company only recently after having tried her hand at other lines of work) has been allowed more freedom in her life than she. Yet there is in May a strong loyalty towards her father born of very strong affection, even to the extent that her view of the world is part-shaped around his behaviour. Her understanding of what it is to be Chinese, for instance, is an explicit account of the kind of man she believes her father to be: hardworking, but aware of his limitations, and never overly ambitious. This affection overrides whatever the disputes or cause for envy which might exist within the company.

We find a similar mixing of warmth, unselfish, intent and money-making in a Filipino company – a string of half-a-dozen or so restaurants and bakeries in Davao. Although it does not trade with China, it buys in foodstuffs from wholesale companies (including 'Welcome') that do and, on occasions, from traders in the city's marketplaces. The company is owned by Noy, a Filipino whose family were all true Dabaweyneans, migrants who, long before the Second World War, had arrived in Davao where they either bought land from the indigenes or married into their families. When old enough his children were brought into the company to experience its working. But only he and his wife (who was its treasurer) and one son were involved in its day-to-day operations. His other children - though directors - had their own lives and professions. They were teachers or lawyers and one owned a business overseas. They were to be offered no discounts or free meals in the restaurants or bakeries, and none were to be offered to their own families or friends. Pay was strictly controlled, and whilst the company would provide medicines for family members, they would be given no cash with which to buy those medicines. And any other businesses in which they might be involved were to be kept financially separate from the company. Indeed, it was made quite explicit to all, that their family relationships should be kept quite separate, emotionally and institutionally, from their work within the company and their interests in it. Once a decision has been made, even if should prove not to have been the best, everyone must rally in support of the company without qualms or bickering; and disputes over matters at work should never be taken into the home. Their relationships with each other, and the warmth and affection which they felt for each other, should be treated as important in their own right. This, Noy believed, was a moral imperative. It would also help to keep the company on an even keel.

This same approach he took to his employees. He allowed himself the luxury of some prejudice. For the uneducated, and especially for the Bagobo to whom he traced his ancestry, he had a soft-spot. They were, he believed, a simple people in whom his values and beliefs could be sown and nurtured with even greater ease. He bought land and houses which he would sell on to his workers (after they had been with him for more than two years) at no profit to himself and by instalments without interest over as long a period as they wanted or could afford. He also provided them with grants for furniture. And as the company expanded, or as workers left or died, and vacancies arose, his employees' children were given preference. This supplemented his employees' wages, and made it more likely that his new workers would be inculcated with the values and practices which he had endeavored to instill in their parents.

Yet he would not be the *ninong* of his workers' children: in that practice he saw favouritism, and favouritism he discouraged. He did not count the hours he worked, and he did not expect them to measure the length of their days either. And though preference may have been given to his workers' children and to the Bagobo, it was his judgment of their qualities and abilities that was paramount: break the

142

rules and you will fire yourself. Just as he had responsibilities to them, they had responsibilities to him; just as he was loyal to them, they were to be loyal to him.

There was an element of *quid pro quo* in these relationships; they were undoubtedly manipulative and stylised to a degree. But also there was in these relationships genuine affection on both sides, and with this came an easy informality. One of his weekly meetings with his key staff to discuss affairs and problems began slowly: they were suffering from a late night and seemed to have no energy to think or speak. On this he commented, adding that they probably needed something to eat. For this he would pay, and on to the table he threw a ragged and dirty bank note of twenty pesos - a derisory amount. They looked at the limp shred of paper on the gleaming table and, with heavy sarcasm and broad smiles, began to discuss what they should buy. The same joking informality with which he treated them, and they he, also marked his relationships with more junior staff. It was not unusual for a young woman to knock at his door, and ask for a contribution to this or that charity, or for some or other function. Always, a feigned grumpy rebuke from him; always the childish pleading and a gentle stamp of the foot in reply; always the burst of laughter and the money produced. Of his lowliest employees, too, he had an intimate knowledge of their circumstances and troubles, such that during birthdays and other celebrations he could wander from one house to the next without invitation, gifts in arms to find himself welcomed at one house after another with a warm respect.

These relationships, then, had something of the personalistic about them, but they were founded upon the affect. It was because social relationships were to be treated *as if* absolute, that family and employees could accept behaviour that was severely professional within the company. Indeed, in Noy's mind it was because of their importance, their almost spiritual quality, that relationships were not to be contaminated by the professional sphere. With religious zeal he gave voice to his belief that there was in human relationships an inherent worth. You should treat others only as you would have them treat you. Fairness, honesty, warmth, and affection - these were good and proper qualities in their own right. Every Good Friday he held a retreat during which he, his family, and a selection of the Great and the Good from Davao, cooked for and served his employees who were compelled to attend. Here he would entwine the spirit of his company with religious teachings for husbands and wives. Then they would pray together. His enthusiasm did not stop there. He organised similar gatherings which were neither compulsory for, nor restricted to, his employees. There was no artifice in these gatherings, at least none of which I think he was aware. For him relationships and the noble emotions were inherently right and just. It was their treatment as such which demanded severely professional behaviour within the company. In this it happened that practical advantage lay, for the greatest advantage, he believed, is to be secured when no advantage is sought.

(ii) The deepening of the affect also brings an understanding that the tensions and disputes which arise within the company are professional matters: they are neither symbolic nor symptomatic of the state of social relationships. Moreover, now that relationships, rules, and roles are treated *as if* absolute, now that their strength is understood to derive from the fact they emanate from each of us, authority is no longer thought to be dependent upon the appearance of perfection, nor is fallibility equated with a threat to that authority. For these reasons, misinterpretations and mistakes, and different views of future problems, solutions, and strategies, may be discussed openly without fear of retribution. There is now considerable freedom to experiment, to make mistakes, and to try other ways.

Let us consider the instance of *Taixi*, an American* family-owned company in Shanghai, the vast majority of whose employees are Mainland Chinese. Policies

---

* The family has German heritage. The company is among the top ten exporters to the Philippines. It is not linked through any investments to any other company in Shanghai. It does not, therefore, appear in any of the figures.

handed down to the company from the US can be extraordinarily dynamic. Quick responses to these, and to the company's customers and suppliers, are essential. Managers and subordinates within the company in Shanghai are given much leeway for action and decision. Very general directions to an objective are suggested (and these often change), but staff are left to find their own ways and means to reach that objective. If difficulties are encountered and cannot be solved by a subordinate, then rather than delay and be forced to explain that delay, the problem, together with a recommended solution, should be communicated to their superior for a decision. When the Deputy General Manager (a highly energetic Chinese woman from Beijing) was asked to put together a quote for a large bespoke order from a US buyer, she instructed a subordinate to provide quotes from two suppliers in Shanghai on the cost of raw materials. The names of the suppliers was forthcoming, but with these came a clear quote from only one, and a confused account from the subordinate for the absence of the other. It took her a number of phone calls to discover the reason: her subordinate's inexperienced contact in that company, reluctant to be turned down, had procrastinated, assuming that the price he would be compelled to quote for materials (which would have to be imported) would be uncompetitive. She then summoned and chastised her subordinate: the incident, a seemingly trivial oversight, or moment of laziness, had meant that a day was lost – a day in which a large order went elsewhere and her attention had been directed away from other pressing matters. But a lesson had been learnt: initiative and drive, openness and speed, were vital qualities in even the most mundane of tasks. And other orders would come.

Freedom of thought and action are not peculiar to family companies. Roles, procedures, and work flows, may be defined more clearly within the larger companies, especially at their lower levels where representations of the company may become more vague, and where mechanistic practices are needed. But we find that even junior managers are permitted considerable freedom of action. It is mostly Koreans who hold management positions down to the level of department heads in *Shanghai Lejin* (上海樂金)*, a large Korean firm. Although some managers lay down step-by-step instructions of work procedures for their mainland Chinese subordinates (mostly junior managers), the majority of senior managers, more laissez-faire in their approach, are happy to let their subordinates find their own way and make their own decisions. In M6†(上海西门字移动通信有限公司) (figure 6, set 3), too, tasks are delegated, and subordinates are left to work out how to meet their responsibilities and achieve particular objectives. This demands imagination, determination, much trial and error, and a deal of mental robustness. Subordinates are to some extent guided informally through open and direct conversations with superiors. Indeed, subordinates often feel that they are expected not only to find a way to meet specific objectives, but also to help the superior narrow down and refine what those objectives should be. Through their easy and relaxed discussion, and in the extent to which they are drawn into the formulation of policy objectives and methods, subordinates are made to feel their superiors' equals.

We find a similar approach within a Taiwanese company. It is a sub-contractor of M14 (飞利浦电子元件上海有限公司) (figure 5, set 2) providing electronic spare parts, servicing and repairs‡. It is one of 8 regional offices in China; its Head Office (China) is in Beijing. Each regional office is fairly self-contained (with their own General Manager and divisions such as finance and operations), and each is responsible for the selection of their own personnel. They are given only very general instructions. Targets are handed down from Beijing, and it is up to the managers of the regional offices to decide how they should be met. The

---

* The company ranks among the top twenty exporters to the Philippines, but it does not rank among Shanghai's top 120 firms nor does it appear to be linked into their investment flows. It is therefore not included in figures 4-15.
† The company is one of Shanghai's leading exporters, and is ranked among the top five importers from, and exporters to, the Philippines. It is largely foreign-owned (European), but mainland Chinese institutions (primarily through a domestic listed company) have a stake.
‡ The company ranks among the top 35 importers from, and top 5 exporters to, the Philippines.

expectation is that they will contact their superiors only if the solution to a problem requires them to step beyond their authority or personal limitations. The Shanghai office is small (around sixty managers and subordinates) and its atmosphere focused and unglamorous. Meetings - informal and brief - are often convened in corridors or work-floors: small groups of disheveled men in shirt sleeves and ruffled suits, come together and break apart, as problems are discussed and decisions are made quickly. They receive only the occasional and short flying visits from superiors either from Beijing or direct from Taipei. There is little sense of hierarchy or monitoring. Their visitors, who are young and whose manner is unconcerned, float in and out of the groups. They do not so much oversee as provide a more detailed and up-to-date representation of the company and its directions. In this atmosphere of concentrated bustle no considerations other than the task at hand seem able to squeeze their way in.

(iii) The deepening of the affect outside the company – and thus an experience of, and interest in, people and their relationships for their own sake – is also conducive to the cultivation of an intuitive understanding of how others are thinking, their capabilities, and their probable behaviour in particular circumstances. This is true both of companies owned and run by families and of those that are not. Within 18 Ifc (table 1), for example, managers form around themselves collections of subordinates, of whose particular abilities and qualities they develop an intimate understanding nurtured in part through regular and distinctly social gatherings and friendships. This they describe as a 'tool box' whose contents may be applied as circumstances change. This 'box' has another, and more sophisticated, dimension: grooming for succession. Driven both by practical considerations, and by a moral and quasi-legal* duty, there is a deliberate attempt to inculcate in subordinates a highly nuanced understanding of their superiors' work, thinking, and decisions. In this, the development of relationships in the social sphere is essential. To first

---

* It is expected that foreign companies will 'Filipinize' their staff.

untangle, and then explain, the reasoning behind their own behaviour and decisions is extremely difficult for the present managers: they are either second or third generation employees of the company, or the children of families who have owned and managed plantations in Latin America or other parts of the world for two generations at least. Their work has become so much a part of them* that their thought and actions have become instinctive. Even when under pressure it seems to them that their decisions simply present themselves in a way that is more emotional and immediate than intellectual, reasoned, and judged. They can, then, for much of the time, and in the most important aspects of their job, teach only by example. Important though it is for managers to know their understudies' qualities, it is just as important that their understudies come to know their mentors. Only then can they begin to sense how and why they make the decisions and behave in the ways that they do.

It is evident from this, that the cultivation of empathy is another aspect of tolerance and creativity: we saw empathy at work in M6 in the behaviour of junior and senior management towards each other; and its nurturing is part of the reasoning behind the employment of workers' kin in Noy's company. This latter practice – which in the Philippines is characteristic of very many companies, large and small – has other dimensions, too. It is seen by some owners and managers as a way of reducing the time and cost needed to train workers, and as a barrier to union activists and others who are, in the mind of the companies' owners and managers, dishonest troublemakers. But most importantly, as it fosters experience and empathy, it also works to coordinate behaviour to the extent that what feels like an instinctive or organic unity of purpose and action may be achieved by those involved.

---

* Perhaps we might say that it has been integrated so closely with their own representations of 'I'?

148

(iv) The deepening of the affect outside the company, and the parallel behaviour that this demands within the professional sphere, also brings the quality of adaptability to the company. Rather than constitute a limited, and limiting, cast into which people and events must fit if they are not to be excluded, rules and roles may now be adapted as necessary to particular instances through common and open consent, without turning the company into a hive of instrumentalism. Indeed, adaptability is often presented quite explicitly as a trait more important than most others.

Haojia * with its Head Office in Manila, with branches also in Vietnam and Myanmar, has some eleven factories throughout China (four in Shanghai, and seven in Ningbo, Harbin, Kunming and Suzhou). Raw materials, most of which originate from the US or Europe, are routed by its suppliers in the Philippines either directly to its factories in China or through the company's Head Office in Manila. Its workforce is predominantly mainland Chinese, though its management comprises some fifty people, largely Chinese-Filipino or Filipino scattered among the eleven factories. Of this fifty, only three are of the owner's immediate family including his son (the President of operations in China); and with them works one of their cousins. The majority of managers are either friends or were referred to the family through friends. As the company has grown and become more complex, centralization and authoritarianism have become neither helpful nor possible. And as competition in Shanghai has intensified, the managerial layer has had to be kept as thin as possible. Thus has a willingness to adapt become the most desirable quality alongside frugality. Leading by example, the cousin of the company's Vice-President has taken on ten different roles in the last two years.

---

* The company is Filipino-Chinese. It is ranked 130th of the strongest companies in Shanghai (measured by sales value). It therefore lies just outside the top 120 companies and their networks of investment in Shanghai shown in figures 4-15; but it ranks among the top 75 importers from, and exporters to the Philippines.

Rules are also treated with a degree of flexibility. Of particular importance to the coherence of this company are those governing appointments and promotion. Viewed as fixed absolutes, criteria for appointment would present only a limited range of obvious candidates for interview. For promotions, too, whilst the criteria are fairly clear in that staff understand what is required of them, those criteria are neither set in stone nor are they framed with absolute precision. This is so partly because it is impossible to capture the balance and dimensions of traits and abilities that might prove valuable. Criteria that are too specific and precise would, in practice, only limit the field while providing an easy disguise for the game-player and button-pusher. It is true that, as a consequence, questions are raised occasionally among subordinates over one or other promotion or appointment. But a probationary period allows for this: a new appointee can demonstrate ability to handle and win round the doubters; for this – the capacity to bring people together rather than make enemies – is viewed as another essential attribute.

(v) We have argued that, for practical reasons, authoritarianism and centralised control tend to give way to decentralisation, collectivism, and interdependence, as practices become more complex. This complexity finds expression in a multiplicity of the rules, roles, and procedures, and in more elaborate training and planning, as shared representations with which to coordinate behaviour are provided to members. We have also suggested that the treatment of relationships *as if* absolute, and the parallel behaviour which this demands in the professional sphere, bring other vital qualities. These qualities, each a dimension of the other, soften our rules and roles, enable more concentrated and coherent practice, and free up thought and behaviour. So valuable are these qualities that they prompt action to strengthen the seal between the professional and social spheres. Were the company to be opened up to relationships that are explicitly social, and the social essence of the company admitted, then the instrumental quality of relationships within the company would have been acknowledged.

The efforts made to strengthen the company's seal against the social sphere are exhibited in the leadership's everyday decisions and behaviour. With the move towards professionalisation, with the deepening of the affect, and with the strengthening of tolerance, creativity, empathy, and adaptability, it is only to be expected that managers, especially at the upper levels, should find that most of their time and energy is spent mediating in, and resolving, disputes. These tensions, however, reflect not only professional creativity. The personal is never absent from our lives. When the young assistant of the President (of M6) was handed the job of setting up and running the company's e-business, and was given considerable autonomy to do so, the manager of the technical division, who saw this new enterprise as being his proper responsibility, was moved to suspicion and envy. Certainly he did not act quickly or with much effect to provide the materials or expertise that his younger colleague had requested. It is also fair to say that, more generally within the company, the champions of new strategies and solutions work hard to garner as much support as they can though a mixture of promises, charm, appeals to loyalty, and, on occasions, criticisms of the less flattering character traits of their colleagues and rivals. And whilst subordinates feel that they are able to talk openly and freely with superiors, they must nevertheless take into account the personalities and changing moods and circumstances of those with whom they are open.

Disputes over professional matters, then, are rarely only professional: the company is always in danger of being turned into material for personal advantage. It is the job of the leadership to prevent this from happening. In *Taixi* competition between two teams – design and logistics – had become intense. In the view of their superior, the leaders of both teams had begun to use a professional interest in their roles as a cover from which to attack and undermine the other. Design, petulant in the face of criticism from logistics, was procrastinating in the name of creativity; while logistics was throwing together supply and delivery chains for the new product more quickly than was sensible or necessary, and was doing so merely in order to make it appear as if design was not up to the job. Their superior's response was swift: the leaders of both teams were called in, and both were told that neither had to like each other or, for that matter, anyone else in the company. But they had to do their work to do, and they should focus on that. If they would not, they would have to go.

The leadership's judgment on the extent to which rules should be adhered is also important in maintaining and strengthening the seal. We have already suggested that the treatment of rules and roles as absolutes will open the company to the social sphere; but an interpretation that is too loose may also weaken the company. A case in point concerns the rules on salaries. Within many companies the range of salary grades and increments for each post are published and disseminated amongst all employees. However, each member's precise grade and income is confidential. Indeed, they are forbidden to make known their salaries to each other. A tendency to treat the exchange of this information as a symbol of trust around which to form relationships has led to the emergence of exclusive cliques and to the spread of resentment.

Strengthening the seal is probably at no time more important than during the succession of a family company – a time when the professional sphere is easily breached, the personal begins to surge, and the company is at risk of being torn apart. In managing the succession of *Haojia*, its leader called on two sets of allies. The first was decentralization, the interdependency of leadership, and the inclusion of managers from outside the family. These were changes which, it seemed to him, were demanded by the expansion and growing complexity of the company. The second was his children's expectations of him. They knew him to be a strong person who asked that his children defer to him on strategic matters. They also knew that if they had had no time to consult him, then they would have to do what he have done in their position, or face his anger. And whilst he had on many occasions said that he would soon hand over the company to the next generation, these pronouncements were met by his children with a smile: he had not yet done so, and he probably never would. These two allies worked in concert. The practical demands for decentralization and an interdependent leadership mitigated rivalries that would emerge among his children; and the presence of outsiders at the highest levels, as well as enlarging the pool of experience, worked to buffer family members from each other. Meanwhile, their expectations of him worked to bind them as the company grew. He was well aware that it had become more difficult for them to defer to him on every important decision, and that it was not a good idea that they should do so, for the circumstances they faced did not always lie within his own experience. He also knew that it was only out of affection, respect, and a desire for a quiet life, that they felt they should defer to him when they could. But with this he was happy. It was their own expectations of him which pressured them to refer to their understanding of what he would do – to representations for practice that he had instilled in them. And as the relevance of that model weakened, as their own experiences mounted, and as circumstances changed, it was their expectations of him which led them almost without knowing it to make of him a figurehead around whom the growing and disparate empire would rally. By allowing decentralized and interdependency to take its course, and by cultivating in his children their expectations of him while in practice standing back, the old leader had, with the lightest of touches, helped to seal the professional from the social. No formal transition would have to be made; far better that the company should be allowed to evolve.

2.3 The diminution of kinship, ethnicity, and other social kernels

We have argued that the deepening affect, through its encouragement of tolerance, flexibility, creativity, empathy, and adaptability, works to soften and seal the professional. It might also be suggested that the affect, and the qualities it brings, increase greatly in value when social relationships, though distanced, are formed among those who are also members of the same company. This layering of the professional life over social life - such that there are close relationships among owners, managers, and employees - may heighten an awareness of the importance of the masquerade. Anxious to avoid breaches of the social and professional spheres, members are especially careful within their own minds to distance the social from the professional. And as they do so, they quickly find themselves moved to cultivate tolerance, creativity, empathy, and adaptability, and to protect the professional from the social.

We might also suggest, however, that there are working in the other direction strong reasons for the removal of this overlap between professional and social spheres. That is, whilst the social quality of relationships within the professional sphere is recognized but left unspoken, and whilst sight of the social sphere is not lost, those with whom social relationships are formed are no longer also members of the same company. The reasons working to remove the overlap are two-fold.

(i) We have implied that as the affect deepens, as our sense in the importance of social relationships in themselves strengthens, and as our relationships and our sense and constructs of 'I' and 'community' are treated increasingly *as if* absolute, so the social sphere defines itself more sharply, and our interest in the affect intensifies still further. With this deepening interest in social relationships - and in 'you', 'I' and 'us' - in themselves, comes a strengthening sense of both commonality and a release from conformity.

Perhaps the most striking instance is that of a young Chinese businesswoman (M18 [上海素广电子有限司], figure 6, set 3). She was clearly very moved by her experience of men and women from American and European companies who gave up their time to various charity organization and clubs (international and local) in Shanghai to help her and others in their careers and in other aspects of their lives; and who did so, in her judgment, for no other reason than the enjoyment they derived from helping for its own sake. This inspired her to do the same, through *Toastmasters* at first. She then set up her own association with the help of her friends who worked (mostly as junior managers) in other companies including M6 (上海西门子移动通信有限公司, figure 6, set 3), M7 (上海通用汽车有限公司, figure 13, set 10) and M9 (上海惠普有限公司, figure 5, set 2). This new association became something of a sanctuary, advising and helping other young Chinese through the pressures and difficulties of competitive education and the early stages of their careers. In this she took much delight. It also changed her outlook on many other aspects of her own life. That relationships and other people were in themselves of interest to her and to others, that she was in herself of interest and importance to others, and that in all this she found enjoyment, suggested to her that we are bound by a commonality. She now had the sense that she could, and should, do and say things without worrying about whether or not other people might think her a little odd: she could choose not to conform. She would no longer accept what her parents told her, nor what she had been told at university or at school. She no longer felt exiled when her parents complained that, at the age of twenty-eight, she had still not married. Her parents might believe that marriage would bring her happiness. But she had her own opinion on this, and on other matters. And if she could not see herself or foreigners as alien and peculiar, then neither could she see any meaningful differences between Chinese from different parts of China. Whichever city or province they came from, the young, she believed, no longer found it difficult to get on with each other; and whereas the Shanghainese may once have been seen by other Chinese as calculating and ruthless, stereotypes such as these were now decaying. For her and her generation, the smallest nuances of behaviour are being released from conformity: in the use of eyes, the turn of the head, the smile, the timbre of the voice, and the touch of the hand, a gentle and natural warmth has begun to shine through, even in public.

It would seem, then, that from the affect something is beginning to emerge: a kind of social ideal which transcends social kernels (even that of kinship) and the sense of allegiance, and the feel of the instrumental, they bear. There are also strong practical considerations that would seem to favour this social ideal. As they fight for survival, it is all too clear to '*The Patriotic Yard*'s' manager that they cannot afford either to limit markets, suppliers, personnel, or creativity; nor can they allow themselves to indulge in disputes. He saw the same demands being made upon the mobile phone company he worked for in Sichuan. And through these demands he sees what seems to him to be a fundamental truth – that there are more differences among individuals and families than between Chinese from one part of China and another, or between Chinese and foreigners. Everyone has their own style of life, so why should he tell his children how to live or what job to take? He is in his late fifties. It is not just among the young that attitudes are shifting.

The attitudinal shift and the practical considerations which seem to have led to this social ideal, together with the freedom from conformity brought by that ideal, are working to reduce, and perhaps eradicate, the coincidence of professional and social spheres. The events surrounding Lucy's company provide an instance of the play of attitude and practice which led to the separation of kinship from company*. Lucy is a Filipina and, as far as she knows, she has no Chinese ancestors or relatives. Her mother started their catering business with a small, open-air stall that offered half-a-dozen kinds of food. Lucy worked with her before and after classes throughout her school and college days. Over the years the business flowered slowly into a restaurant, with its own branch, and a livestock division which bought and sold live pigs and cattle in Davao, Cebu and Manila. The practices and techniques which her mother had used as the businesses grew Lucy adopted and continued. Profits were kept small but the turnover was high. Most importantly they worked hard at their reputation for cleanliness, good food, and good service - a reputation which spread by word of mouth through their customers, through Lucy's relationships and those of her mother, her brothers and her sister. In this way they established a sound and ever-growing core of patrons who returned again

---

* The company does not trade with China, nor does it rank among the top 120 company's in the Philippines. For these reasons it does not appear in tables 1 or 2, nor in figures 1-3. But it does buy foodstuffs from Chinese wholesalers who trade indirectly with China and directly with Davao's street markets.

and again. Her own children she dissuaded from entering the family business. Her eldest son was encouraged to read medicine; the others studied agri-business and marketing. She lent her eldest son money to set up his clinic; and she was saving to give her other children the same advantage once they had qualified in their chosen professions. She wanted her children to be independent. There was also a desire on her part to broaden the family's base: resting her future and that of her children upon the vicissitudes of the catering business was not in her view a wise strategy, and would not provide them with the status that she wished for them. Above all, perhaps, was the concern that her relationships with her children, and their relationships with each other, might be tainted - much as her relationships with her brothers had been - by arguments over the business. As Lucy's mother aged, she let the livestock division fall into the hands of Lucy's brothers, and gave Lucy authority over the core of the business - the restaurants. The two parts of the company remained under one business license (registered in Lucy's name) but were run independently. To her brothers the arrangements seemed unjust. As if to add insult to injury Lucy would not favour their supplies of live pigs over those of their competitors: she would only buy what she thought to be the best meat at the best prices. And whilst she had, to begin with, lent them money, she had not received the return she had expected and was reticent to lend them any more. The livestock trade may well suffer from the difficulty of late payments, she had said, but the catering trade was also risky. She would not add to her risks at a time when she had, for the first time, borrowed a large sum of money to set up a new branch that was only just beginning to break even. All this, too, caused bad feeling. Then her brothers acted clumsily.

Lucy had been careful to renew her business license and pay her taxes. After 30 years she had learnt that rather than play them for fools, it was always better to establish good relationships with officers of the Bureau of Internal Revenue who, in any case, with their strong *corps d' esprit* and deep pockets, made good customers. And she and her mother had indeed built up a sound understanding with them. They would take into account the vagaries of her trade, the loans she now carried, and the news that she had until recently been subsidizing her brothers. They appreciated that she was only trying to make a living in an uncertain world; and she knew that they needed to bring in a reasonably convincing stream of revenue. They would negotiate with her in a calm, friendly, informal manner, and reach a settlement in which she would be allowed to under declare her sales, and stagger her tax payments. Her brothers, however, had under-declared their sales, and had tried to hide it from a Bureau official who she did not know. When the official examined the port authority's records of shipments, and found that the volume of trade was far greater than her brothers had made out, the lie was discovered. As holder of the business license under which her brothers operated it was Lucy who was liable to pay their back tax and penalties. There was also the possibility that it might seem as if she had gone behind the back of those officials with whom she normally dealt. So she paid for her brothers' cack-handedness and explained to her friends in the Bureau what had happened. She then turned on her brothers: she had lent them money and received nothing in return; now she had paid their taxes and their fines; and she had had to patch up relationships with the Bureau that she and her mother had worked hard at over many years. She instructed them to apply for their own permits, and she made arrangements to turn her side of the company into a corporation. She would hold 50% of the shares. Of the other half, her sister was given the majority and the remainder were divided equally among her brothers who were thus left with a small stake in a business from which they were effectively insulated and would find difficult to tear at after their mother's death. In return for this reprieve (Lucy had toyed with the idea of giving them nothing) they could expect no help in their own business affairs.

There was much bitterness now, and much sorrow. Lucy had seen her mother struggle all her life to give her family something, and she had struggled with her. Her brothers, she thought, had been remarkably selfish in their actions and had threatened to undo all that had been done. By distancing her own children from the business and by encouraging their independence, she hoped to spare their future from the heartaches of her past. She had not ruled out a successor. If there was to be one it would be her eldest daughter. But her daughter was interested in other things at the moment and Lucy would not press her into a business which guaranteed nothing.

Probably as pernicious in its limitations upon market, supplies, personnel, and stability, is ethnicity. Indeed, as the affect deepens and as professional life sharpens, those individuals and groups whom we might identify as belonging to certain ethnic categories do not themselves look favourably upon ethnicity as a useful kernel in social or professional life. Much care is taken within companies in Shanghai not to separate out different groups. In *Haojia*, formal meetings (few though they are) are conducted in Mandarin, and the minutes are recorded in both Chinese and English. Managers who do not yet speak or read Chinese well – and these include Filipino-Chinese - are taught to do so. Indeed, notions of 'Filipino', 'Chinese' and 'Filipino-Chinese' are quite consciously dissolved into the company's creed of flexibility and frugality. Almost by definition those people who are able to fit into the company are those who neither match, nor play to, ethnic categories.

This determination to override ethnicity is no less true of companies staffed predominantly by mainland Chinese. For instance, the concern in *Taixi* is to make sure that the company employs Chinese from many different parts of the country. This widens the pool from which competent employees who are able to work independently may be drawn; and guards against the emergence of destructive cliques built around, say, place of origin, language, former employment, or attendance at the same educational institution. This spread of personnel - combined with tight work schedules which leave the staff with little energy to do anything other than go home after work - also helps to maintain the company's focus.

Although they may leave work together at the end of the day, staff keep to their own social lives.

The overlap between the social and professional spheres is seldom removed completely: friendships, sometimes very close, are still forged within the company. But an atmosphere is created in which it is implicitly understood that social relationships are to be distanced very clearly from professional life. In many companies in the Philippines, too, attempts are made to foster such an atmosphere, and to prevent the emergence of relationships formed around ethnicity and other kernels, such as fictive or actual kinship, mutual friends, language, hometown, education, and experience. Within I79 (figure 1), workers within the same unit or division are not permitted to take on the role of *ninang* or *ninong*, while lovers, whether or not they marry, will be reassigned to separate divisions. Nor, then, may relatives be appointed to the same division. These rules apply equally at managerial levels, though the need for them is rendered less likely by a stringent regime of interviews, exams, training, fieldwork, and a one-year period of probation.

3.0 The company's external dealings.

We have argued that professionalisation and the deepening of the affect – the treatment of relationships as important and valuable *in themselves* – demands the performance of a masquerade. In order to protect the social sphere we must treat our relationships (and our rules and roles) as absolute while silently admitting that this is not in fact the case. It is only then that the social and professional spheres of our lives begin to sharpen. We have also argued that from the deepening of the affect, a social ideal (a sense of profound commonality) emerges; and that there are for the company various problems associated with the formation of social relationships around kernels such as kinship, ethnicity, place of origin, language, mutual friends, or shared membership of an institution (such as a school, university, or association). A concomitant of this ideal, and of these problems, is

160

that social kernels come to be seen increasingly as irrelevant or deleterious to both professional and social spheres. As a consequence, a gap between those with whom we might deal in business and those with whom social relationships might be formed, begins to open up. We now look as much outside our own narrow professional life for those with whom we might strike up relationships explicitly social in quality. Our relationships are no longer only psychologically distanced: those who are part of our social sphere are now also physically separated from our professional life.

Professionalisation and the diminution in the significance of social kernels are also characteristic of the company's external dealings. These transactions are almost always legally binding. In the view of those involved, their legal status makes these deals more predictable; time and money is saved; and merchants are no longer compelled to perform what is, in the words of one Filipino-Chinese businessman, a 'dance of relationships' that would otherwise be necessary both as a precursor to, and as means to sustain, those business dealings. The movement of goods from China to the Philippines is therefore preceded by a traffic in documents. In the case of 'Welcome' these documents include a letter of credit (from their bank in the Philippines) guaranteeing payment in China. The money may be claimed in China only once the goods are in transit to the Philippines. The company in the Philippines is then informed that payment has been made. The physical movement of goods, and the payment of customs duties to customs, is handled by a broker. The broker makes a partial payment to customs prior to the shipment leaving China. Once in transit, the broker informs 'Welcome', the party in China makes a claim on the letter of credit, and the bank informs 'Welcome' that payment has been made. The broker follows the arrival of the goods in the Philippines, and payment of the balance of duties is made.

Despite their legal weight, however, these are not a-social transactions. Just as the social quality of rules, procedures, and roles, that make up the frame and walls of the company is kept in sight, so the presence of the social quality of these transactions is kept in mind. Far from being an absolute and rigid phenomenon which commands us to behave in a certain way, it is silently admitted that the contract, the exchange, and our behaviour, emanate from us and can be given meaning only by us. Of this social dimension we remind ourselves through an explicit distancing of the contract from the social sphere: it is 'impersonal', 'legal', separate from my relationships with you, or 'just business'. It is from this masquerade – from its treatment *as if* absolute – that the contracts' greater strength, precision, and reliability derives. Without this masquerade, legal contracts, transformed into pure absolutes, would become brittle instruments adhered to publicly, but constantly broken, circumvented, and manipulated in private. Constant monitoring and enforcement, and so the gradual ossification of activity, would soon follow. Social relationships are not a substitute for a legal framework: imbued with the affect, social relationships are the *substance* of that framework.

The view to which we are leading, then, is that the contractual agreement, treated *as if* absolute, is symbolic of the affect. The deepening of the affect demands that social relationships no longer form the explicit basis of business deals; while the emerging social ideal, and the problems associated with social kernels, move us toward the physical separation of professional and social spheres. There now remains only an understanding to treat any agreement reached between trade partners in the same way as we would treat rules and roles within the company – *as if* absolute. The contractual agreement does not substitute impersonal legality for social relationships: its essential social quality is silently admitted; and it is silently recognised that the true strength of the contract derives from the fact that it emanates from us. In short, the contractual agreement replaces personalistic relationships with those that are more affective.

Given that relationships are not the explicit basis of trade, and given the strength of the social ideal, the weakening of social kernels, and nature of the contractual agreement, then it should be no surprise that there is little correspondence between ethnicity, kinship, language, place of origin and direct trade links with mainland China. We noted in chapter 3 (section 3.1 and 3.2) that the Philippines' direct trade with China's mainland is by no means dominated by 'Chinese' companies, and that connexions with southeast and southern China are not as strong as we might have expected. We can add that, in some instances, even when overseas Chinese are first generation migrants, and even though they visit their relatives in China fairly regularly, these social relationships do not overlap with business. Although the owner of 1C (table 2) will make the trip every year to see his relatives in Xiamen (Fujian), where he was born, his business dealings are limited to Tianjin and involve no ties of kinship or friendship. The owner of 'Welcome' also travels to Fujian three or four times a year to see his relatives. At the same time he will arrange orders with the factory manufacturing the ceramic tiles that his daughter sells in Davao, and tackle any problems with goods, supplies, and timing. But the factory is not in the same town as his relatives; and again his dealings with the factory involve no ties of kinship or friendship. There is also no contact between his daughter and the factory (her spoken Chinese is not good enough) though she, too, will visit Fujian once every two years or so. Her relationship, and that of her sister, with their father's relatives in China are not close: the two sisters make the occasional journey partly to keep in touch, and partly to please their father.

Nor should it be any surprise to find that although they remain 'distanced', social relationships tend to emerge out of business deals rather than form the basis of those deals. The physical separation, as well as the psychological distancing, of social and professional life, together with the broadening of markets and suppliers which follows the weakening of social kernels, create the incentive - and open up opportunities - to form suitably 'distanced' social relationships with people outside one's own immediate professional sphere. Take the case of 1C (table 2): most of the agricultural chemicals in which it deals originate from Indonesia and Malaysia, and are coursed through one supplier in Singapore. From this long-standing trading arrangement a friendship emerged between 1C's owner and his supplier – a friendship that would draw in their children who would later attend university together in Australia. The bond between the two men strengthened each time 1C's supplier went out of his way, and well beyond any contractual duty, to chivvy the shipping companies and expedite deliveries to Mindanao. Had it not been for those interventions at a crucial time when 1C was attempting to build its name and clientele, the company would have been placed in a very difficult position from which it may not have been able to recover. Indeed, it was partly his friend's example that had led 1C's owner to make 'service' his company's creed: even if shipments are late, the company will provide materials from its reserve stocks and ask no payment from its buyers until the original cargo has arrived. Their friendship is explicitly distanced from, and is not confused with, the professional. It does not put an end to the traffic in documentation; nor is it transferable. The owner of 1C may have initiated contact with China Chemicals* through his friend's father (who had once worked for that company) after China Chemicals had made a blind appeal to him (through mass postal advertising) for his custom. But although China Chemicals provided him with good quality samples (produced by its sub-contractors), the fertilizers subsequently delivered were, to all intents and purposes, quite useless. The consignments were quickly returned to him by his most important clients, including 2Fi, 13 F, 18Ifc (table 1) and 8Ifc (table 2). There then followed visits to China Chemicals' plush offices in Tianjin, and much plain speaking with middle-ranking officials. Meanwhile, his desire to bring in goods from America grew more urgent.

Kinship, too, might also emerge out of business deals. The most important of 11If's (table 1) buyers in Korea, which itself receives substantial investment from an American company, entered into a joint venture with a Chinese partner in Shandong, specializing in the manufacture in volume of lower quality musical

---

* The company has indirect connexions with companies shown in figures 4-15 through, for example, Shanghai Huayi (上海华谊[集团]公司) (RR, figure 11, set 8).

instruments. The venture in China (*Saehan*) is managed predominantly by Koreans and its Chinese labour force has been trained by Koreans. To keep abreast of technical demands and likely changes in specifications and orders, 11If's owner visits Shandong two or three times a year. On one of these visits he was accompanied by his daughter who struck up a relationship with *Saehan's* operation manager. The two were later married. But although 11If's owner had now partially drawn his trade partner into his social sphere, their social and professional lives remained quite distinct. There are no mutual investments between the two companies; and their trading arrangements remain strictly contractual and open to competition.

This is not to say that kinship does not precede trade links. And it is again this Korean family company, 11If, which provides one of the few such instances. The company's primary market is Korea, and the owner channels his goods through an import-export company owned by his wife in Korea. His wife's company is only an intermediary; and most of his final buyers are other companies (with whom he has no kinship connexion) in Korea, Japan, or the US. Shipments through his wife's company are contractual; and no subsidies or favours are given. But if any company is to make profit from his need to ship his goods, then why should it not belong to his wife?

A more common precursor to trade links overseas is friendship. Again, however, there is no suggestion that trade is being directed or shaped by this or by other social kernels. AT*, in common with 1C, supplies agricultural chemicals to Davao. It is owned and managed by Filipinos but, like 1C, it regularly imports materials from China, this time from Zhuhai. The trading links came together by chance: an old school friend (a Filipino) of the owner was approached by *Zhuhai Qiaoji* in China to work as its agent in the Philippines. It was he who, trawling through his

---

* The company imports chemicals from China, but the value of its imports are too small to appear in table 2. However, the company does figure as a source of goods for market traders.

address book for possible customers, approached AT with prices quoted by his Chinese employer; and who arranged for the material to be routed through Manila. Goods are ordered and money paid with no direct contact between AT and *Zhuhai Qiaoji*. AT's most important sources of agricultural chemicals, however, are the US, Colombia, Malaysia and Thailand. Here again the supply channels, though set up seven years earlier, remain strictly professional. Though prior friendships happened to present themselves in the course of attempts to find suppliers and buyers, they were not, at least in the view of those who were involved, the catalyst for, nor did they secure, those deals. Price, quality, and reliability are the only considerations.

Relationships that are openly social, then, do not guide trade, though they may provide occasional opportunities. But they do have another significance. The distanced presence of these relationships within the professional sphere provides a symbolic reminder of the social dimension of the contractual agreement between companies.

What we have said of international dealings we may also say of companies' external dealings within the Philippines. Short, simple, and legally binding, written contracts usually follow verbal agreements that are often treated with equal or greater importance. Part of the reason for this is the speed at which transactions must be made. Prices are often moving up and down from one moment to the next. If a supplier, over the 'phone, commits to sell at a certain price, that price is understood to be fixed. And both sides, buyer and seller, accept that on that day only one of them will be lucky: prices are likely to move one way or the other before money is finally paid from one account to other. Following this verbal agreement, faxes are usually sent. These are not so much clumsy statements of commitment as they are attempts to avoid any confusion when so many figures are being quoted and so many deals are being made. The merchant's word, then, is important because it is a contractual agreement in a form that allows merchants to work quickly and effectively. There is, however, another reason for the importance of the spoken word: it is immediately understood as having emanated from us and, therefore, as being symbolic of the contract's social dimension.

Gifts may be understood in a similar light. In Davao 'Welcome' has been supplied with rice, coffee and cocoa from Calinan and Digos regularly for more than ten years by a small core of companies. These trading arrangements remain contractual, but are layered with 'distanced' social relationships. This 'distanced' presence is a reminder of the social dimension of mutual business dealings and contractual agreements. It is, however, the exchange of simple gifts (such as T-shirts and calendars at Christmas, on birthdays, and on other occasions) rather than the social relationships themselves, that have come to symbolise the unspoken social dimension of these deals. The transference of this symbolism from social relationships to gifts may have become necessary for the simple reason that social relationships are too close to an open admission of the agreements' social quality to work reliably as symbols preserving the affective. Should the social dimension of agreements be made too obvious, the instrumental quality of relationships would be made plain, and the move back towards personalism would have begun. In the case of smaller dealers - who, every now and then, either directly or through agents, supply Welcome with, at most, one or two sacks of rice, coffee or cocoa - there are no contractual obligations or agreements, verbal or written. There is, therefore, no need for any gifts.

4.0 Conclusions

We have argued that underlying descriptive and analytical categories of the company - such as 'traditional', 'modern', 'Chinese' or 'ethnic' - is a greater complexity rooted in the play of representations, attitudes, and relationships. We have suggested that the distancing of social relationships from the company is realised initially through authoritarianism. For various practical reasons this gives way to professionalisation or, in other words, to the clarification of rules and roles, and to the coordination of practice through shared representations of the company. At the same time there is a shift in attitude from the personal to the affective. We argued in chapter 1 that this shift from instrumentalism, and towards the treatment of social relationships *as if* absolute (as if important and of interest in their own right), is inherent in the human condition. But it may also be prompted by the sense of alienation which authoritarianism and personalism stirs in us. The corollary of the affect's deepening is the creation of a social sphere quite distinct from that of the professional sphere.

Although the one does not cause the other, there exists a synchronicity or sympathy between attitudinal shifts and professionalisation. This synchronicity describes the parallel behaviour present in both social and professional spheres. Since we hold that our social relationships are distinct, important, and of interest in their own right, then, if the social sphere is to be protected, it follows that our rules and roles within the professional sphere must be of a different order, and that they, too, must be treated *as if* absolute.

We are, in effect, asking ourselves to perform a kind of masquerade both within and outside the social sphere of our lives. Although within that sphere we treat 'you', 'I', 'us', and our relationships, as absolute, we must admit to ourselves that they are not in fact absolute. If we did not make this admission, then we would have turned our relationships and representations of 'I', 'you' and 'we', into rigid phenomena independent of us. In doing so we would have robbed ourselves of a true appreciation of the affective. And we would have made ourselves over to those of us who claim both to understand these phenomena and, therefore, to be capable of interpreting and directing them accurately. However, this admission - that our relationships are not in fact absolute - must be made silently. If it is not, we would lead ourselves, through open admission of their social quality, to destroy the mystique of the rules and roles of the professional sphere; and, through the implicit admission that our social relationships have an instrumental quality, to breach the integrity of the social sphere.

This treatment of our social relationships *as if* absolute brings tolerance, empathy, and flexibility to the professional sphere. So valuable are these qualities that our desire to perform the masquerade deepens, prompting greater efforts within the professional sphere to protect it from the social. This strengthens the seal between the two spheres still further.

The performance of our masquerade, and the synchronicity which exists between the affect and the professional, encourage the affect to deepen to the extent that a kind of universal social ideal emerges. Bound by a sense of commonality, there is now within the social sphere a diminution both in the desire for exclusive relationships and for conformity (to the greater difference of the group); and, therefore, in the significance of social kernels such as kinship and ethnicity. This social ideal, and this reaction to conformity, are again paralleled in the professional sphere where they hold practical advantage. Here, within the company, there is a tendency to remove any suggestion of instrumentalism; social relationships, though distanced, are formed not so much among members of the same company as with people outside it; the use of social bases such as kinship, language, and ethnicity, comes to be regarded as being either less important as a prelude to business, or as a limitation; and an emphasis on creativity and independence grows heavier.

At the same time, as the professional and social spheres become more sharply defined and distanced, the need for a reminder that we are only performing a masquerade intensifies. For were we to loose sight of the true social quality of the rules and roles of professional life, and were we to treat our relationships as absolutes, we would have begun the move back towards the personal, breaching the two spheres. These reminders can take many forms, but they may include the merchant's 'word' and gifts.

What the details of particular instances appear to show, then, is that the practice of trade and business provides its own stimulus for professionalisation; and that this is accompanied by a more affective attitude to social relationships. What these particular instances also show is that professionalisation and attitudinal change are not clear cut or unidirectional; nor do they begin or end at a particular moment in time. Attitudes are constantly shifting, creating uncertainty even within each of us. Upon this we must layer the additional complication of changes in practical considerations and representations. Together, attitudes, practice, and representations, work to sharpen, pull apart, and breach the professional and social spheres, generating ambiguity within and among companies. Thus does the overlap between the social and professional spheres seem to be moving in opposite directions simultaneously among parts of the same company. In *Haojia*'s Shanghai branch, the Shanghainese workforces' relatives are excluded from any possibility of employment in the company, while the appointment of employees' kin to other branches of the same company in the Philippines serves as a means of informal and inexpensive training, induction, and political screening. Even within the same branch of a company we may find ambiguity. In I8 Ifc (table 1) and 8Ifc (table 2) the appointment of employees' kin and the inheritance of jobs are seen to hold distinct advantages in certain areas of the companies' operations, but are expressly forbidden in others. Even where management and family ownership has been separated, the overlap of the professional and social finds expression in the form of other practices. In AT (to which we also referred above) family ownership is completely separated from management, responsibility for which rests in the hands of the General Manager. However, he has known the family well for more than fifteen years; and whilst many companies in the Philippines and Shanghai do their best to eradicate both *padrino* managers and the cliques which form around other familiar social kernels such as language and place of origin, he is the *ninong* of many of his subordinates' children, and he does his best to foster those groups. For this is a sales company: the presence of these cliques helps to sharpen competition; and his role as *compadre* helps him to convey the impression to each clique that they have a special place in his heart. The Chinese company 1C, in common with AT, also sells agricultural chemicals, but here we find that the owner (and a very active President and manager) will not become his employees' *compadre*. Social relationships are very clearly and explicitly distanced. 'I will do my job and you must do yours'. But his wife, who among her other responsibilities is in charge of personnel, sees value in encouraging the succession of posts within the families of her employees; and she is happy to take on the role of their children's *ninang*. In this instance, perhaps, we are seeing reminders of the unspoken social quality of professional roles taking a symbolic form stylised enough to keep it from being understood as an open admission of those roles' social quality.

There does appear, then, to be a strong move towards the professionalisation of companies that dominate the Philippines' economy and its trade with China; and towards the physical separation of social and professional spheres. Whatever the advantages that an overlap of professional and social spheres may bring, its risks and limitation are seen to be greater still. But as we turn our attention to the particular we find always exception, ambiguity, and contradiction. Set against this fluid complexity, notions such as 'tradition', 'modern', 'Chinese', ethnic', 'hybrid' and 'convergence' seem awkward and limited descriptions of features that apply to some part of all companies at some time.

Chapter 5
Political Transformation? China

1.0 Introduction

In the previous chapter we continued with the dis-aggregation of particular instances of trade and business in the Philippines and China. We argued that from our attempt to tease out the play of representations, attitudes, and relationships, there has emerged what appears to be an association between the professionalisation of the company, and attitudinal change. We also suggested that authoritarianism may in itself demand a measure of professionalisation, and stimulate a deepening of the affect.

Can we, perhaps, also see something of these shifts in attitude reflected in the merchants' own representations of 'the Chinese' and other groups? From the point of view of many of those (including overseas Chinese in the Philippines) whose experience is centred in Manila, there seems to be little, if any, difference between the ways in which the overseas Chinese run their companies, and the operations of Filipinos; and this is a view which, as we noted in chapter 3, is often shared by those who staff the more technocratic institutions of government. Nor do those Chinese-Filipinos who have had several years of experience in Shanghai see much difference between family-owned businesses there and Chinese or Filipino family businesses in the Philippines.

These views correspond with the comments on ethnicity and its diminution that we made in chapters 3 and 4. It is only as merchants recount their experiences in those parts of China or the Philippines with which they are least familiar that the bold lines of caricature thicken, colour drains away, and dimensions flatten. Even those overseas Chinese with the most sophisticated, nuanced, detailed, and particular understandings of Manila and Shanghai, are quick to paint images of Chinese from other parts of China in awkward strokes of black and white. The northern Chinese reach agreements easily and seem to be content with a small profit; but they will rarely keep to their word. Meanwhile, the southern Chinese, determined to make the bigger profit in any transaction, will duck and dive in the face of their responsibilities and all manner of legal and moral constraints. Equally comfortable with their own descriptions of the Shanghainese as being lazy, concerned only with their pay, sensitive to criticism, irresponsible, calculating, and cut-throat, are those Chinese recently posted to Shanghai from the north, south, and west of the country. In the Philippines, too, the sophisticated corporate businessmen and businesswomen (whether Filipino, Chinese, or International[*]), find their caricatures strengthening as they cast their mind back to their experiences in the provinces. The Filipino dislikes responsibilities, and is slow to make decisions, most especially over financial matters. They are an outgoing and friendly people who sing well, dance gracefully, and know how to enjoy life; but they are undisciplined, poorly focussed and, rather than work hard, they prefer to depend upon political connexions and patronage to make a quick profit. The Chinese, on the other hand, are clannish, secretive, and family oriented; and although they have an ability to view the bigger picture with clarity and objectivity, they are manipulative, untrustworthy, ruthless, and locked into their traditions.

There is a notable contrast between these flat caricatures and the highly nuanced descriptions of particular instances which merchants are also more than capable of providing. The latter are so full of detail and dimensional commonalities that it is impossible either to generalise or to point to any fundamental differences between ethnic groups. The contrast is most striking when it issues from the same mouth. We might, perhaps, imagine a gradation in the complexity of representations as, in

---

[*] See chapter 3

their minds, the more cosmopolitan merchants travel away from Manila and Shanghai to the rim of their experience and find there only simplistic and negative caricatures. After all, the decline in the significance of ethnicity and kinship as we move towards Manila, and the deepening of professionalism and the affect noted in chapters 3 and 4, would lead us to expect a concentration of attitudinal change as we approach centres of business organisation. As they move from those places where they feel most comfortable, do the merchants experience a sense of disorientation? This, we suggested in chapter 2, may be the origin of our notion of difference. Is it through this sense of disorientation that they interpret their own frustration with what they perceive to be a weakening, both in the affect, and in the level of professionalism, among the people they are talking about?

The suggestion is intriguing, but the complexity and fluidity of instances on the ground make very uncertain any notion of a 'mappable' geography of attitudinal change. We noted in chapter 4 instances of those, both young and old, who see more differences among families and individuals than they do either among Chinese from different parts of China, or between Chinese and non-Chinese; and who therefore seem immune to the attractions of caricature. We also noted in both chapters 4 and 3 that there are in Davao instances of the affect deepening, and of moves towards greater professionalism. And we suggested in chapters 1 and 2 that a constant state of ambiguity in attitude, as well as being inherent in the human condition, describes a practical response to the relationships formed around us. Consequently, we should not be surprised to find among businessmen and women at the centre (and in the provinces in the Philippines) an ambiguity in their representations of self and group, both over geographical distance and as their immediate circumstances alter. Owners, managers, and workers (whether they be Filipinos or Chinese) will constantly change their minds: they will, as circumstances seem to require, adhere to one or more of the many, and often contradictory, concepts of 'Chineseness' or 'Filipino'. When faced with envious criticism of his success a 'Chinese' merchant (2 C, table 2) will, for instance, say 'we, the Chinese, unlike Filipinos, rely upon our word of honour in the conduct of business'. But he will, in the same breath, recognise that Filipino merchants depend upon their word of honour and operate as effectively by word of mouth in the conduct of trade, and he will extend lines of credit to other 'Chinese' and 'Filipinos' alike. The successful Filipino merchants will lament the inability of 'Filipinos' to succeed in business; Chinese merchants who turn to Confucian explanations of their success see no differences between the way in which Chinese and Filipinos conduct business; to be 'Chinese', it is claimed, is to be an extension of being 'Filipino', and yet 'the Chinese' are inherently different because of their culture; a farmer will not trust 'the Chinese', and yet he will associate with, trade with, and rely upon, close Chinese friends rather than another Filipino to buy his crops; a Filipino whose great-grandfather was Chinese will complain about the clannishness, secrecy, and dishonesty of 'the Chinese,' and yet he is proud to bear a surname which is Chinese; 'the Chinese' are fundamentally different from 'the Filipinos', it is claimed, and yet there is no point in trying to make a distinction between these groups. It would seem that the generalised representation 'Filipino' and 'Chinese' which the merchant sometimes creates is often at odds with the dimensional commonalities of the merchants and customers he actually deals with in particular instances.

Arguably, then, the extent to which ethnicity as a social kernel diminishes in importance while an awareness of the details and dimensional commonalities of particular instances, and a suspicion with generalisation, correspondingly increase, may well constitute a barometer of attitudinal change. This change, we have said, is conducive to, and is a concomitant of, professionalisation. It may also be encouraged by, and lead to, the erosion of authoritarianism and centralised control within the company. But it is a barometer of change in particular instances and at particular times rather than in the general atmosphere across geographical space. Indeed, so dynamic are their representations of self and group that those who might be defined as Chinese, Filipino, Korean, Japanese or Indian, appear to have left behind those of us who would attempt to enumerate, assess, describe, and explain them. And it may only be sensible that we should accept this. For, as we noted in chapter 3, the more we attempt to enumerate and assess, the harder our concepts may become, and the more we risk lending our interpretations to misrepresentation and abuse. This problem is not unique to the study of the Chinese or the Philippines. If the intentional and unintentional construction of identity by academics has political repercussions for these two countries, then similar repercussions will be felt even more deeply by those who have only recently survived war, or who are riven by political divisions, or whose intention is to dismantle particular regimes if not the home nation itself (Fandy, 1999; Bernal, 2004). We can take this argument still further. The treatment of 'I', 'you', 'us', and our relationships, *as if* absolute - and the masquerade and the compact which this affective attitude demands of us - is evidently sympathetic to democratic values and to the professionalisation of democratic institutions. Bold caricatures, if drawn into the practice of relationships and used to create exclusive and hostile groups, will only block formalisation and frustrate political change.

In view of the deepening of the affect, the emergence of the social ideal, the diminution of ethnicity and kinship, and the complex variations in the presence and strength of representations of ethnicity, surely we are now bound to ask whether or not shifting attitudes have begun to find wider expression in the polity, both in China and in the Philippines?

2.0 Merchant, bureaucrat, and politician.

It is a common view that doing business in China is difficult and that it is especially difficult for foreign companies owned and managed by those who are not Chinese. Foreign, non-Chinese, companies may have the capital, but they do not have in place the relationships to compete effectively; nor do they have the knowledge and experience that will allow them to establish such relationships. However, we noted in chapter 4 that owners, managers, and employees, including those who are overseas Chinese, are frustrated when they find that even the simplest task is weighed down by personalistic considerations and when, as a consequence, they feel compelled to follow an elaborate choreography simply in order to establish and to maintain business arrangements or agreements which, in their view, should have no need of constant nurturing.

Those who are attempting to break into the domestic markets (whether or not they are Chinese) are often faced with three especially difficult problems. The first is to buy space on shelves in the supermarkets, in department stores, and in shops and warehouses of the smaller retailers and wholesalers. The second is to find reliable distributors who will search out and secure that space, broker deals, and move the goods – and who will do so at prices that will still leave the foreign company with some profit. So intense is the competition, and so exasperating is it to see shoddy goods beating their better-priced and higher quality products onto the street, that *Shanghai Lejin*'s (上海樂金) marketing division (pushing for lower quality, lower-priced goods) and its technical division (determined to maintain and improve quality) have begun to turn on each other.

A third problem has been the collection of revenue. For instance, 18If (table 1) whose primary export market from the Philippines is Japan, Korea and the Gulf has found it relatively easy to establish an office, a ripening room and a cold room in both Shanghai and Dalian, and to sell their fruit at good prices. But it has proved far more difficult to collect revenues from distributors; and this has prompted the company to attempt to trade directly with the supermarkets and retailers who then raised their charges for shelf space.

In more recent years, then, competition has become especially cut-throat; and access has, in the view of some, more to do with establishing the right contacts within the bureaucracy and polity, and with paying suitable kickbacks. It is partly for this reason that companies are having to treat different parts of China as quite distinct markets, each of which requires its own dedicated and well-connected marketing teams. Even those overseas Chinese who have learnt the ropes well enough in Shanghai admit to having come unstuck when they venture beyond the Municipality's boundaries. Out there, they say, officialdom is strongly instrumental. In one instance a Chinese-Filipino merchant who, having rented a factory from a state company together with its 300 workers, discovered, much to his surprise, that he had taken on far heavier welfare responsibilities than he had bargained for, including the pension and medical expenses for one employee who, only 6 months after the deal had been signed, was invalided out of the company with a chronic, but not life-threatening, medical condition.

However, dealings between companies and officialdom are more sophisticated than these kinds of problems might seem to suggest. We noted in chapter 4 that in companies in Shanghai the affect does seem to be deepening, and that there do appear to be moves towards greater professionalism within the company and in its external dealings. Foreign companies are able to find the more reliable and effective distributors. It may take time (often years), but it is possible, through trial and error, to weed out the unreliable; and simple practical measures, such as paying and collecting in cash rather than through cheque or bank transfers, will help to keep the distributors in line. And companies do work to contract. Take the instance of *Taixi*: three quarters of its buyers and suppliers are overseas (mostly in the United States), and the remaining quarter are in mainland China. We noted in chapter 4 that most of the company's staff are mainland Chinese, and that it is they who arrange the deals. In common with practice in the Philippines, deals are made verbally at first. These are followed up with written contracts in the form of promissory orders. Here in Shanghai, as in the Philippines, particular importance is attached to the merchant's word: it allows speed, and it is symbolic of the contract's social dimension. The merchant's word is therefore equated implicitly both with the protection of the professional and social spheres, and so with predictability and reliability. To break one's word is to damage one's own reputation and business now and in the longer term. So powerful are these sentiments that the legal dimension is often regarded as superfluous: such is the confidence in their word, and in the quality of their products, that *Taixi* issues contracts guaranteeing supplies during a one-month period, but orders in raw materials based on a two-month forecast of the customer's requirements. If, during the first month, the company is late with its deliveries, the company will pay for the cost of the raw materials used during the second month. Thus the company is committed to their customer for two months, but the customer is committed to the company for only one month.

Shipbuilders, state and private, also work to clear contracts. In this competitive international market, profit margins have become so thin that the *Patriotic Yard* has had to move away from the manufacture of container ships, to the production of smaller, higher quality, and more specialized vessels. Delivery dates are built into contracts, and broken deadlines incur heavy financial penalties. The aim here is not merely to meet deadlines, but to deliver early. Although this earns no financial reward, the reputation of the yard and its word grows.

Contractual agreements, then, are observed. We suggested in chapter 4 that these are not a substitute for social relationships: to the contrary, social relationships are the substance of those agreements, though recognition of that substance is left unspoken. Symbolic reminders of those agreements' social dimension may take many forms, including gifts or the merchant's word. But whatever form they take, those reminders are essential to the masquerade: otherwise rules, roles, and relationships, as they ossify, and are turned into instruments of the personal, will lose the strength and flexibility which derives from their treatment *as if* absolute and from our common compact.

It is in this light that we might also understand the relationships between companies and officials in Shanghai. These are usually formed with district officials. They will do their best to help foreign interests negotiate bureaucratic and legal constraints and guidelines surrounding everything from location to employment conditions, tax and customs. In return the company is expected to do its best to keep the official informed of its decisions and problems. From the officials' point of view this is only good manners: the company has received much help from officials who are held to account by their superiors for what goes on among, and within, businesses in their jurisdiction; and the district officials' superiors have a natural and legitimate interest in the possible effects which the company's behaviour and decisions might have on the local economy. It is precisely in order to keep the contact between company and official on a professional footing that the masquerade is performed; and that, as part of this, the unspoken social dimension of that contact is symbolised, commonly in the form of ritualised gifts, meals, and social gatherings. For instance, *Haojia*'s owners and managers spend much time and energy socialising with officials, though there is very little socialising among the company's own employees. Meanwhile *Taixi*'s managers will send cards, calendars and perhaps a company pen or some other present to officials at Christmas with thanks for all their help, guidance, and corrections, over the past year. The intention here is not to foster what is sometimes called 'social capital' or, less pretentiously, obligation. Indeed, not only is there no intention to foster a sense of obligation in the official, but every effort is made to avoid conveying the impression that the company harbours any such intention. To do otherwise would appear to represent a breach of both the professional and the social; and would introduce a sense of instability, uncertainty and suspicion into the mind of the official. Were the merchant to allow the social to encroach into the professional sphere, the social would be tainted, and professional life would have been made expensive and more complicated. The number of officials who would have to be drawn in to keep the illicit deals hidden would snowball; and if an official is moved on, the merchant would have to begin all over again with the official's replacements. All this only makes for sleepless nights.

Whilst there always exists the opportunity to weave together personalistic relationships through which rules might be circumvented and favours dispensed, the rituals and the gifts are neither inherently corrupt nor are they necessarily a precursor to corruption. To the contrary, they often mark genuine attempts to preserve the integrity of the professional and social spheres. They are to say, very simply and directly, 'lets keep our dealings professional, and tackle problems when they arise'. The kinds of problems which do emerge, while bureaucratic, are potentially damaging. The *Patriotic Yard* works to very tights deadlines which must be met if it is to avoid heavy financial penalties on profits that are already marginal. The delivery of a completed vessel has to be accompanied with a bundle of documents whose processing through various government departments can take up to four or five days – as period of time that can make the difference between a small or still smaller profit, or between profit and loss. Through their relationships with district officials in those departments, the whole procedure can be completed in one morning. In this instance, the flexibility brought to rules and roles brought by the unspoken social dimension is in no sense theoretical: it keeps people in their jobs.

Some measure of attitudinal change would appear to be taking place at the lower reaches of the bureaucracy. In view of this - and given the authoritarian quality of China's polity, the close links between the economy and polity noted in chapter 1, and the apparent shift towards professionalisation and the affect noted in chapter 4 - then should we not expect that more professionalised, formalised, and stronger practices and institutions, are emerging more widely in China's political life? Might we not also expect that, however modest, some momentum for democracy is beginning to build up? We noted in chapter 1 that there are today many commentators throughout the social sciences who see in China's polity evidence of such transformation, though coming through their writings is a strong sense that the emerging patterns and qualities of institutions and values will be Chinese and not western. China's democratic forms, it seems, will be coloured by Chinese characteristics. One inference which might be drawn from this literature is that culture plays a greater role in China than in the Philippines. This is curious from an intellectual standpoint, though understandable. The images of China's difference and uniqueness, and the presence of a truly ancient dialectic between scholarship (domestic and foreign) and the Chinese polity (a dialectic whose influence has also been felt in the literature of the overseas Chinese), have endowed the scholars' cultural representations of China and 'the Chinese' with considerable political meaning.

The problem we face is that until we are able to disaggregate in the field particular instances of the representations, attitudes, and relationships, which together comprise the organs of China's central government, it will remain unsafe to attribute much authority, either to our beliefs about the leadership's motivations and its representations of the world and China's place within it, or to our assessments of the extent and nature of such informal-formal transformation as may be underway. Nevertheless, we might be able to see political change reflected indirectly in those economic institutions and practices that are of special political significance. Among the most important of these, perhaps, are flows of investment. Statistical and documentary materials suggest that the devolution of investment flows among the strongest* industrial enterprises - and these include Shanghai's largest importers from, and exporters to, the Philippines†– is clearly institutional in

---

*As measured by sales.

† More than half (about 60%) of the top fifty exporters (and they account for the majority of exports by value) from Shanghai to the Philippines fall into three categories. The first comprises companies which rank among the top 300 (and most of these companies are in the top 120). This includes, for example, M6 (上海西门子移动通信有限公司), set 3 (*see figures 4 – 14*); M7 (上海通用汽车有限公司), set 10; M14 (飞利浦电子元件(上海)有限公司), set 2; M29 (上海氯碱化工股份有限公司), set 8; M94 (东芝电脑[上海]有限公司); M120 (飞利浦亚明照明有限公司), set 2; M226 (上海亿人通信终端有限公司). The second comprises those companies which receive major investments from groups or companies (such as G6 [中国华源集团有限公司], set 9; and M28 [上海广电信息产业股份有限公司], set 3) which rank among the top 120, or from those ranking companies' and groups' subsidiaries (such as 沪东中华造船[集团]有限公司上海中华造船厂长 [related to G11 {沪东中华造船集团有限公司}, set 11]). The third category comprises those companies which receive investments from entities who are not ranked among, but have

182

character. This discrepancy between the growing personalism often commented upon in China's economic and political life (see chapter 1), and the institutional quality of investment flows, is curious. Might it indicate the beginnings of deeper, if longer-term, political reform?

3.0 Investment patterns

The strongest 50 industrial groups and 120 industrial enterprises - which together comprise Shanghai's industrial core - and their investment flows are shown in figures 4 - 15[*]. Also shown in these figures are those industrial enterprises (another 160 or so in number) which rank among the next strongest 380 enterprises and which are linked through investment flows, interlocking board chairs or lines of subordination[†] to other industrial enterprises within the core or strongest 500 enterprises. Among the top ten investors in each core group or enterprise are other

other major investments in, companies and groups that do rank among the top 120. This includes, for example, V (上海久事), set 2. Nearly three quarters of all exporters (including those who are not linked into the webs of investment shown in figures 4 -15) are either foreign companies or have a substantial foreign component. Of these foreign, or substantially foreign, companies, only 10% are overseas Chinese.

The figures for importers are somewhat lower. Only just over a third of the top fifty importers (and they account for the majority of imports by value from the Philippines into Shanghai) may also be placed into the first two of those categories. The first category includes , among others, M10 (上海惠普有限公司), set 2; M6 (上海西门子移动通信有限公司), set 3; M20 (惠普计算机产品[上海]有限公司), set 2; M14 (飞利浦电子元件(上海)有限公司), set 2; M168 (英特尔科技[中国]有限公司); and, again, M226 (上海亿人通信终端有限公司). The second includes, for example, 上海市医药有限公司 (related to G4 [上海医药{集团}有限公司], set 8). None can be put into the third category. And of all these importers, a little under 60% of them are foreign or substantially foreign. Of these foreign entities, just over 10% are classified as overseas Chinese. (*Sources:* SSG (上海市工商管理局) 2002-3; SSTJJ (上海市统计局), 2002-3; SHHG (上海海关综合统计处) 2003-3.

[*]The information on investments from which these figures were constructed was supplied in large part by SSG . Other sources include SSTJJ (2002 & 2003) (various records); ZCZP 中国诚信证券评估有限公司, 中诚信国际信用评级有限责任公司 (2002); Li Zhaowen (2002); ZQLZQX 中国企业联合会, 中国企业家协会 (2002)

[†]This latter type of connexion represents, in most instances, both a superior's financial interest in its subordinate as well as the remnants of the pre-reform organisational hierarchy. Within this hierarchy, enterprises fell under companies that were in their turn responsible to bureaux and ministries.

core entities and 'supplementary' units. These supplementary units refer to: administrative or political bodies; and to other enterprises that either lie outside the strongest 500 industrial enterprises, or are not classed as being 'industrial' in character in official Chinese materials. The supplementary units shown are: those which are the sole investor, or the prime originator of investment, in core enterprises; those which invest in, or receive investment from, more than one core entity; and those that have an investment connexion with another supplementary unit which itself invests in, or receives investment from, core entities. Included among these supplementary units are those listed[*] companies that invest in, or receive investment from, only one other supplementary or core entity.

A simplified overview of these investment connexions is provided in figure 15. The core (but excluding the top 50 industrial groups), though it represents less than 1% of the total number of industrial enterprises in Shanghai, is responsible for some 45% of total industrial sales within the municipality. The share of municipal sales accounted for by the core, together with those industrial enterprises which rank among the next strongest 380 enterprises and which are linked to other industrial enterprises with the strongest 500, rises to 53%. Taken as a whole, the strongest 500 industrial enterprises comprise less than 3% of the total number of industrial enterprises but account for just under two-thirds of sales.

3.1 Coalitions and hierarchies

What appears to have emerged from industrial reform over the last twenty-five years or so is not so much a single web but a series of webs or, more accurately, coalitions with lose internal hierarchies, connected to one another at different levels in those hierarchies and with varying degrees of intensity. These coalitions comprise clusters of mutual investments which take place among the top 500 enterprises within similar lines of activity. These clusters are often centred on

---

[*]Companies listed on the Shanghai or Shenzhen stock exchanges.

formal groups, such as: G1 [Baoshan] (上海宝钢集团公) (set 5); G4 [Shanghai Medicines] (上海医药集团有限公司) (set 8); G6 [China Hua Yuan] (中国华源集团有限公司) (set 9); G2 [Shanghai Auto Industry] (上海汽车工业集团总公司) (set 10); G15 [Shanghai Construction Materials] (上海建筑材料集团总公司) (set 1); and G8 [Shanghai Nonferrous Metals] (上海有色金属集团有限公司)(set 1). Some of the industrial enterprises ranked among the top 500 shown in figures 4-15 are formally a member of these core industrial groups, but most are not.

The stronger - and usually core - industrial enterprises (and especially those listed on the China's stock exchanges) also serve, in effect, as secondary nodes. These include: M28 (上海广电信息产业股份有限公司) [Shanghai Guangdian] (set 3); M371 (上海广电电子股份有限公司 (Shanghai Guangdian Dianzi) (set 3); M59 (上海汽车股份有限公司) [Shanghai Auto] (set 10); M3 (上海市电力公司) [Shanghai Power] (set 6); M4 (中国石化上海石油化工股份有限公司) [Shanghai Pechem] (set 6); and M5 (中国石油化工股份有限公司上海高桥分公司)[China Petrochemical] (set 6). M28, for instance is secondary to G7 (上海广电集团有限公司) [Shanghai Guangdian] (set 2); M3 is secondary to SE(国家电力工会司华东公司) [State Power] (set 6); and M4 and M5 are secondary to the SDB (国家开发银行) [State Development Bank] (set 6).

The most important kernels, however, are those which reach both within and across lines of activity. These tend to be supplementary units, and may be placed into various categories. The first are bureaucratic and political units, particularly those involved in the administration of state assets. At municipal level they include SA (the State Asset Administration Office [上海市国有资产管理办公室] and the State Asset Administration Committee [上海市国有资产管理委员会]); and at central level, they include PRFT (Ministry for Trade and Economic Cooperation [中华人民共和国对外贸易经济合作部]), and the State Council [国务院财政部]).

The second are those companies charged with the administration, supervision, and direction, of those assets. These include: V (Shanghai Jiushi [上海久事公司]); SS (Shanghai Industrial Investments [上海工业投资集团有限公司]); MM (Shanghai Municipal Government Asset Management Development Co. [上海市政资产经营发展有限公司]); NN (Shanghai State Asset Management Co. [上海国有资产经营有限公司]); Ii (China Xinda Asset Administration Co.[中国信达资产管理公司]); Ii2 (China Eastern Asset Administration Co. [中国东方资产管理公司]; and jj (China Hua Rong Asset Administration Co.[中国华融资产管理公司]). The third are trusts, such as W (Shanghai International Trust and Investment Ltd.[上海国际信托投资有限公司]. The fourth are holding companies, such as QQ (Shanghai Light Industry Holdings (Group) Co. [上海轻工控股集团公司]), TT (Shanghai Textile Holdings Co. [上海纺织控股集团公司]), and X (Shanghai Electronics Holdings [上海仪电控股集团公司]). Finally there are those other groups and listed companies which lie outside the core and top 500 such as OO+ (Shenergy [申能股份有限公司]), UU+ (Dragon Group[上海龙头集团股份有限公司]); and the banks, such as the Transport Bank (交通银行上海分行). There exists, then, the appearance of a hierarchy: state organs and its commercial arms feed each other, the industrial groups, listed companies, and enterprises.

A little more precision and definition can be given to these statements and to the hierarchy. If we begin by looking at the number of flows and their direction, then investment flows can be broken down into two categories: those which occur within similar and related lines of activity; and those which take place across those divisions.

The first category is the larger: some 67% of investments - that is, about two-thirds of the number of investment flows shown in figures 4-15 - occur among entities within the particular lines of activity identified. Of these about one third flow from supplementary units to industrial enterprises (more than half of which are either ranked within the top 50 or are listed companies or both). Another third flow among entities ranked within the top 500 enterprises and 50 groups, and most of these (about four-fifths) flow from groups and listed companies to industrial enterprises. About 15% of investments within lines of activity flow from supplementary units to groups, and another 10% flow among supplementary units.

It is also among entities within lines of activity that most instances (close to 80%) of the larger and medium flows of investment are concentrated; and half of these investments flow from supplementary units to the stronger enterprises, listed companies, and groups. Another third take place among enterprises and groups; and about a tenth take place between supplementary units.

The second category, then, is the smaller one: only about a third of the number of all investment flows take place between entities across different lines of activity. About 30% of these flows occur among supplementary units; a little under a quarter of investments flow from supplementary units to industrial enterprises. Only about one tenth of flows between units across different lines of activity occur among industrial enterprises and groups. But whilst the proportion of flows among the upper echelons (supplementary units) across different lines of activity is greater than the proportion of flows among the upper echelons within the same line of activity, the vast majority (70%) of all smaller flows occurs between units across different lines of activity. In other words, not only are there fewer instances of flows across different lines of activity, but the proportion of smaller to larger flows across different lines of activity is higher than between units within the same lines of activity. Across lines of activity there are also, in comparison with intra-sectoral flows, a greater number of small flows and fewer larger flows among supplementary units.

In sum, within particular lines of activity there is a greater focussing of the sources of investment in fewer originators towards the upper end of the hierarchy; and a slight fanning out of originators among the lower ends. This fanning out becomes more pronounced across sectors and some two-thirds of these flows are small or medium. Indeed, investments received from units in other sectors, though they may rank among the recipients' top 10 investors, may account for as little as 1% of the total in some instances.

A further observation which may be of some importance is that even within sectors, links - such as those emanating from M14 (飞利浦电子元件上海有限公司) [Philips Electronics Components] and M10 (上海惠普有限公司) [Hewlett Packard] - may be tenuous. Many of the stronger enterprises are free-standing or coalesce in small clusters around local government units (see sets 9 and 11).

3.2 Industrial parochialism

These oligarchic coalitions appear to exhibit rather weak connexions between Shanghai's industrial enterprises and those in the rest of China. Leaving aside for the moment the involvement of the various organs and commercial arms of the central authorities, there is relatively little investment by provincial enterprises in Shanghai's core industrial entities; and there is relatively little investment by those core entities in provincial enterprises. In less than 1% of core entities (excluding listed companies) do provincial entities rank as the sole, major, or main (top 10), investors. Nor are the main investments by Shanghai's core enterprises directed towards provincial enterprises.

Even among Shanghai's listed companies (in all sectors) we still find manifestations of what appears to be a marked degree of parochialism, at least as far as the rest of provincial China is concerned. Shanghai's listed companies are listed only on the Shanghai stock exchange (none appeared on the Shenzhen bourse); and they form by far the largest proportion (20%) of all companies listed on the exchange. The next largest proportions are 7% each for Jiangsu and Zhejiang, followed by Beijing (6%), Shandong to the northeast, and Hubei and Sichuan to the west *(ZCZP, op.cit.;* Li Zhaowen, *op.cit.).*

Investment in Shanghai's listed companies by provincial enterprises (listed or otherwise) is comparatively light. Only in about a third of Shanghai's own companies do provincial interests figure among the main (top 10) investors. The majority (some three-fifths) of these investors do not hold more than a 5% stake, and most are much smaller (under 1%). Only in 6% of instances did the provincial share either exceed a third or constitute the majority share holding. Only in one instance (M267 [上海宽频科技股份有限公司]) was the enterprise subordinate to another provincial authority (Jiangsu).

The interests of Shanghai's enterprises (listed or otherwise) in provincial enterprises (whether or not listed on the Shanghai or Shenzhen exchanges) are also comparatively light. Only in about 20% of provincial companies do Shanghai enterprises rank among the main investors. Again the majority of these holdings (some four-fifths) do not exceed 5%, and most of these are much smaller (less than 1% or 2%). And in no more than 5% of provincial enterprises do Shanghai companies hold more than a fifth of shares.

Very few of the industrial enterprises shown in figures 4-15 rank among the main investors in provincial enterprises. Indeed, only 2% of the provincial enterprises listed on China's stock exchanges receive significant (within the top 10) investments from any of those companies shown in figures 4-15. Most of the main investors from Shanghai are either not classed as industrial, lie outside the core or top 500 or, more commonly, are trust or security companies, such as Q [国泰君安证券股份公司]. As might be expected, investments by these entities are spread widely and, in any one instance, are relatively small (*ibid.*; SSG, 2002-3).

Looking more broadly across the Municipality, a number of other figures seem to confirm this parochial tendency. The figure for the accumulated total of provincial enterprises (in all economic sectors) which have operated in Shanghai at one time or other over the past decade, is a little over 20,000; and their accumulated investment is estimated at 160 billion *yuan* (SNBW [上海年鉴编纂委员会], 2002). These figures do not compare favourably with those given above for foreign entities; and whilst most of that accumulated total is accounted for by fairly dramatic increases in the number of provincial enterprises operating in Shanghai in recent years (from just over 3,500 in 2000 to a little over 4,000 in 2001), the contribution of provincial enterprises to municipal economic growth fell from 9% in 1998 to under 5% in 2001-2. Procurements outside the municipality by Shanghai's wholesale and retail enterprises have also fallen from 17% of those enterprises' total procurements in 1995 to 6% in 2001/2 (*ibid.;* SSTJJ, *op.cit.*).

In the other direction, the number of Shanghai enterprises investing in other parts of China is only marginally higher: some 4,200 enterprises with investments of some 18 billion *yuan* for 2001-2) - a little above the average for annual investments into Shanghai. The number of industrial enterprises with their headquarters set up outside Shanghai in other parts of China amounted to just 0.04% of the number of enterprises and a very small share of sales (at least with respect to municipal sales) of just 0.1%. Sales outside the Municipality by Shanghai's wholesale establishments have also fallen (*ibid.*).

3.3 Local-central-foreign coalitions

It is clear that while connexions with the rest of provincial China are weak and weakening relatively, connexions with the outside world are strengthening. Whilst foreign entities are the originator for only 17% of the flows within and amongst sectors illustrated in figures 4-15, they do represent substantial inflows of investment (especially in high technology) at the lower ends of the hierarchy, a good proportion of which have made their way further up that hierarchy.

Furthermore, although these foreign enterprises tend to cluster towards the lower end of the hierarchy and around the kernels dominated by supplementary units and groups, some do appear to serve as nodes, including: M17 (上海永新彩色显像管股份有限公司) [Shanghai Novel Colour Picture Tube Co. Ltd.], set 3; M215 (上海贝岭股份有限公司) [Shanghai Beiling]; M18 (上海索广电子有限公司) [Shanghai Suoguang Electronics], set 3; M25 (上海索广映像有限公司) [Shanghai Suoguang Visual Products], set 3; and M4 (中国石化上海石油化工股份有限公司) [Shanghai Pechem], set 6. We should also note that a fifth of supplementary groups (a proportion that excludes administrative units) and a fifth of groups are foreign, including: Aa (汉诺威亚太投资有限公司) [Han Nuo Investments Ltd.], set 2; Z (惠普{中国}投资有限公司) [Hewlett Packard Investments], set 2; Bb (飞利浦电子元件{上海}有限公司) [Philips Electronics], set 2; L (可口可乐[中国]投资有限公司) [Coca-Cola Investments], Dd (索尼{中国}有限公司) [Sony (China) Ltd], set 3; KK+ (大众交通集团股份有限公司) [Volkswagen Transport], set 6; LL+ (上海大众科技创业{集团}股份有限公司) [Volkswagen Science and Technology], set 6; G18 (上海海立{集团}股份有限公司) [Shanghai Hai Li], set 7; and G35 (中国第一铅笔股份有限公司) [China First Pencil Share Holding Co, Ltd], set 7. Together the foreign entities shown in figures 4-15, not all of which are ranked among the top 500, account for about 31% of municipal industrial sales. More broadly, nearly two-thirds of the core industrial enterprises and just under two-thirds of the remaining 380 strongest industrial enterprises within the Municipality are foreign - that is they are either wholly owned by foreign interests or are classed as some form of Sino-foreign venture. Taken as a whole they account for a little under 40% of Shanghai's industrial sales.

Coalitions are also oriented towards the centre. Across the municipality some 6% of industrial enterprises are classed as state-owned; and 1% are directly subordinate to the central authorities. Together these state-owned industrial enterprises are responsible for the lion's share (about two thirds) of the output value by the entire state sector whose share of Municipal output value has fallen steadily from 65% in 1991 to 33% in 1996 to 14% in 2001/2, while the share of foreign entities has risen over the same period from 8% to 52%. Within the core industrial groups and enterprises, however, the proportion of the number of state-owned entities is higher. More than half the groups are state-owned; and some 13% of enterprises (and 14% of the strongest 500) are state-owned and account for some 12% of total municipal sales. And whilst just about all of these in practice fall under municipal jurisdiction, the proportion of enterprises (regardless of ownership classification) which are directly subordinate to the centre is also higher by some 4-5%. If the origins of investments are taken into account, the percentage of the centre's direct interests rises. Some 16% of groups and 26% of core enterprises either receive substantial (sole, majority or main) central investment or are directly subordinate to the centre and are responsible for some 21% of municipal sales (a figure which excludes groups). And nearly half of these entities also receive substantial foreign investment. Indeed, many are 'foreign' as defined above; and if these entities are taken out of the equation then the contribution of entities receiving substantial investment from, or who are subordinate to, the centre falls to just 10% of municipal sales. As a proportion of entities shown in figures 4-15, then some 13% of enterprises (including supplementary listed enterprises) receive direct central investment from, or are directly subordinate to, the centre. If originating units (often bureaucratic units) are included, that proportion rises to about 15%.

4.0 Transformation?

In chapter 1 we briefly outlined the pattern of industrial organisation as commonly presented in the literature. New coalitions (a term used here to describe the relationships among informal collections of enterprises as well as formal business groups) were loosely hierarchical and themselves became kernels of association for newly-formed enterprises. Rather than compete with one another and duplicate each other's activities within provincial and sub-provincial areal administrative divisions (and thereby weaken their ability to compete with the networks and combines that were forming in other parts of China), these expanding alliances chose instead to coalesce, establishing strong positions within particular sectors of local economies. More cooperative than competitive, these coalitions together dominated local economies and turned their attentions to the outside world for money and markets. And while they presented a formidable barrier to enterprises from other parts of provincial China, they looked to the centre both as a source of money and as a possible route across barriers set up by similar arrangements in other parts of China, providing them with a reach across the national market that foreign partners would find attractive.

The investments traced above would appear to indicate that the pattern of industrial organisation which has emerged in Shanghai does not diverge to any great degree from this generalised pattern. The Municipality's coalitions are latticed to one another with varying degrees of intensity, and are parochial in their view of the rest of China. This parochialism is reinforced by the sheer size of China and, more importantly, by the need for money, markets, contacts, technology, ideas, practices, and experience. The centre of economic gravity lies at the lower or outer edges of the hierarchy, for whilst these enterprises appear to rotate around key nodes (groups and supplementary units) in these coalitions, these nodes are often widely recognised as ineffective, unprofitable, and beset by many other kinds of problems (see, for instance, *ZQLH, op.cit)*. Their significance as indicated by sales does not reflect their market performance, but rather their position in a political-cum-economic hierarchy. Their saving grace is that they are conduits for investment and political connexions into foreign concerns that are more effective economically. These coalitions, then, are heavily dependent upon foreign concerns, not only as reflected in economic figures, but also in their organisational fabric. They are also strategically connected to the centre by a shared interest in foreign money and markets.

Economic power is thus localised; and it is shared among local coalitions broad enough to ensure that no single cabal is able to dominate, yet concentrated and coherent enough to work as an agent for interests at the centre. Arguably, this method of cohesion is more subtle and sophisticated than anything that has emerged in Shanghai since 1949. Whilst state-owned enterprises as a specific institutional category have come to be seen widely not only as less important to the economy, but as an impediment to its growth, it would seem that the interests of the state's central and local officials, once represented by those state-owned enterprises, are now represented in part by the distribution of investments in varied forms and at various levels through like-minded sets of relationships. The events into which relationships are now shaped may have altered, but the hold of the state's officials over their interests has, if anything, been strengthened.

Although the pattern of industrial organisation indicated by investments has not produced any surprises, we can draw from it two observations which may be of some importance. First, it appears that the reach of business groups extends far beyond their formal boundaries, and that combines of enterprises without group status are equally powerful. A similar observation was made of Taiwan's industrial organisation some 15 years ago; and it was regarded then as a quality which made Taiwan's 'related enterprises' quite distinct from Korea's *chaebol* and Japan's *kigyoshudan* (Numazaki, 1991).

The second and perhaps the most striking quality of these investment networks is their strongly institutional appearance. It might have been expected that in a personalistic context ownership and investment would rest more heavily with individuals, cliques, and families, and would probably be defined less clearly by sector. This is certainly the case in the Philippines where, as we have said (chapter 1), strongly personalistic social relationships are the *sine qua non* of any consideration of the country's political economy; and where overseas Chinese and mestizos are said to dominate the economy (Skinner, 1996; Wickberg, 2000, 1999;

Palanca, *op.cit.*; Chua, 2003). Yet only two of the top 500 companies in Shanghai are classed as domestic private companies; individuals investors do figure among the top 10 or 20 shareholders of a number of listed companies, but their holdings are, in the vast majority of instances, nominal; and very rarely do individuals figure among the top 10 or 20 investors of the other companies shown in figures 4-15. Why, then, are investment networks in Shanghai so strongly institutional in quality?

(i) One possible explanation is that this quality reflects an attempt by comparatively impermeable and rigid sets of relationships and expectations (those of local and central governments and Party and enterprise managers), to hide, disguise, suppress, control and direct their competing personalistic and preferential interests (individual, cliques and possibly family) by moulding their interests into a facade of institutional channels (Shanghai's coalitions and those investment networks).* This behaviour might be read as symptomatic of the emergence of the kind of state-guided relational capitalism which, despite the recent economic crisis, has proved so successful in East and Southeast Asia; and which, according to some writers (such as Keister, *op.cit*; Wang, *op.cit;* and Yan, 2000*)*, has clear economic advantage in China. Or it might be construed as a distinctively Chinese form of bureaucratic entrepreneurialism produced by China's communist institutions (see, for instance, Gore, 1998). Either way, whilst the practice of particularistic relationships has in general become more open, officialdom still has difficulty in admitting openly the exercise of those relationships in this key area of economic life. The subordination of the domestic private sector to the coalitions may also partly reflect the ambiguity with which the pursuit of individual or private collective interests are still viewed. If so - and here we are following Pye's (*op.cit.*) argument that open factionalism is crucial in the emergence of a modern and democratic political economy - then it might be suggested that a continued

---

*Hertz's (*op.cit.*) analysis of Shanghai's stock market would seem to point in this direction.

reluctance to acknowledge, and to deal with, particularistic relationships and interests openly, may represent an obstacle to the development of a more predictable and stable political economy. Unless the state is first willing to acknowledge the practice, then little can be done to tackle those of its aspects which are inimical to the emergence of a more effective and prosperous political economy over the long term.

(ii) On the other hand, the fact that there are now available data on investments (including investments made by individuals), not only in listed companies but even in non-listed entities, may suggest that, however grudgingly, politicians, bureaucrats, and managers, are becoming more open. Such candidness is certainly intriguing when it is viewed as part of a context of still broader change. For instance, there is some evidence to suggest that more than nominal separation of state ownership from control has been taking place slowly over many years (Dong and Hu, 1995; Ruskola, 2000) such that even though ownership categories remain blurred, enterprises are slowly being insulated from state favours and interference. This may be more true of those enterprises with substantial foreign participation and of listed companies; but it may also be true of other companies whatever form the expression of state interests might take. These changes, we should add, are coincidental with what is regarded by some writers as the professionalisation of the bureaucracy and enterprise management (Bian, Shu, and Logan, 2001), and with what appears to others to be a decline in the use of the law by the Party for political ends, and a strengthening of the rule of law as a framework for economic modernisation (see, for example, Lo, 1995; Chen, 1999; *cf.* Tao and Zhu, 2001; Lubnam, 1999). Still broader social change may be suggested by the apparent decline in the traditional family in urban China as young adults with the financial wherewithal leave the nest and set up their own households, and as equality between generations and the sexes appears to strengthen (Logan and Bian 1999; Logan, Bian and Bian, 1998). Relationships among these atomising families may remain strong, and they often continue to live near each other and help each other out. Yet taken-for-granted and obligatory particularism may be weakening even now.

Could it be that such representations have tuned in to deep and widespread shifts towards the affect and greater professionalism within Chinese society? If so, then might not the political sensitivity associated with devolution of investments, the critical role assumed by foreign entities within these flows, and the formalisation of these arrangements, suggest that professionalisation and the affect have also begun to find voices within the leadership? This is so, we might argue, because, as in business organisations, authoritarian control has shown itself extraordinarily labyrinthine and limiting when exercised within the polity. The leadership has been moved ineluctably both to clarify rules, procedures, and roles, and to emphasise shared (and therefore more open) representations. At the same time the affect has deepened such that a concentrated and well defined social sphere has begun to emerge. Decades of tight control in which 'community' justified what was, certainly under Mao, highly personalistic rule, amounted to a denial of much of what we are (see chapter 1). Once the party loosened its grip over economic affairs, the sense of extreme alienation which had built into a head found grateful release as people began to search for, and to create, a social refuge.

In the polity, then, as in business, practical requirements, and the practice of authoritarianism, may be stimulating professionalism and a deepening of the affect. In political life, as in economic life, it is coming to be realised that the treatment of social relationships, and of rules and roles, *as if* absolute, is necessary to guard both the social sphere and the efficacy of professional life. We might also suggest that attitudinal change within the polity is being hastened by the very close links that exist between government and business in China. Read in this light, the institutional hardness of investments, and the broader political, economic, and social changes noted above, take on a particular saliency. Now that the affect is deepening, rules and roles are being regarded less as a political instrument; and business is being insulated from politics to the extent that the devolution of investment flows (in which foreign interests have a vital role) has been formalized. If Pye (1995) is right in his belief that social relationships in the polity are hidden, then this behaviour, rather than constitute an obstacle to political development, might suggest that for some time now the leadership has being taking part in a masquerade - a pattern of behaviour which we suggested earlier (chapter 4, section 2.2) is vital to professional and social life. Meanwhile, with the social sphere better defended, the family has become a smaller and more concentrated expression of the social refuge and the affect. As an initial stimulus to attitudinal change and formalisation, communist rule may have been at least as strong as the practice of trade and business organisation.

(iii) Professionalisation, the deepening of the affect, and the transmission of attitudinal change into the polity, may also have been encouraged by other dimensions of political necessity. To understand this we must outline the political features rooted in the pattern of industrial organisation in Shanghai described above.

(a) First, it is clearly difficult for independent (private) merchants to be seen as anything more than adjuncts to those coalitions that dominate the local economy. The key nodes (the holding companies, the asset administration companies, the groups, the listed companies, other enterprises, and the banks), may often be inefficient. Yet they are vital to a sense of cohesion, and they distribute investments into the more important, often foreign, enterprises at the lower end of the hierarchy. Whilst there are attempts to pare down these nodes and to make them more efficient, the interests of the state's officials which they represent may simply be transfigured into other forms (Ding, *op.cit;* and Hertz, *op.cit*). Shanghai's own independent entrepreneurs are tolerated and encouraged just so long as they soak up the unemployed, serve as out-workers and sales agents for the oligarchies, and fill whatever other gaps that may open up in economic life. They also continue to

198

form extensive networks and combines amongst themselves, mimicking the large central-local-foreign coalitions. However, they face many difficulties, the most damaging of which are those experienced in their attempts to secure credit and investment (SCXQFXB [上海市促进小企业发展协调办公室], 2002; Chen Naixing, 2002; SHRZ [上海荣正投资咨询有限公司], 2002). Their growth, either individually or as combines, seems to depend upon how far they are willing to work with the coalitions; and when they do meet with success and grow in size and influence, then they should expect to be absorbed by those coalitions sooner or later.

The blurring of forms of ownership (private, state, and collective), and the degree to which state and collectives smother independent enterprises, also finds expression in the marketplaces. These have evolved since the late 1980s into modern, and usually multi-storeyed, buildings now dominated by textiles rather than by wet and dry agricultural goods. Most clothes and other manufactured goods are brought in from other parts of China, especially from Guangzhou, Shenzhen, Hong Kong, Wenzhou, and Hangzhou, as well as from other cities in Jiangsu, Zhejiang, and Fujian; though, as in the late 1980s, Shanghai remains an important source of such goods for traders in the marketplaces*. Whether goods are produced in Shanghai or elsewhere in China, most of the traders in Shanghai (about two-thirds) are either employees of factories producing the goods they sell, working either on fixed salaries or for commission or for both; or they are in effect private operations (commonly registered as 个体户 [individual households]†) contracted by a factory to work, often exclusively, as its agent. Most of the

---

* About 18% of traders obtain their goods from Shanghai's own factories. Guangzhou is the source of the majority (55%) of traders' stock. The other figures are 9% for Hangzhou, 8% for Wenzhou, 4% for Hong Kong, 2% for Shenzhen, and a little under 1% for Beijing.) Around 500 markets traders and wholesalers in Shanghai were surveyed (mostly in the Zhabei district).

†These entities normally comprise less than eight people. Those with more than eight people are usually classed as 私营企业 (private enterprises).

factories are state or collective or some blend of private, state, and collective. Another third of the stores in the marketplaces are private businesses, usually family affairs, selling goods produced by factories owned by themselves or by their close relatives (brothers, sisters, children, parents, husbands, wives and cousins). A few of the factories are Shanghainese; most, however, are to be found in other parts of China, especially in the south and southeast. Split-family businesses similar to these also trade with the Philippines: in Manila, particularly around Divisoria and Baclaran, small agglomerations of shops have formed, selling goods (usually textiles and some leather goods) manufactured in their relatives' factories in China (again, mostly in the south and southeast of the country). The presence of these entities may well help to entrench street representations of 'the Chinese' in the Philippines, but their significance pales in comparison with the main streams of trade between the two countries. More generally in Shanghai, whilst the numbers and economic indicators of independent businesses have strengthened dramatically over the last twenty years[*], and whilst the financial rewards for entrepreneurs are great, they remain small fry.[†]

(b) Second, the status of foreign entities also remains complex and ambiguous. There is no doubt of the vitality they bring to business in Shanghai, and of the industrial economy's very close dependency upon them. There is also no doubt that they often prefer as little entanglement as possible with officialdom (though this is more true of those enterprises acting largely as export platforms), and certainly as far as joint ventures are concerned they prefer majority equity shares (Yan, 2000). But there is also no doubt that they find it difficult to operate without bureaucratic and party contacts, most especially if they have ambitions within the national or local domestic markets. They therefore have no choice but to allow themselves to be drawn into Shanghai's coalitions.

---

[*] Private businesses now account for about 53% of all small enterprises in Shanghai (SCXQFXB, op.cit.).

[†] Small, private enterprises account for less than a fifth of the receipts earned by all enterprises classed as small, and for less than 1% of sales within the Municipality (ibid.).

(c) Third, the relative insularity with respect to the rest of provincial China cannot but worry those with a broader view of China's interests. Just as long as the interests of any particular group at the centre are spread across different localities and local coalitions, then China's disunity will remain inconceivable within the minds of those who comprise those relationships. But it would be surprising if there did not emerge a desire for enterprises in more successful areas of China to expand their regional economic kingdoms either for the sake of ambition or in order to reduce economic disparities. If closely matched by political factions at the centre such that the interests of those factions were to follow the grain of these expanding coalitions, then we might have good reason to reconsider the likelihood of China's disintegration more closely. Certainly, it is often thought that the beginning of the end of China as a united state is signaled by the orientation of local economies towards the outside world, their parochial view with respect to the rest of provincial China, disparities in material wealth across the regions, the occasional recalcitrance of provincial authorities over such matters as tax and spending, and the subordination of legislation to political expediency.

One effect of these three features is to dampen practices - such as vibrant family businesses, and open competition among large companies – that may stimulate the affective and a move towards greater professionalism. Another is to concentrate power and wealth in the hands of relatively few coalitions closely integrated with state officials. This appears to have evident, though possibly short-term, benefits that we have already commented on. Yet another effect is to further strengthen China's dependency on foreign markets and money (such that the outside world also has a very real and common interest in China's stability and success). This is clearly of great economic and political advantage to China and its trading partners. But the opportunities provided by the expansion of markets overseas may also lead to the concentration of still more power in existing coalitions, to wider inequalities regionally, to greater economic and political vulnerability, and to a higher risk of instability. Moreover, it is estimated that the economic costs associated with a weak legal system or, more specifically, with poor enforcement already outweigh the benefits of informal methods of transaction (Tao and Zhu, 2001): unless businesses take into account the rules of WTO membership with some degree of spontaneity, then the state, and companies, will be burdened with still more cumbersome and expensive supervision as criticism from overseas mounts with China's trade surplus.

The leadership may therefore reason that whatever risks might be associated with the dispersal of economic power among many small and independent domestic family businesses, these risks are in the long run more preferable to those inherent in concentrating wealth and power in a few coalitions, however well connected with the centre they may be (see, for instance Chen and Feng, 2000). We may, for instance, already be witnessing many more smaller family businesses moving with greater confidence and certainty to the centre of economic life. The recent admission of private entrepreneurs into the ranks of the Communist party towards the end of 2002 and recognition of the problems they face (SCXQFXB *op.cit.*), may be symbolic of just such a move. The leadership's political concerns may also prompt them to take measures which, quite fortuitously, will also help to transform large companies and coalitions into important catalysts for attitudinal change. Reducing the concentration of power in favoured companies by separating state from enterprise, or state ownership from state control, and by attaching more significance to rule of law, seem likely to place those organisations in circumstances where they will have to professionalise if they are to survive and prosper. Encouraging the larger businesses in Shanghai, as well as the smaller family companies, to expand their operations, markets, and investments, to other parts of China (and *vice versa*) may have a similar effect. Whilst the relative significance of investment and procurements by Shanghai's enterprises in other parts of China, and by provincial enterprises in Shanghai, have, if anything, been declining, absolute levels of investment and procurements have been rising. There are also concentrated efforts underway to develop the Changjiang valley (embracing the provinces of Tibet, Qinghai, Sichuan, Yunnan, Guizhou, Hunan, Hubei, Jiangxi, Anhui and Jiangsu) with Shanghai at its 'head' (Lu Bingyan [ed.], 1999; Yang Wanzhong [ed.], 2001; and CLFY [长江流域发展研究院], 1999) Moreover, it is companies which belong to Shanghai and to the rest of the Changjiang Valley that make up close to 60% of all companies listed on the Shanghai stock exchange (*ZCZP, op.cit.*; Li Zhaowen, *op. cit*; *SSTJJ, op.cit.*; *ZQLH, op.cit.*).

5.0 Conclusions

We have argued that authoritarianism and practical considerations are stimulating professionalism and the deepening of the affect in and around China's industry. This experience may be feeding attitudinal change within China's polity, and may have found expression in the institutionalisation of investment flows. Further impetus to attitudinal change may come from various political considerations: the risks associated with dependency upon a relatively small number of large companies, and upon foreign markets and investment, may suggest to the leadership that they both encourage larger numbers of small family companies to move to the centre of economic life, and insist on the professionalisation and fragmentation of the larger companies and combines. If this assessment is accurate, then we might expect to see fairly shortly the dispersal of economic power among a much larger number of smaller companies and the braiding of investment flows into finer and more complex channels in which individuals and small corporations have a larger stake.

We are, then, likely to see national economic life becoming dependent upon a blanket of small family businesses that will gradually unfold across the country. Set within this blanket will be a comparatively small number of large companies. These will be more genuinely national in scope or oriented to the international economy. The interests of local and central governments, and of bureaucracies and Party, in these companies will be significant; but those interests will be more transparent, and the companies themselves will be more effectively insulated from the favours and control of the state in its various guises. We might also expect that as professionalisation and the affect find a stronger voice within the polity, political institutions and practice will become still more regularized and predictable. The polity may also become more liberal. For there is, we have implied through much of this book, a strong and reasoned sympathy between, on the one hand, democratic sentiments and, on the other hand, the affect.

The shift in attitude towards the affect, and the associated formalisation and liberalisation of the political economy, may prove to be comparatively rapid. As we noted earlier, neither the debate over, nor the practice of, 'distancing', nor the ideal of institutional probity and the rule of law, are new to China. And it is often suggested (see, for example, Pearson, 1997) that memories of past (pre-1949) institutional patterns and qualities may work their influence upon the institutions and practices of the present. Dong and Hu (*op.cit.*), for instance, suggest that ownership never automatically implied control in China; and (as we noted earlier in chapter 1) Ruskola (*op.cit*), has argued that the clan corporations of Imperial China met most of the corporate criteria of Anglo-American law. If memories such as these really do have a bearing upon current events then they would indeed be extremely influential.

These forecasts are not particular remarkable. It is widely acknowledged that China should reduce its dependency upon foreign trade and investment, stimulate demand in its own domestic market, encourage small businesses, re-value its currency, and observe its own commercial laws more carefully. It is also widely hoped, and expected, that mutual dependency and openness will encourage political freedom in China. However, our attitudinal perspective does attempt to specify how and why such measures and tendencies* carry such profound meaning for the quality of many aspects of Chinese society. It also suggests that unless we can examine at first hand and in detail the representations, attitudes, and relationships, of the politicians and bureaucrats who make up China's leadership at the highest levels, then our chances of being able to put together fair assessments of how they might think and behave are, at best, poor. Can we be sure that, despite the hopeful signs of informal-formal transformation we see in China, a cleavage is not opening up between the mass of the populace (among whom professionalism and the affect is strengthening) and the leadership? Would it be naïve to think other than that the leadership remains strongly personalistic? Is the desire of China's rulers to build a massive economy driven by a concern for their subjects? Or is that desire motivated largely by a wish to foster in other countries a dependency upon China greater than China's dependency upon them; to build a strong military with global reach; and to turn China into the greatest political and military presence the world has ever seen? And can we be sure of how the leadership might react in the wake of severe economic downturn or political crisis either at home or abroad? It is conceivable that such crises might drive home the belief that democratic politics is essential if tensions are to be defused, and if continuity and stability are to be realised over the longer term. But if some future crisis should be viewed in a personalistic frame of mind, then it would seem equally possible that China's leadership will only lash out at those at home and abroad whom it believes are frustrating its will and ambitions.

Unless we are able to dis-aggregate particular instances of the leadership, then our interpretations of the Chinese polity may tell us more about ourselves than they do about China. Those who fear China may fear intolerance and weakness in themselves. Those who see in China something better than anything to be found in

---

* That is, if those measures and tendencies are sustained, and to the extent that they find expression both in the encouragement of family companies and in the professionalisation of large companies whose relative economic significance is declining.

other civilizations may see only a reflection of what they believe to be their own distinctiveness, perceptivity, and morality. For others, the comfort and power brought by the market to the US, Europe, and many other countries around the world since 1945, make it tempting to ascribe a connexion between trade and democracy. Still more certain does this connexion become when an implacable enemy seems to commit itself to your game and to play by the rules of international commerce,

There is the danger, then, that we will proceed too confidently upon very little understanding of what we do and why we do it. If we begin to view our academic representations – our explanations and ideas – of the Chinese leadership with more authority than they deserve, then we are likely to misdirect ourselves and others. If we become convinced of the crucial link between trade and democracy, or of the righteousness or evil of the Chinese way, then those beliefs might be used to steal advantage. Fear of the West's eclipse, and the hope that trade will ignite democracy in China, might both be used in equal measure to justify trade and investment contrary to the broader and longer term security interests of the West. At the same time the Chinese leadership, while turning China into the centre of gravity for trade and investment, may be more than happy to encourage in their western counterparts a belief in the inevitable victory of democratic values. If China's leadership feels that wealth and power is all that determines the popularity, acceptance, and moral certainty of democratic ideas and practice, then why should they not also feel that China's still greater wealth and power will legitimise the Party's own form of government and its own vision of civilization? When most countries begin to look to China for opportunity and favour, democracy will be a lost cause, and the US a spent force. Only then will the Chinese leadership believe that they have guaranteed their position at home.

* * * * *

Our attitudinal perspective suggests that there are sound reasons why trade and business will transform China's political economy fundamentally. That change, it would seem, has already begun. But this perspective also suggests caution. Change is ambiguous and never certain; and without first-hand analyses of the relationships, attitudes and representations played out within the leadership, our assessments will amount to little more than guesswork. The simple truth is that none of us has experience of a large and authoritarian state with economic and military power equal to, or surpassing, that of the United States. We must hope that leaders of democratic nations will bear that fact in mind over the next twenty years or so as they encourage trade and investment with China.

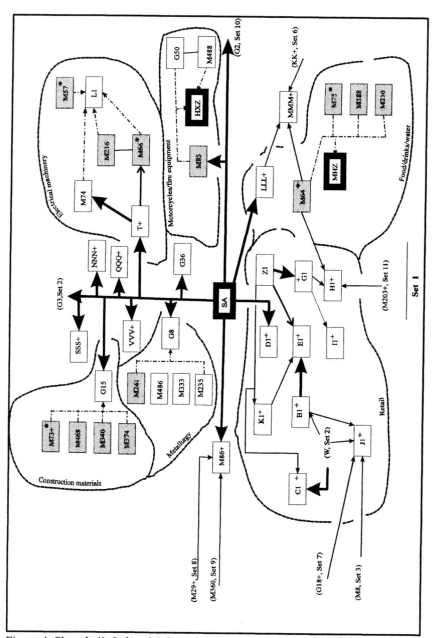

Figure 4. Shanghai's Industrial Organisation, Set 1. *Source:上海市工商管理局*

208

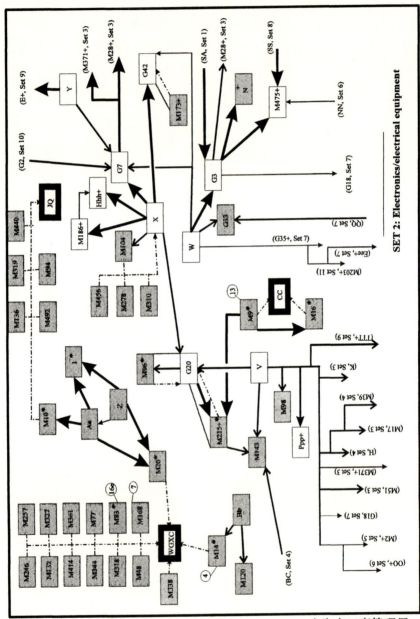

Figure 5. Shanghai's Industrial Organisation, Set 2. *Source:上海市工商管理局*

209

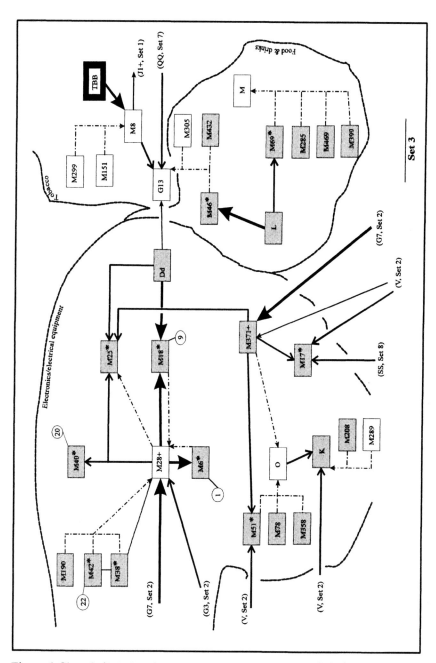

Figure 6. Shanghai's Industrial Organisation, Set 3. *Source:上海市工商管理局*

210

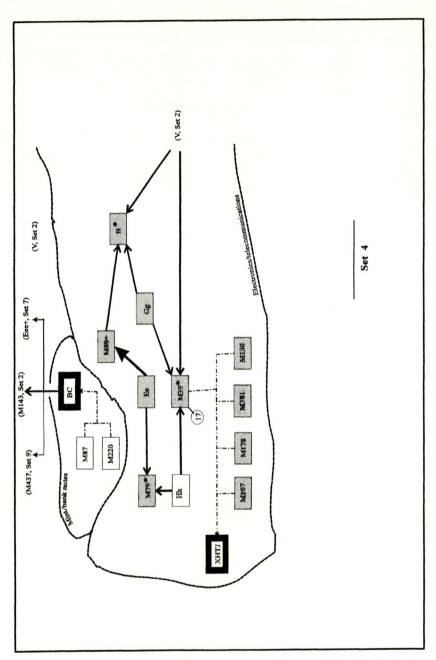

Figure 7. Shanghai's Industrial Organisation, Set 4. *Source:上海市工商管理局*

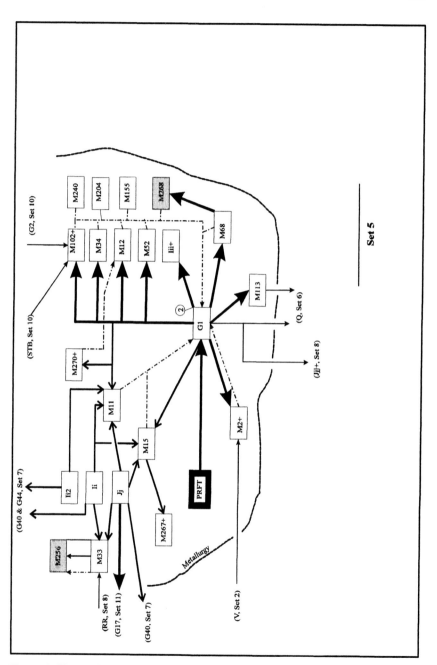

Figure 8. Shanghai's Industrial Organisation, Set 5. *Source:上海市工商管理局*

212

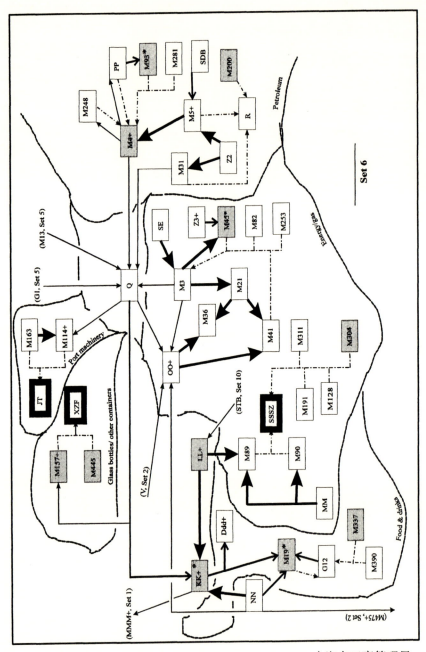

Figure 9. Shanghai's Industrial Organisation, Set 6. *Source: 上海市工商管理局*

213

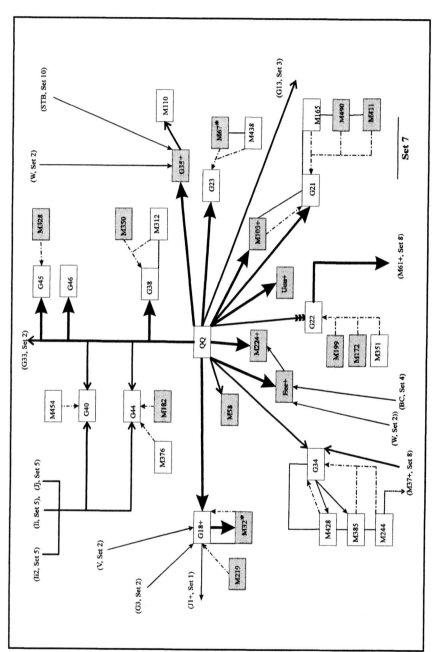

Figure 10. Shanghai's Industrial Organisation, Set 7. *Source:上海市工商管理局*

214

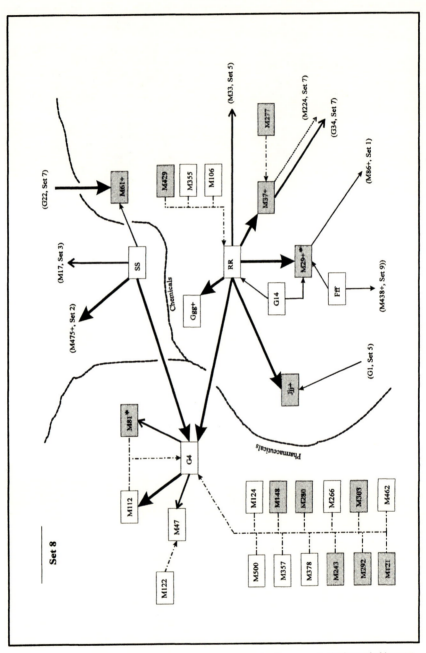

Figure 11. Shanghai's Industrial Organisation, Set 8. *Source:上海市工商管理局*

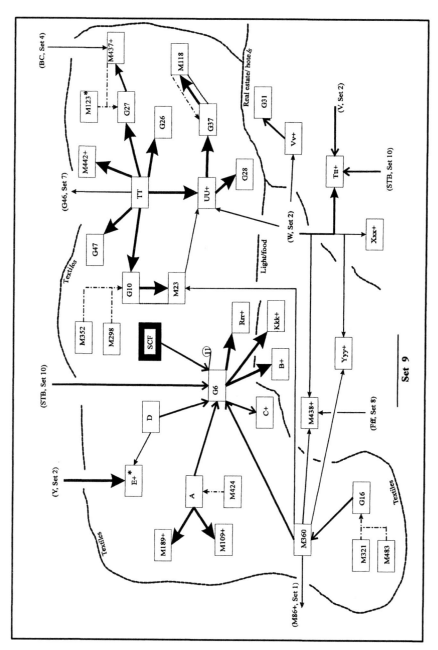

Figure 12. Shanghai's Industrial Organisation, Set 9. *Source:上海市工商管理局*

216

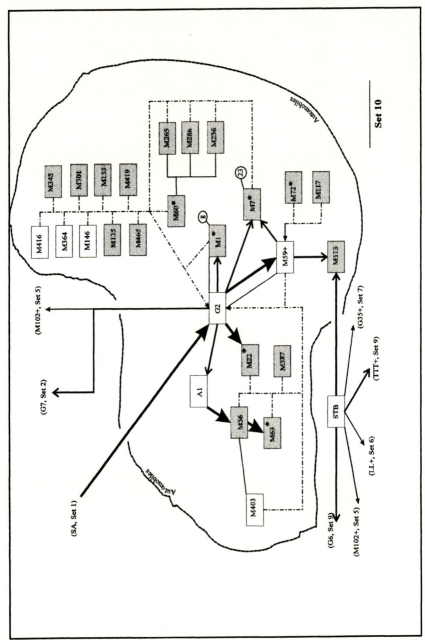

Figure 13. Shanghai's Industrial Organisation, Set 10. *Source:上海市工商管理局*

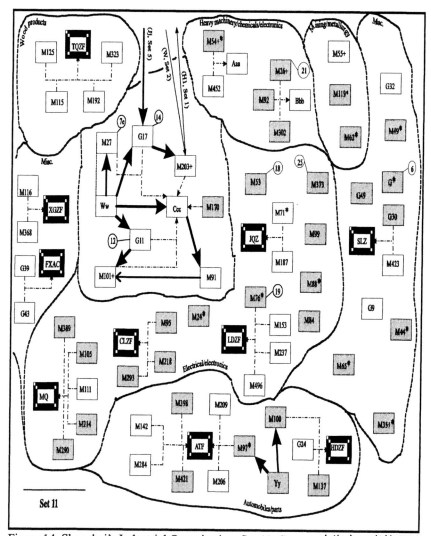

Figure 14. Shanghai's Industrial Organisation, Set 11. *Source:上海市工商管理局*

218

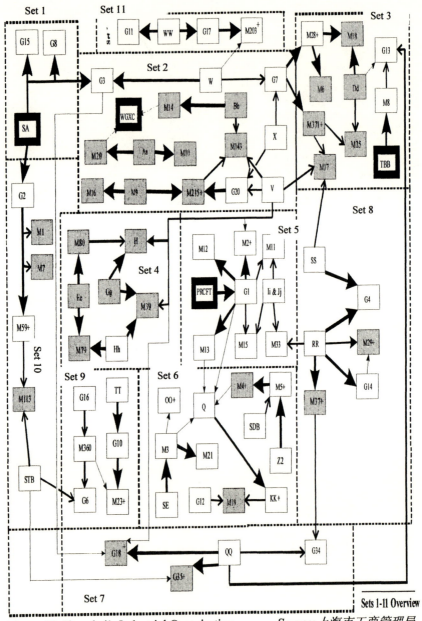

Figure 15. Shanghai's Industrial Organisation.   *Source:上海市工商管理局*

219

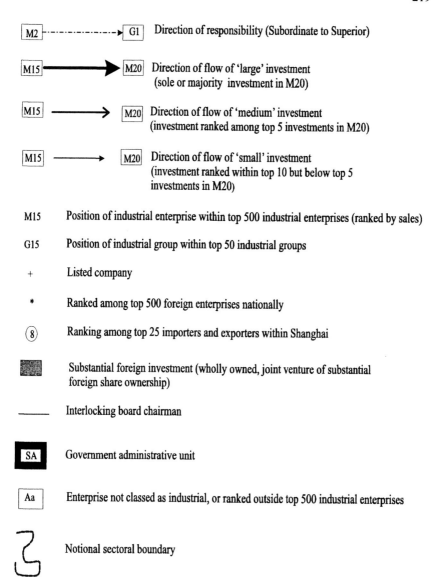

Key to Figures 4 – 14. The information on investments from which these figures were constructed was supplied in large part by 上海市工商管理局 (2002 & 2003). Other materials include: 上海市统计局 2002 & 2003; Li Zhaowen, 2002; 中国诚信证券评估有限公司, 中诚信国际信用评级有限责任公司 (2002); 中国企业联合会, 中国企业家协会 (2002).

Chapter 6
Political Transformation? The Philippines

1.0 Introduction

In previous chapters we argued that cultural and structural representations of the Chinese have worked to erode the confidence of Filipinos in themselves, and to obscure the dimensionality of trade and business. We have also suggested that there is an association between the professionalisation of companies and a shift in attitude towards the affective; and that, in China, this association between attitude and organisation, together with the authoritarian quality of China's polity, may be working to stimulate transformation towards a more formal and liberal polity. We argued further that there are indications of attitudinal change at the lower ends of China's bureaucracy; and that such change at the upper levels of the polity may be reflected indirectly in economic institutions and practices of special political significance.

Similar comments can be made of the Philippines' polity. At the lower reaches of the polity and bureaucracy (and, as we shall see, at its upper levels too) there is, as in China, constant manoeuvering, circumvention, and corruption, most especially in connexion with taxation and customs. Lucy's difficulties, referred to in chapter 4, exemplify the kinds of problems that businesses and officials face almost constantly. Yet from the point of view of those merchants with experience in Manila and Shanghai, relationships in the Philippines are more clearly distanced than in China. In Manila, social relationships between manufacturers and their suppliers are as important as in Shanghai; though in contrast with Shanghai, manufacturers have little or no contact with the distributors and consumers of their goods. As for officials in Manila they are, if anything, disinterested in companies and their overseas trade. For their part, too, companies prefer to have as little contact with officialdom as possible, unless government and bureaucrats are willing to provide tangible help. The reasoning here, as in Shanghai, is to keep life simple and energies focussed on the business. But there are occasions when contact with officials is unavoidable or essential. When, as part of their attempt to ease the flow of traffic from the city along its main thoroughfare towards the port and airport, local government agencies in Davao restricted the movement of heavy vehicles along a branch road between 1C's warehouse and the port. Finding his main arteries threatened, the owner turned at once to his contacts within local government, asking them either to lift the restriction or to grant him an exemption. In this case, as in many others, companies are careful to avoid conveying the impression that either the official or the company is in the other's debt. It is in this respect that associations – especially those who serve not their own interests but those of the wider community – are of some importance. The manager of 3 CF (table 1) joined the Masons and a number of the other more cosmopolitan associations. Here he could meet bureaucrats from Customs and the Bureau of Internal Revenue, and politicians from local and national governments. Help was given and received, and friendships made for their own sake. And if at some later date he had a problem with the supply of electricity he could ring the president of Davao Light and Power; if he needed to expedite shipments, or protect them from the red tape of greedy bureaucrats, he could always have a word with politicians who were always willing to help a thriving company that earned dollars. Rather like the merchants' word, or their rituals and gifts, associations such as the Masons, Rotary, Lions, Kiwanis, and JCs, are not only forums within which deals are made or officials collared. They are also a reminder of the unspoken social dimensions of the contacts made among merchants and officials in their everyday professional lives. When merchants outside the association appeal to the official or ask for advice or information, or when they strike their deals among themselves, their mutual membership of the association is symbolic of that unspoken common compact that binds each to the other.

However, unlike China - where we must rely on indirect signs of possible attitudinal change at the polity's heart – we may look directly at the upper reaches of the Philippines' polity, and there attempt to tease out the play of representations, attitudes, and relationships. Indeed, we can even look past the decisions and actions of government with regard to the Philippines' direct trade with China (which remains of small if growing interest to national government, at least in comparison to trade with Japan and the United States) and concentrate on the workings of Congress and its relations with the Executive. For it is Congress that sets the legislative framework, and which sits at the heart of most scholarly representations of the Philippines polity.

2.0 Legislature and Executive: dependency, influence, and bargaining

Members of the Lower House (the House of Representatives) are of two kinds: those who represent districts; and those who are admitted under the Party List system. The vast majority of members are district Representatives whose constituencies are clearly defined geographically. Members admitted under the Party List system are fielded by particular sectors that have garnered enough votes*. These sectors are reasonably discrete. For example, APEC (Association of Philippines Electric Cooperatives), whose members buy (rather than generate) electricity from the National Power Company and distribute electricity throughout the country (mostly in the rural areas), comprises 120 cooperatives, each of which is made up of consumers, employees, officers, and a board of directors.

The relationship between district Representatives and their constituencies, whether through elected local government officers (mayors, vice-mayors, councilors, and *barangay* captains) or directly with voters themselves, are complex and fluid. But when all is said and done, Representatives are under considerable pressure to secure as large a share of the national budget as they can, and to deliver material

---

* Two percent of the national vote for Party List candidates is required for each list seat.

improvements to their districts. To this end they must, for certain kinds of projects - such as converting a local school into a national high school - secure the passage of legislation in the form of local bills. As with all bills, these must be passed not only in the Lower House but also in the Senate, just as bills passed in the Senate must be passed through the Lower House before they can be enacted. District representatives must also do their best to ensure that as large a share as possible of funds held by departments of the Executive (such as the Departments of Health, Education, and Public Works and Highways) are spent in their district; and that their share of the community development fund - which is one component of the 'pork' that Representatives may distribute within their own district and at their own discretion - is indeed released as and when required. Thus, although it is the Lower House alone that has the power through the budget to raise taxes and allocate funds required by the Executive, the Lower House is dependent upon the Senate for the approval of projects and upon the Executive for certain categories of funds, for the release of funds, and for implementation.

In common with Representatives, Senators are also provided with discretionary funds. But these are necessarily spread thinly, for unlike Representatives, Senators are elected nationally and have no clearly defined constituencies. They are normally 24 in number, and each is elected for a term of 6 years - a period equal to that of the President, and twice that given to a member of the Lower House. But whereas the President is restricted to a single term in office, Senators are permitted two consecutive terms, and Representatives three, before they are required to take leave; and both Senators and Representatives may run again after their enforced absence. Senators are expected to take a broader and longer view of national and international affairs (it is the Senate alone that has the authority to approve international treaties), and to pursue more substantial legislation of national importance. The Senate, however, is, as we have said, dependent both upon the Lower House for the passage of its legislation, and upon the Executive for the effective implementation of that legislation.

The Executive, centred upon the Office of the President, is thus dependent upon the legislature for budgetary appropriations, and for the passage of such legislation as is needed to implement its policies. As a consequence of this mutual dependence, each body acts to strengthen as far as possible its bargaining position and influence over the other .

2.1 Executive and Lower House

In an attempt to secure its legislative agenda, the Executive may certify its proposed bills as urgent. Certification carries more weight if set within a clear policy framework, and if accompanied by persuasion and explanation. The Legislative-Executive Development Advisory Council (LEDAC) to some extent institutionalises these attempts at garnering support. Certification, however, is a convention: it may hasten the passage of a bill, especially if the President holds a majority in both Houses; but it cannot in itself compel members of the legislature to yield. And if this symbolic appeal to the national good were used too often, its moral authority would be devalued.

More direct and gritty influence lies in the Executive's hold over the timing and release of funds, over the bureaucracy which implements projects, and over preferment. Although the Lower House approves the apportionment of funds, the Special Allotment Release Order is dependent upon the President's approval. And whilst the President may be commanded by the budget to release funds, in practice the President may either disperse funds held by particular departments such that they benefit some districts and not others; or delay the release of, or impound, funds, including those classified as 'pork'. Also within the gift of the President are appointments, the most important of which are subject to scrutiny and approval by the Commission on Appointments.

The demands and wishes of the President, and the views and ambitions of the Representatives, are transmitted between the Lower House and Malacañang via the

Presidential-Legislative Liaison Officers (PLLO). They are organised according to regional divisions*; and their head, who holds Secretary rank, is usually to be found prowling the Lower House, attending meetings and hearings. He is known colloquially as the 'spy boy'. Informal relationships run alongside the PLLO between the Palace and individual Representatives who, because they are known to have the ear of the President, can have a deal of influence in the House. Through the PLLO and her more informal placements, the authority of the President in the Lower House is considerable; and, once the election of the President is confirmed, there is often a migration of members from opposition parties to the administration's coalition.

However, the authority of the Executive is not certain. Much depends upon the ambitions of Representatives. Those whose concerns are limited to their own district, from whom little is heard on the floor or in the committees, and who have little interest in national affairs, are more willing to toe the line; and this is true even of those members who remain in opposition parties. Members with more ambition, and with an interest in national events, while acting to secure their base in their district by delivering materially what they can, will also maneouvre to create a bloc within the Lower House. For within the House, power, relative to that of the Executive, depends upon the creation of these blocs. These groups are fluid and, despite their best efforts to stay together, shift with issue and personalities, and reach across party lines. Party-list Representatives, as their numbers rose in an unsympathetic House from two to twenty-four, have had a particular incentive to work together in order to secure from both majority and minority parties promises of funding†. Yet they, too, will switch allies and break apart as and when their diverse sectoral interests, and their judgments about how these may be served best, seem to demand.

---

* Northern Luzon, Central Luzon, Southern Luzon, Visayas, and Mindanao

†Interview with Rep. Valdez, August 2004

With their own legislative agendas, and with their attractiveness to, and position within, power blocs in mind, Representatives - both district and party list - will fight tooth and nail to secure membership or chairmanships of the more important House committees. These committees select and mould proposed legislation, carry out oversight functions, and, in the case of the Commission on Appointments, shape the personnel of the Executive and Judiciary. In the selection of a committee's members and chairmanships, a number of considerations come into play - expertise, seniority, preferences, tradition, the view of the Speaker (whose position is dependent upon the wishes of the President), and the party make-up of the Upper and Lower House*. In addition, the authors of the proposed legislation have the right to sit on the committee scrutinizing their bill. Indeed, although they cannot vote, any Representative may take part in the discussions of any committee, and may be able, if particularly influential, to change the flow of the debate. This is especially true if the chairman is either weak or inexperienced.

2.2 Executive and Senate

The attempt by the Executive to exercise influence over the Senate is a similar matter, but only to an extent. A wish to be re-elected; a desire to see their own legislative agenda enacted; their dependence upon the Executive for the release of funds and implementation of legislation; and an ambition either to serve in the Executive or to build up a base for their own bid for the Presidency: all these, and other considerations, may figure in a Senator's negotiations with Malacañang, and may provide the Executive with leverage over a Senator. As in the Lower House, forming power blocs is part of the game. But Senators have other cards to play. The fact that they are elected nationally and are not directly accountable to a specific constituency, and the relative longevity of their terms in office, affords them the luxury of patience and time, weakens any hold the President may have, and dilutes

---

* Conversely, the chairmen of minor committees often have difficulty in attracting enough members.

any inducements that might be offered. It is therefore expected, and it is indeed the case, that Senators are more independent minded, less easy to sway, and more difficult to read. Naturally, any President would prefer to have a majority in the Senate, though neither a majority nor the machinations of the PLLO provide any guarantee of control. Senators, opposition or majority, cannot be compelled to follow a particular line. Indeed, not only are they less susceptible to the charms and threats of the President, but, both as individuals and collectively, they can be distinctly aggressive and robust in dealing with the Executive.

2.3 Senate and Lower House

Understandably the relationship between the Senate and the Lower House is somewhat unequal. Senators, from the point of view of the Lower House, treat local bills most unsympathetically. The leadership of the Lower House, through the Speaker, may be obliged by convention to badger the Senate President to take action; but much humbling lobbying is still required of Representatives, and even then there is no guarantee of success. Of the three thousand or so local bills passing out of the Lower House during the 12th Congress, less than 5% saw the light of day. The low success rate is accounted for partly by the sheer number of local bills: this puts a great burden on a treasury that is already over-stretched, and robs national legislation of its time in the legislative calendar. Reducing the chances of success also increases the value of any support that may arise from the Senate. So valuable is this currency to Representatives, that Senators may safely ignore any *quid pro quo* that Representatives may feel has been established. For instance, even after a group of hopeful Representatives (mostly of LAKAS) had kept their side of a bargain to support and expedite the Absentee Voting and Dual Citizenship bills through the House in return for Senatorial support of those Representatives' own local bills*, the Senate did not think twice about off-handedly reneging on that agreement.

---

* Interview with Rep. Zubiri, September 2004

The importance of local bills to Representatives, the fact that Senators can restrict their passage, and the relative length of a Senator's time in office, provide Senators with considerable leverage over Representatives. In pursuit of their own legislation, Senators will rarely be seen at dinners and lunches in the Lower House to press their case. The Senator only need go to the leader of a bloc or, through the Speaker, cut a deal with Malacañang and let the Palace wring out the necessary support from the Lower House. At the same time, a Senator may draw on the support of other Senators, and through the media or through their own personal road shows, drum up support among NGOs and voters across many constituencies. In this way Representatives are caught between the Senate, the Executive, and the Representatives' own constituencies.

3.0 Tension, splintering, and distortion

There exists, then, considerable tension between the Executive, the House, and the Senate. From the point of view of the Executive (and this is especially true of those who have also served in the Senate), the legislature appears to be something of a free-for-all. From the Lower House (whose members' concern is, first and foremost, to bring home the bacon) emanates an overwhelming flow of bills: most are local, and the few which are more nationally oriented reflect the gamut of special interests. From the Senate, meanwhile, spring individual manifestos written in proposed legislation, as if each Senator is their own administration-in-waiting[*]. When looked at in their entirety, bills originating in the Senate and House, if they achieve any coherence, do so only by chance. The sheer volume of legislative traffic - and the accompanying competition, bargaining, and compromise - make it extremely difficult for the Executive to realise their visions and ambitions. Viewed from the Lower House, the Senate's cavalier and summary treatment of local bills

---

[*] The defense often raised is that authoring and generating publicity for legislation on well-defined issues throughout one's term is the cheapest and most effective way of keeping down election costs. Interview with Hon. Sen. Biazon, July 2004.

is exasperating. The Representatives' frustration is made still more acute by the slow passage through the Senate even of bills that are of material and national importance, such as those granting franchises to airlines, television stations, and telecommunication companies. Bills which may find their way through the Lower House in matter of months may linger on in the Senate for two years. Whether the fact that the Senators are only twenty-four in number should be thought to slow down or speed up the passage of bills (the same number of which are scrutinised by the Lower House with its two hundred or so Representatives), depends upon the initial degree of frustration with which the Senate is viewed. The Senate is similarly frustrated by, and often contemptuous of, the Lower House where time and money is washed away in torrents of petty legislation.

The views which Senate, the Executive, and the Lower House have of each other are, then, direct and unflattering. Senators are, as a body, commonly regarded by the House and the Executive as a lazy, obdurate, odd, and selfish gaggle of egotistical little presidents who 'behave as if they feel they owe you nothing'. The Lower House is viewed by Senate and Executive as ineffective and parochial. And both House and Senate see the Executive as already too powerful and greedy for more. These frustrations, and the language, are only to be expected given the intended division of interest and authority in this tripartite system of government (Executive, Legislature and Judiciary). The problem, however, is that political parties - which would otherwise bridle and direct these frustrations, temper bargaining, focus energy, and impose across both Houses and the Executive a sense of cohesion and direction - are weak, and are commonly regarded, quite openly and unashamedly, as electoral vehicles*. The consequence is a splintering of interests, and a search for other methods of control and cohesion. The methods to hand are obvious. But - in the absence of the relatively clear ideologies, values, principles, manifestos, codes of conduct, and discipline, of strong parties - the use of policy,

---

* Interview with Hon. Sen. Jinggoy Estrada, August 2004.

funding, the legislative process, legislation itself, and preferment to secure leverage, only makes still more uncertain the alliances that gather round the transitory issues of the day. The need for leverage becomes still more intense; and soon the politicians' manoeuvering begins to take up so much time and energy that securing leverage becomes an end in itself. Thus the procedures of government are fouled, and political vision dissolves. The more specific ramifications of weak parties, and the splintering of interests, are numerous.

3.1 Cabinet and bureaucracy

A sense of considerable insecurity is created in an Executive that is faced with the unenviable task of cobbling together the larger number of supporters within the legislature. Not only might individual Senators (who are already difficult enough to read) become kernels of opposition, but so might members of the Executive itself. And both, if not effectively isolated in time, might be capable of turning shoals of Representatives against the incumbent. The Office of the President must also bear in the mind, in particular, the views of the Armed Forces of the Philippines (AFP) and the Church, whose own factional divisions make uncertain their support for the President. With these doubts in mind, the President, surrounded by a small and informal group of trusted confidants, is prompted to take into her hands as much power and authority as she can, for she believes that otherwise she can neither hold together a strong enough base for support, nor begin to provide for her policies and their implementation any sense of direction whatsoever. The effect of the President's insecurity on the cabinet and bureaucracy is particularly damaging. Members of the cabinet must look over their shoulder at the President for whom they work to please, and in fear, as they manoeuvre to secure leverage, win support, field criticism, and compete with each other (and with members of the Legislature) for time in the legislative calendar. Such an atmosphere does not allow departments to be run independently; it does not foster the judgment needed to make good or hard decisions; nor is it conducive to the formulation of imaginative solutions, or to the transmission of reliable information. It is also likely to prove most unattractive to anyone with administrative ability and flair.

The stern reach of an insecure President is also felt by the civil service. Whatever their claim to independence, and however much bureaucrats might wish to see themselves as being independent, the Executive treats its civil servants as a political extension of itself. Bureaucrats down to the level of bureau heads are removed and appointed with a change in President; and for their subsequent careers they are dependent upon their political masters. This has a considerable effect on the lower ranks, both at the centre (in the National Capital Region), and in the provinces. In the provinces, most especially in the south, civil servants feel somewhat isolated- a sentiment enhanced by linguistic differences and by what they feel to be the center's rather dismissive view of the *provincia*. The centre is, from their point of view, a political jungle. Partly for this reason, and partly because of the cost of living in Manila, civil servants in the provinces are often reluctant to seek advance beyond the rank of Director. After that point, they are afraid that their prospects will be even less dependent upon competence, and even more dependent upon uncertain connections either with politicians or with higher ranking civil servants who are, to all intents and purposes, political appointees. For those within the service who are both highly educated and committed, it is particularly disheartening to find oneself under the thumb of politician with neither of those attributes; and the possibility of languishing in such a position for much of one's career discourages others from joining the service.

It is largely in response to the Executive's influence, and its willingness to open the bureaucracy up as a political battlefield, that both the Lower House and the Senate also have an interest in seeking to extend their influence over the bureaucracy. The Representatives' intention is to ensure that projects within their district are indeed implemented such that they benefit their constituencies or themselves or both*. Contacts with bureaucrats are also useful in the event of crises of one kind or another such as an outbreak of dengue. It is therefore always useful to know, in particular, the Secretaries of the Departments of Public Works and Highways, Budget and Management, Education, and Health. For Senators, too, influence over the bureaucracy is necessary for similar reasons. In the face of competition from many other priorities and items of legislation, a Senator with an interest in seeing his own favoured bill have its intended effect, will need reach into the bureaucracy. Still more important for Senators is that this reach will unlock the accurate information needed when drawing up their legislation and when exercising their oversight functions. Without that reach, bureaucrats are likely to let the Senator know only what they wish the Senator to know. But unlike Representatives, Senators do not need to cultivate personal relationships within the bureaucracy (though this will do no harm). They may, of most levels of the bureaucracy, simply demand. This authority derives not only from their office, but also from what a Senator can do to the bureaucrat. Senators can - and this appears to be a standard technique known to both sides - have an anonymous constituent file a complaint with the Ombudsman against a civil servant. Alternatively, a Senator may report the bureaucrat's uncooperative behaviour to a superior, knowing that the superior, with an eye on forthcoming attempts to gain a better share of budgetary appropriations in the annual round of negotiations, will tend to favour the Senator. Or the Senator can simply drop hints that a Congressional investigation may be launched on this or that matter. From the point of view of the Senate, then,

---

* Kickbacks through the tendering process, either to Congressmen or to local politicians and bureaucrats, are incorporated in the calculations of costs made by companies, and cut into both quality and profit. Neither is propriety on the part of companies encouraged by the late release of funds. This is a common problem and can create additional costs for companies who will also build this into their assessment of costs and quality. The complex procedures and institutions (such as the Regional Development Council) which have evolved in order to bring coordination and integration to development efforts across regions, provinces, cities, and municipalities, well intentioned though they may be, often work only to complicate matters. These various considerations, together with the use of funding as political leverage, make for rather uncoordinated attempts at development.

bureaucrats tend to be compliant. The only time they balk at cooperation is when the President attempts, for whatever reason, to stop or restrict the flow of information. Then the bureaucrat must be imaginative in the way these conflicting pressures are dealt with.

The extent to which the civil service may become a political battleground should not be underestimated. Neither should the ferocity with which the bureaucracy can be wielded as a weapon. This is true even, or perhaps especially, of the Ombudsman. Although the Ombudsman is a prosecutorial arm of the Judiciary, the latter has no jurisdiction over the former; and it is also implied within the constitution that the Ombudsman should be independent of the Executive. In practice, however, the Ombudsman looks to the President and is marshalled for political ends - a role made easier by the fact that the Ombudsman alone has authorisation to follow up allegations made anonymously. Thus, for example, Senator Defensor-Santiago, who refused to concede to Ramos in the 1992 elections, and who continued to accuse him of electoral fraud, found herself in hospital facing criminal charges of corruption brought against her as she lay in hospital seriously injured after the car she was riding in was hit by a military vehicle on Ramos's order*. It was not until three years later that, in the absence of any evidence, the charges against her were dropped. One cannot bring true rigor to a consideration of these kinds of allegations and counter-allegations; but certainly in the regional offices younger anti-graft officers (who are qualified attorneys) are well aware of political influence both upon their case loads, and upon the direction of those cases.

The influence of the President upon the Ombudsman derives in part from the latter's need for funding. Although as a constitutional commission its funding is supposed to be guaranteed, in practice it suffers perennially from shortages of staff,

---

* Interview with Hon. Sen. Defensor-Santiago, August 2004.

low morale, and a backlog of dockets. Moreover, should the Ombudsman have ambitions to become, say, a justice of the Supreme Court or to run for the Senate, the support of the President will be needed. And it is to the President that the Ombudsman owes his position in the first place.

This brings us back to the Commission on Appointments - another body through which the Executive and legislature attempt to counter one another. As we have said, the Commission approves key appointments to both the Executive and the Judiciary,* and to other constitutional commissions including the Ombudsman and the Civil Service Commission. The Commission on Appointments - an organ of legislative power - comprises 12 Senators and 12 members of the Lower House. Were members of the Commission willing to put their own interests to one side, and were they suffering the discipline of parties who recognized that a non-partisan and corporate (rather than personalistic) outlook was, on occasions, of the utmost importance, its political composition need not prevent it from being impartial, nor from appointing candidates who are themselves independent. In practice, however, the Commission is - from the point of view of those who have both sat on it, and have had to bear its scrutiny - a bargaining shop of some interest to legislators, particularly during the first two years of an administration when most of the key appointments are made. It is in this forum that Representatives will attempt to extract from candidates as much as they can for their own districts; and that both Senators and Representatives are likely to ask candidates about pending contracts, applications for the conversion of land, or about their willingness, once appointed, to favour the placement of the legislators' allies in posts that will soon be within the candidate's gift. It is also here that old scores are settled as

---

* More precisely, it is one of the Commission's twenty-three standing committees that has the authority to approve (or reject) the President's selection of members of the Judicial and Bar Council (Senate, 2003 [June 4th]). It is the Council which is responsible for the appointments of judges and justices of the Supreme court.

candidates who once denied favours, now have their own appointments blocked; and where new grudges are formed.

3.2. Kinship and business

The absence of strong parties and the insecurity that arises, also provide the space, and plenty of incentive, for the intrusion of kinship and business as politicians scout around for dependable allies. Extensive webs of relationships exist within the Lower House; and these extend into both the Senate and provinces. Links with the provinces are largely vertical - that is, relatives holding elected local offices concurrently with the Representative, generally do so within the Representative's district or, if not, within the province where that district is to be found. And, as one might expect if they are working to secure the Representative's political base, the offices most commonly occupied are those of mayor and vice-mayor, counselor and *barangay* captain. About two-thirds of the relatives of members of the 9th Congress holding elected offices concurrently with Representatives were to be found in these posts. This proportion rose to around three-quarters during the 11th and 12th Congresses*. If we then include the relatives of members of both Houses who have held elected public office at any level and at any time in the last century, then another dimension of the picture emerges: more than half their relatives served in the Lower House, Senate, or highest posts of the Executive. This historical view also reveals that the proportion of members of the Lower House with political ancestry hovered around 60% during all three Congresses. The proportion of Senators with political ancestry is higher still, and ranged from between two-thirds and more than three-quarters.

---

* Material derived from the Philippines Center for Investigative Journalism (PCIJ), 2004; Securities of Exchange Commission, 2002-3, 2004. Thanks also to Ricky Castillo of the Congressional Staff for piecing together many of these links. The pattern of kinship links and business interests for the 10th Congress are very similar, and are published elsewhere (Hodder, 2002). However, that material on the 10th Congress excludes the help of Congressional Staff and the PCIJ's (2004) use of the government officials' own declarations of interests. For the sake of consistency, details on the 10th Congress have been omitted.

One cannot dismiss altogether the possibility that these dynasties reflect the transmission of interest and experience from one generation to the next; and it must be noted that they are not uncommon (though, for the most part, not as prevalent) in the democracies of the US and Europe. However, even within the Senate and the Lower House, many are more unforgiving. They are scathing of these scions of political families who never attend sessions; whose wealth is sufficient to enable them to delegate such that they need never appear in their districts (preferring instead the comfort of their homes in Manila); and who now hold office only because their name, connexions, and money, allows them to sway the results of the elections. They are, it is said, determined to keep the office within the family or, when circumstances require, to hand it temporarily to a close ally over whom they have a strong influence. They desire power, both for its own sake, and because they fear that they and their family might suffer all kinds of retribution were their office to fall into the hands of their opponents. Indeed, those Representatives and Senators from more professional, but more modest, backgrounds, and some with revolutionary credentials, see its domination by political dynasties as the crux of the legislature's problems, and as the main deterrence to the true reform of public institutions more generally.

As for business interests, we find that around four-fifths of all Representatives in all three Congresses have interests of one kind or another, from minor share holdings and directorships, to ownership. Some of these interests were acquired during Marcos's rule when - as in the case of Enrile's Jacinto group or Cojuangco's stake in various agribusinesses and in San Miguel - many elected representatives and ministers were awarded direct control of particular companies or large parts of whole industrial sectors (Celoza, 1997). But there are other more immediate reasons for the extent of the legislators' interests. Low salaries (the equivalent of a few hundred pounds sterling every month even for the President) and the absence of state funding of elections leave politicians with little choice but to fend for themselves and their families. By implication they are expected to solicit funds to

238

cover election costs. A large donation for a campaign cannot but have an influence upon the subsequent actions of a politician. And it is said that there are Representatives who are heard from only in those debates which impinge upon their own businesses, or upon the businesses of small cliques of merchants who, in effect, sent the Representatives to Congress, and for whom the Representative works. Antonio Floirendo Jr., for example, a member of a prominent merchant family in Mindanao, is commonly viewed as a placement for Mindanao's banana exporters. Other merchants, it is commonly alleged, operate upon a far grander scale. Cojuangco, though he sat neither in the Senate or Lower House, helped to fund the campaigns of members of the National People's Coalition and rival parties*. Lucio Tan, who seemed to be even less discriminating, was said to finance most of the campaigns of most of the representatives from Luzon (12th and 13th Congresses). Indeed, practically all the members of the tax-writing committee (Ways and Means) were in his pocket. Consequently, he escaped P20 billion of documentary stamp tax and avoided excise tax, while a proposal to index tax on cigarettes in the wake of the depreciation of the pesos could not even get out of the committee stage of the Lower House. A still more serious allegation concerns the strengthening flow of dirty money into the administration. Money from illegal gambling which found its way into the pockets of President Joseph Estrada, has now been joined by a flow of unlaundered narcotics money† into the coffers of the Arroyo administration.

3.3 Media storms and electoral fraud

Weak parties, the splintering of interests, the insecurity of the Executive, the politicization of the bureaucracy, and the intrusion of kinship and business, have worked together to enhance two further problems.

---

* Interview with Rep. Ocampo, August, 2004

† Interview with Hon. Sen. Angara, September 2004.

(i) The first is a tendency to by-pass the whole legislative arena and play directly to the street through the media. This is seen to be vital to election success for those politicians who need a high national profile; and it is part and parcel of building support for certain kinds of bills. Whipping up a maelstrom of allegations may also help to create additional leverage. So common is this practice, however, and so proficient have its practitioners become, that rather than by-pass the legislature, members of the Executive and both Houses have drawn the media into their world and turned it into a mere extension of the polity. The press corps to be found in both Houses (the larger in the Lower House) provide one route through which stories may be channeled. Seeding stories in this way may require some payment to the journalist or to their desk editor or to both, especially if those stories are placed 'anonymously' and are clearly serving the political ends of the source. Members of Congress, and their relatives, with ownership or part ownership of newspapers and other media organisations, or with personal connexions with individuals working in those organizations, provide other routes. Alternatively, if the allegations are of sufficient interest, then press releases, public statements, privilege speeches, or debates on the floor of the chamber, may be all that is needed to generate enough coverage.

The stories supplied and the charges made are limited only by the imagination. They vary from doubts about the sanity of colleagues, to the invention of problems in order to claim easy credit for their solution, to charges of widespread corruption. A case in point concerns the allegations made by Enrile following Arroyo's proposal to raise taxes in 2004 in response to the deepening fiscal crisis. Enrile's argument was one that many had made: citizens should not be asked to pay more taxes until existing taxes were collected and used properly. To do otherwise simply shifted intolerable burdens on to the honest. An illustration of the kinds of problems which the government had not only failed to deal with but had also had a hand in, was the development of a lucrative secondary market in tax-credit certificates. Fictitious companies - armed with raw material import complements, export documents, and bank credit memos purporting to record inward remittances of export proceeds - had applied for, and had been granted, tax-credit certificates. The certificates were then sold on: the largest buyers had been Petron and Shell whose stock of illegally acquired certificates amounted to somewhere between P2.7 billion and P8.4 billion. So extensive had the market become that efforts to conceal it had become half-hearted. In one instance a newly established company (TEC) had secured certificates worth P125.4 million, even though it reported annual sales of only P8.4 million. Once these certificates had been sold on to the oil companies, TEC folded.

The collusion of the Executive and bureaucracy in this market was extensive: the one-stop-shop in the Department of Finance responsible for issuing the certificates was involved, as were the Board of Investments, Customs, and the Bureau of Internal Revenue. The Inter-Agency Committee - an *ad hoc* body set up to investigate this illegal market and to bring prosecutions - was also implicated. Very few prosecutions were in fact brought, and those that had (against the Director of the one-stop-shop, and against an undersecretary in the Department of Finance) had either failed or stalled as a consequence of the deliberate incompetence of government prosecutors, or so Enrile alleged. Had not the Executive also provided many of the key players in the market with other forms of protection? Most cynically, the Executive had first impounded much of Chingco's real estate property (it was he who had engineered the market) and then sold those properties to companies owned by Chingco's in-laws.

We cannot know whether, or how deeply, these allegations are rooted in truth. The system for tax collection is very weak; corruption and evasion is undoubtedly widespread; and, even by themselves, tough bank secrecy laws make investigation and conviction extremely difficult. Yet, for many - and particularly for those in the Central Bank who argued that whilst a more efficient collection was always needed, so was a tax increase - there was little doubt that Enrile and others were attempting to fashion a stick which could then be laid aside should certain aspects of the proposals be withdrawn.

(ii) The second problem is electoral fraud. In such fissionable conditions, there is little means or incentive to restrain ambition; and while the legitimate costs of elections alone continue to rise (a single t.v. commercial of 30 seconds on prime-time national channels will cost P182,000), there remains no state funding of the politicians' costs. The need for a good result after so much money has been spent is therefore pressing. The kinds of practices that emerge vary somewhat with the office. In general, the first hurdle for candidates is to ensure that their names appear on the ballot. This often requires some form of payment to be made over to local political leaders (governors and mayors), and this is so even if the candidate and local politicians are of the same party. Direct personal advances, or promises of funding for local projects, are also necessary if the support of the *barangay* captains is to be secured. Bearing promises of projects and incentives of other kinds, the *barangay* captains and their *purok* leaders will work through their networks of kinship and friendship to solicit votes from the heads of families. They, in turn, will exert what influence they can over their family and friends, though perhaps in return for some consideration - a job for their son or for a friend who has been out of work for some time? Once the pitches have been made and the deals done, the *barangay* captain will report back on the number of streets that can be delivered. In this way, candidates may build up a picture of the districts, municipalities, cities, and provinces they might be able to count on. Local merchants, too, may exert considerable influence on votes, either through their employees, charity work, social rounds, and membership of associations, or by organizing and directing local campaigns. And again, some *quid pro quo* may be expected and given - perhaps a seat on an influential planning body or on the board of a bank or government corporation? Some of the haggling for votes can be more unseemly than illegitimate. But it is into this greyness that the blacker arts of the electoral process can blend more easily. The provincial certificates of canvass, which are rather commonplace documents, are particularly vulnerable to counterfeit. For the election of the President these documents, as they arrive at Congress for scrutiny, trigger a new bargaining spree as candidates attempt to buy up members who they hope will be less than vigilant and offer their support in numbers sufficient to allow the eventual winner a hold over Congress.

Both these problems - the use of the media and electoral fraud - may weaken parties further. The use of the media to pursue political ends and vendettas, simply highlights the irrelevancy of parties. And election fraud, by undermining the confidence of the President in the support she commands both in Congress and in the country at large, is likely to deepen her sense of insecurity such that the emergence of any strong party, even within her own camp, will be regarded as a threat. In 1998, when LAKAS-CMD had control of the House and could have formed an effective counter-balance to President Estrada, the party was decimated by the migration of its members to the administration. Following the 2004 election, LAKAS-CMD, though it was now the President's party, suffered another exodus of its members who - lured by promises of funding, influence, and financial and legal solutions to personal problems - joined another party, this time within the coalition. This party, Kampi, founded by Arroyo in 1998 before she joined LAKAS as its President, had been revived by her husband together with his brothers (one of whom served as a party whip). Her husband denied involvement; but the general consensus was that his was the guiding hand, motivated very likely by fear of, or doubts over, the loyalty of LAKAS in the bumpy times ahead. Kampi would be a second string to his wife's bow. The Liberal Party, too, which, in the view of its members, had propelled Arroyo to office as Estrada fell, also found itself increasingly marginalised by the President. Disillusioned, the party had continued to support her in 2004 only after some persuasion that they would indeed have an influence over policy making. But with an offer of deputy speakership made to Nonynoy Aquino, came the proviso that he should be willing to fall into line when asked.*

4.0 Constraints

Arising from this account of some of the problems with the Philippines' Legislature, are two comments of some interest. The first is that these problems often seem to derive from the institutional arrangements in themselves or, in other words, from the observance of rules, roles, and procedures. The contrasting nature of constituencies and of the role of Senators, Representatives, and members of the Executive; the permitted length of their terms in office; the budgetary procedures, especially with regard to the funding of local projects; the respective functions of Senate, Lower House, Executive and civil service; and the position of the legislature within the tripartite division of government: all go some way to explain certain problems (such as incessant bargaining, the pressure on the legislative timetable, the splintering of interests, and the politicization of legislative and funding process). It is also clear that weak parties not only exacerbate those problems, but also provide the room and - by sharpening a sense of insecurity - the incentive for politicians to send out tendrils of personalistic relationships in order to isolate and forestall each other, to politicize the bureaucracy, and to draw in family and business interests. This serves to weaken parties still further.

In short, we are led to the suggestion that weak parties are perpetuated by the problems they exacerbate or help to create. And indeed, by the mid 1990s, Landé (1996) had reached a similar conclusion: personalism and particularism were the result of the weakness of parties, and that weakness could be explained in part by the write-in system of voting and by a lack of ideology or programmatic glue (pp.131-133). Although the structure of clientalism and machine politics are not so very different from each other, the former was being supplanted by the latter.

---

* Interview with Rep. Aquino, B.S., August, 2004.

244

If this is right - if many of the problems with the legislature do indeed derive more from the institutional and procedural arrangements in themselves - then institutions have the potential, if reformed, to offer some hope of improvement in the political economy. Strengthening parties and restricting or prohibiting dynastic succession, for instance, may not be wholly dependent upon first dealing with the deep personalistic quality of Philippine society. Legislation may well have a positive effect.

The second comment, which is a corollary of the first, is that the legislature and other institutions and their rules, procedures, practices, and conventions, do seem to constrain the behaviour of legislators and the people they help to govern. This appears to be indicated not only by the problems referred to above, but also in a number of other respects. These are outlined below.

(i) Although tensions occasionally spill out onto the street where blood is shed, they are for the most part contained within political institutions and procedures. Securing political leverage may have become an end in itself, and legislation and the legislative and funding process may have become the means to that end. But at least the battles take place for the most part within institutional bounds. There are also attempts to reclaim the polity's dignity through the use of existing institutions, procedures and conventions, and, when this seems insufficient, to introduce reform. The more frequent use of LEDAC and the PLLO in order to improve coordination and to sharpen a sense direction, are small examples. There are also attempts underway to introduce a Party Development Act which, if realised, would strengthen political parties, transform them into accountable public bodies with legal personalities, and end the periodic migration of their member *en masse*[*]. There are also efforts to draw up legislation to put an end to political dynasties, to limit the flow of local bills and, most dramatically, to change the constitution.

---

[*] Interviews with Hon. Senators Lim and Angara, July 2004.

Whether these changes will be realised, or work as intended, is another question. Yet the fact that something is being tried, and that tensions, disappointments, and frustrations, are being routed through such discussions and measures, is surely an important sign of maturity and tolerance.

(ii) A similar observation is that sharpening class divisions are being played out within the legislature. The divisions seem to be three-fold: between the educated and often, though not always, wealthy and established families with a political heritage; the educated professionals, often from modest families, with relatively modest incomes and, in some cases, revolutionary credentials; and those with little formal education from poor families who have either made 'new' money outside politics, or risen through the ranks of the army, police, or local government, and who have turned the poverty from which they emerged to their advantage. Across these divides lie other cleavages: between those who see a strong man-of-action, capable of bringing unity and direction, as a solution to the country's problems, and those who believe the future lies in the reform of institutions, and in shifts in values; and between those who are *of* the political dynasties, and those who are not.

There is always present the inevitable risk of oversimplifying the complexities of sentiments and very fluid perceptions. But whilst some divisions are often more stark within the mind than they are in practice, they do inform the thoughts and actions of legislators, electorate, and members of the Executive, and in this sense they have a truth about them. They certainly feel very sharp. Lapid was clearly stung* by Enrile's description of him as the 'Little Senator'; and by the dismissive remarks circulating in the Senate and Lower House about his poor education, complete lack of professional training, and inability to participate in formal debates (which are conducted mostly in English) on the floor and in committees.

---

* Interview with Hon. Senator Lapid, August 2004.

Thus, from the point of view of the educated professional with comparatively modest bank accounts, the rich have had it too good and have been too comfortable for too long to ever contemplate true reform, while the uneducated populist, if they are not merely a less sophisticated version of the old elite who will protect and build up the influence of their own families at the expense of the country, are thought likely to be seduced by the simplistic formula of the left. And indeed, the populists' clarion call is decisive action and unity. They have contempt for the complacency of the old establishment, they see themselves in their stead, and they believe that they can bring to the poor, from whose ranks they have emerged, more of what the rich have kept for themselves. Meanwhile, the more open and progressive of the old elite understand the impatience and attraction of the populist, sympathize with the professional, and see danger in the growing divide between the 'haves and have nots' in the country at large. But danger also they see in moving either too quickly or too slowly.

What is most interesting and telling, however, is that views and sentiments such as these, and the presence of people from such varied backgrounds, should find a place in political institutions. Perhaps as valuable a contribution as any other that politicians make during their times in office, is to play out political dramas often touched by personal tragedy and, in so doing, to create true theatre. There, upon the stage, represented by the sacrificial politician, citizens may be content to leave their own frustrations, grievances, disappointments, prejudices, fears, and hopes, rather than give vent to them on the street. In this sense, too, the personal relationship between individual citizens and the politician – central to which is the exchange of tangible benefits for political support - makes democracy incarnate, if only for a moment. Were the citizens' walk-on part to be written out, or were cynicism to become so intense that the theatre began to seem like a tawdry charade designed to fool, then it may be that citizens will indeed turn to what they believe to be the easy solution of the strong man.

(iii) A third possible expression of the constraint on behaviour might be indicated by the influence of political dynasties and business interests which, though still strong, may be weakening. The 'class war'; hostility to dynasties and to business; charges of corruption, and the willingness of the media to broadcast such allegations; recognition within the legislature and on the street of the problems created by the intrusion of kinship and business; and what appears to be a genuine desire among some businesses for a level playing field: all may be taking their toll on dynastic politics and the influence of business.

(a) If we give a little more attention to kinship links among those members of the legislature, local government, and the upper levels of the Executive who are serving in elected public office concurrently, we find a complex picture. (As an illustration, figures 16 - 21 provide a simplified outline of these networks for the 12th Congress). Some 12% of Representatives of the 9th Congress, 15% of representatives of the 11th, and 9% of the 12th, are inter-related; and these relationships exist among Representatives both within the same provinces and regions, and between different regions and provinces. The proportion of Representatives related to Senators is somewhat lower at 5.5% (9th Congress), 6.5% (11th) and 5.6% (12th). Both groups (that is, those Representatives who are related to one another within the Lower House, and those who are related to members of the Senate) overlap to some extent, but by no means completely. About a quarter of Representatives (in the 9th Congress) with relatives in the Senate had no relationship with other Representatives. This figure rose to nearly a half during the 11th Congress; and to just over half during the 12th Congress. Nor is there a complete overlap between these two groups and those Representatives with relatives in local government within the provinces in which their districts are to be found. Nearly half of those Representatives who are related to each other had no relatives serving in local government. The proportion rises to 2/5 for the 11th and to just over half for the 12th. And of those representatives who are related to Senators, only 1/5 had relatives serving in local government within their own province. This proportion rises to 28% for the 11th Congress and 30% for the 12th Congress. More broadly, around 20% of Representatives of the 9th had relatives serving in local government, but no relatives serving in the Senate or Lower House. This proportion is 21% and 26% for the 11th and 12th Congresses respectively. And two-thirds of Representatives had no relatives serving concurrently either in local government or in Congress (9th, 11th and 12th). In short, most members of the Lower House had no relatives serving concurrently either in the Lower House or in Senate or in local government; and those with relatives serving concurrently, tended to be found *either* in the Senate *or* in local government.

A consideration of the survival of Representatives across the three congresses, also raises doubts about the significance of political dynasties. We find that fifty members survived all three Congresses. The number of relatives (serving concurrently in elected posts) of each of these Representatives was on average only a little higher than the average number of relatives (serving concurrently) of those Representatives who did not survive all three congresses. We also find that those Representatives who survived all three congresses had, on average, the larger number of relatives who had served in elected office at one time or other during the last century*. However, about two-thirds of those who had survived either had no relatives (serving concurrently) at all, or less that the average number of relatives (serving concurrently) of those Representatives who did not survive. In short, pedigree does not hurt, but it would seem that survival is not dependent upon it.

If we turn now to the Senate, and consider Senators' relatives serving concurrently in other elected posts, we find that kinship appears to be more prevalent than among members of the Lower House; but in some respects it is less significant

---

* The proportions were 3.06:3.09, 4.4:3.52, and 5.34:3.69 for the 9th, 11th and 12th Congresses respectively.

than implied earlier. There were no kinship links among Senators in the 9th Congress, though during the 11th and 12th Congress the proportion rose to 16%. The proportion of Senators with relatives in the Lower House and local government also rose from 16% (9th) to 38% and 46% (11th and 12th Congresses respectively). Another 16% of Senators in the 11th and 12th Congresses had relatives in local government *only*. The average number of relatives of Senators serving in elected office concurrently is also higher than the number for Representatives: a little over two for the 11th and 12th congresses. The figure for the average number of Senatorial relatives who served at some time in the past is also higher (at 4.33 and 4.43), as is the average number of relatives (concurrent and historical) of Senators who served in both Congresses (5.33 and 6).

Looked at in the round, kinship is more significant in the Senate than in the Lower House; and whilst there is some overlap, kinship links tend to be oriented *either* between the Senate and the Lower House, *or* between the Lower House and local government. It would seem that membership of political dynasties does not hurt and may often help, but it is not a precondition for initial election success or survival. Similarly, whilst political dynasties in local government may help to secure political bases, they do not necessarily propel members into the highest political offices. The hostile views within the Senate and Lower House towards political dynasties, and the emergence of what appear to be class tensions within political institutions, would seem to fit this interpretation.

(b) We can also find a more complex picture of business interests than our earlier observation (that 4/5 of representatives have business interests) might seem to imply. (Figures 22-25 provide an illustration of these interests for the 12th Congress). During the 9th Congress some 19% of members had mutual business interests, but only for 3% of members did these business interests and kinship links coincide. These proportions rose to 21% and 4% (11th), and fell back a little to 19% and 2% for the 12th. Among those members in the 9th Congress with shared business, only two members had interests in companies ranked among the top 100 nationally; and neither members was a major shareholder or held ranking positions in those companies. Another two members, however, held ranking positions in a subsidiary of Manila Electric. Another eight members held interests in businesses which ranked among the top 2000, and in which no other member had a direct interest; and of these companies, two were ranked among the top 100.

During the 11th Congress, among those members with shared business interests, twelve had interests in companies that ranked among the top 100. Of these twelve members, eight held ranking positions. Another twelve members had interests in companies which ranked among the top 2000, and in which no other members held interests. Of those twelve, one held a ranking position in a business ranked in the top 100. During the 12th Congress, of those members with shared business interests, thirteen had shared business interests in companies that ranked among the top 100. Of those thirteen, three members held ranking positions in their respective companies. Of those members with shared interests, three also had interests in businesses in which no other members had business interests. Two other members, who had no shared interests with other members, also had interests in businesses among the top 100; another ten members had interests in businesses which ranked among the top 2000, and in which no other members had an interest.

If we take into consideration all members with business interests (including all those with no mutual business interests) then we find that 17% of members of the 9th Congress had interests in companies ranked among the top 5000. That figure of 17% embraces the 13% of members with interests among the top 2000, and 6% of members with interests in the top 100. The nested proportions for the 11th Congress were 21%, 17% and 6%; and, for the 12th Congress, 15%, 13% and 6%.

Within the Senate we find that during the 11th Congress, only three members had mutual business interests; eight members had mutual business interests with members in the Lower House; and in only one instance did kinship and mutual business interests coincide. But there also existed kinship links with seven members of the Lower House who held interests in companies that ranked among the top 5000. Two of these companies also ranked among the top 100. During the 12th Congress, seven members of the Senate had mutual business interests, and, altogether, ten had shared business interests with members of the Lower House. Only in two instances did kinship and mutual business interests overlap. As a whole, five members of the Senate had business interests in companies ranked among the top 100; and seven had interests in companies ranked among the top 2000.

In sum, mutual business interests within the legislature were a more significant kernel of association than kinship; but it would seem that most business interests of most members of both houses in all three Congresses were, as far as the broader economic picture is concerned, fairly small, local affairs which did not rank among the top 5,000 let alone the top 2,000 or 100 companies that dominate national economic life. Whilst there are exceptions, there would appear to be no simple correlation between political office and business prowess: the translation of political office into business empires, or of business success into political office, is no easy matter. This would seem to fit the more critical view of business held by members of the legislature. It might also reflect something of the way in which merchants look at their own profession and that of the politician.

5.0 Towards the formalisation of the Philippines' polity.

The view to which we are leaning, then, is that formalisation has found expression in the legislature's many problems, as well as in its more positive tendencies. Rules and roles are now being observed. The presence of such constraints upon behaviour is nothing new. It was, in Thompson's (1995) view, precisely their removal by Marcos which led the country from 'clientelism under democracy' to 'sultanism' or, in other words, to unencumbered personal rule. And it was Aquino's defeat of Marcos in 1986 and its immediate aftermath that marked a breakdown in the patron-client system (see Wurfel, 1988; and Thompson, *op.cit.*).

Read through our attitudinal perspective, we begin to see practices in which the strengthening of professionalisation, and a synchronous deepening of the affect, would appear to be quite open and explicit. There is, for instance, an unwritten convention within the Senate that one should not take umbrage at disputes over political (or, in other words, professional) matters. The convention is not an easy one to adhere to. Senators are small in number; they are divided by education, past careers, experience, personality, belief, and ego; and they are thrown together for many years. Inevitably disputes will flare up on the floor and in the media; accusations will fly; attempts are made by some to undermine or destroy others politically; and each may in their heart of hearts detest and despise their colleagues. After political opponents had first briefed the press that Defensor-Santiago was losing her mind (and this was after she had suffered a family tragedy), and had then asked her not to take their comments personally, she had wondered bitterly how should she take them? How was Lapid to put to one side Enrile's biting taunts? And what, asked some, were Jinggoy Estrada and his mother doing in the Senate if not solely to protect the disgraced ex-President? Yet Senators must find some way of working together if only for their own self-interest and self-respect. Each will, at some time, need as much support within the Senate as they can muster; and the pursuit of personal vendettas will only prove to be expensive financially as each side briefs and counter-briefs the press. One cannot afford to be bound by personal relationships, or by a sense of personal obligation or grievance. And so, as a matter of necessity, there is about the Senate something of the atmosphere of an elite club in which the social and the professional are, or appear to be, kept separate. To their constituents it seems like rank hypocrisy as Senators first clash, then shake hands and smile. But without that compartmentalization, the institution would cease to function.

It is true that this distancing is more about a practical civility than propriety. The more noble still have little choice but to heed Machiavelli's words to the Prince that those 'who act virtuously in every way necessarily come to grief among so many who are not virtuous.' And relationships formed around kernels such as school, class, mutual friends, membership of associations (such as the Rotary Club), as well as kinship, are still the *sine qua non* of any level of political life: they are the means of information and of the trade in favours. When the Central Bank was asked to appear before a Congressional committee at a particularly busy time, a 'phone call to the committee's Chairman (who happened to be the fraternity brother of a member of the Bank's Monetary Board), was sufficient to re-schedule the hearings and to pare down much of preparatory work required from the Bank for the hearing*. But might practicality and politeness mark the turning of excessive personalism into taboo? Even the more unscrupulous (for whom the ends justify the means) must alter their behaviour such that they give at least the impression that they are abiding by convention and have a more urbane outlook on life. Even for them, politeness and practicality within the Senate can count for more than personal relationships. And more generally within the legislature, the bureaucracy, and business, it is important, certainly among the sophisticates, not to give the impression that one is trying to foist a sense of obligation upon another. The more professional technocrats would regard it as rude and churlish not to reply to a question asked by a Senator in the course of everyday social conversions at, say, a party or on the golf course; but they will not volunteer information to a Senator before the question asked, lest this convey the sense that something is expected in return.

We can also find what appears to be open recognition of the need to distance social relationships at the level of constituencies. The sense of *quid pro quo* between

---

* Interview with Melito S. Salazar Jr., Monetary Board Member, *Bangko Sentral ng Pilipinas* , August 2004.

legislator and constituents is easier for the Senator to shake off. They will think nothing of dismissing a constituent who turns up at their office asking for money to cover their fare back to their home province; and they will think nothing of the constituent who, once rejected, threatens to turn the votes of family and friends against the Senator. Representatives, however, have a much harder time of it. The expectation among constituents that, in return for their votes and support, the Representative should deliver everything from jobs and medical and legal help, to new roads and (during a fiesta) brass bands, is powerful and difficult to move against. As we have said, members of the Lower House are under considerable, and legitimate, pressure to deliver material benefits and improvements to their constituents. And it is with a deal of exasperation that both Representatives commonly recount how, in the minds of their constituents, such local concerns are of paramount or exclusive interest. Imposing party discipline and the priorities of national policies upon Representatives might only cost them electorally. Given this fact of life, Representatives and Senators might as well make the best of opportunities for dissent and ambition opened up by the lack of strong parties; while the Office of the President, inured to its need to bring more coherence and order through other means, is likely to view with distrust the emergence of a strong party even within its supporting coalitions. Many Representatives are content with the status quo. But others believe that, quite apart from any benefits that might accrue to political parties, they, as Representatives, would gain an enormous sense of freedom if 'pork' were cut, the sense of a personalized *quid pro quo* between themselves and their constituents weakened, and constituents inculcated with the realisation that, regardless of how they might vote, Congress and government have a duty to serve all citizens.

Through our attitudinal perspective we can also begin to see various stimuli and blocks to change, and, therefore, possible solutions to the problems faced by the legislature. We have argued that the distancing of relationships is, to some extent, a practical response that enables the legislature to work. The inculcation of intellectual thought in which the distinction between social and professional spheres is strong, might play its part in attitudinal shifts among the many highly educated legislators. That many legislators have personal experience in, and contacts with, family businesses and large corporations, may also help to explain those shifts. We must also consider the possibility that attitudinal change has been imported by those legislators who, before entering politics, made their way through the ranks in the army, police, or intelligence agencies - institutions which, despite their reputations, contain pockets of disciplined staff who either are, or who aspire to be, highly professional*.

Of the blocks to change, perhaps the most damaging and difficult to deal with is a lack of confidence. Were the diminution of a sense of worth and increasing instrumentalism the only assault on confidence, then it might be possible to look elsewhere for material to shore up a collective belief in the Philippines and Filipinos. These attacks, however, are coming from many directions. It is a nation whose history, rooted in colonialism, has no strong or convincing sense of pre-colonial traditions. Its political institutions are modelled upon the world's greatest power: yet its people have laboured under martial law; the performance of its economy has, at best, been modest in a region of miracles; and such economic success as it has achieved is often attributed in no small measure to the ethnic Chinese. It is a country better known internationally for its migrant workers and domestic servants, its sex trade, and mail order brides. And many of its younger and best people are leaving the country at the rate of 700 a week†. It would be remarkable, then, if people and government did not look at each other with a jaundiced eye. This crisis of confidence fosters, and is in turn fuelled by, the

---

* According to Casper (1995) a more professional attitude was to be found within the military. It was among the lower ranks who retained their institutional allegiances that opposition grew to Marcos and his tendency to promote officers to the highest ranks on the basis of their personal loyalty to him (see also Thompson, 1995).

† The figure does not take into account returning migrant workers.

polity's failings, locking it into a perpetual state of hopelessness. This corrosive circle lowers expectations: the starting point is the likelihood that whatever is attempted will be desperately ineffective. More pernicious still is that those in politics with hope, idealism, and righteousness, have the sense that they are on their own, and that they cannot place much faith in the world around them nor in the hope that the institutions and procedures of government will work more or less as they should. The best will feel that they need to compromise, and are soon worn down; the less robust will have long-since had their personalistic view of the polity re-affirmed. Most deadly, perhaps, is that the erosion of confidence blinds one to what good there is, and to what is now a little better than it once was. Thus the strengthening of the professional sphere and the synchronous deepening of the social sphere, the presence of integrity, and a degree of economic progress - the very things which could break the cycle of despair and cynicism, and restore confidence - are left unrecognized.

Solutions to the problems with the Philippines' polity will depend ultimately upon political leadership at all levels: for the task is to break the gyre of cynicism, and establish a virtuous circle of confidence and hope. This will entail supporting and strengthening hot-spots of attitudinal change when and where they occur; and linking them together such that individuals and groups with a less instrumental view of the world no longer feel that they are on their own. These hot-spots of change are to be found both within and without the institutions and activities of government. But they are probably most evident within constitutional commissions (such as the Civil Service Commission, the Commission on Elections, and the Ombudsman) which, for all their faults, contain highly educated staff who - were they given encouragement and made to feel less isolated - would act to radiate attitudinal change throughout those institutions and beyond. It may also be, as we have already implied in this chapter, that the legislature is itself capable of prompting attitudinal shifts among its own members. The introduction of measures to strengthen political parties and weaken dynasties would have some effect, as would measures to strengthen the writ of the constitutional commissions. Reforms of these kind would mitigate the splintering of interests, the intrusion of kinship and business, and other problems (such as electoral fraud) noted above. They would also would strengthen attitudinal change within these bodies, and have a signal effect on confidence within the country more generally. Eliminating or reducing 'pork'[*], and encouraging in constituents a more national outlook, a more nuanced understanding of their walk-on part, and a more realistic expectation of their Representatives' ability to deliver material benefits locally, might also help to reduce the mismatch between constituencies and legislature, and make it easier to build up more robust party machines. Stronger support for small and medium businesses, and for Filipinos overseas; more concentrated and focussed attempts to encourage overseas Filipinos to return to, and invest in[†], the Philippines; and the deliberate presentation of small businesses and overseas workers as heroic elements of Filipino society: all would do much to energize these catalysts of attitudinal change, shore up confidence in the polity, and improve the self-image of Filipinos. In this regard, too, turning to practical advantage the newness and variegated cosmopolitanism of 'the Filipino', and doing so with pride, might be of greater value than attempts to manufacture a unity of kind and ancient origin (Anderson, 1994). Drawing associations and Church still more closely into government institutions where they may participate in the formulation and implementation of policy, especially with respect to small businesses and overseas Filipinos, would also help to build confidence and propagate attitudinal change still more widely.

Change will not be fast; but as social relationships are increasingly distanced from professional life and as confidence returns, presidents, senators, representatives, and members of the judiciary and civil service, may find that their willingness to

---

[*] One element of this pork - the priority development assistant fund - was slashed in 2004-5 (*The Economist*, March 26 2005, p.96)

[†] The passage of the Dual Citizenship Act was part of just such attempts.

observe the limits of their own authority, will reward itself with the strengthening of the state and of their own standing at home and abroad. At the same time, they may find that the influence of association and the Church, against which politicians today so often rail, will decline while the separation of business from state, the weakening of the country's formidable bank secrecy laws, the improvement of revenue collection, and a toughening of government's ability to mediate effectively between the interests of its own citizens and those of corporations, will become a matter of course.

6.0 Conclusions

In this chapter we have argued that positive tendencies are present in the Philippine polity. For instance, growing tensions between rich and poor may be finding some expression, and release, in the legislature. The influence of kinship and business interests may be diminishing: and if this is to be explained partly by concealment, then it might reflect both a measure of shame as well as concerns about legal action and public criticism. Rules and roles and being observed, and there is a synchronous deepening of the affect. Still more significant indications of this deepening professionalism are to be found among the many problems with the Philippines' polity. Some of these are, to an extent, part and parcel of the cut and thrust of ordinary democratic politics. In the Philippines, however, they are exacerbated by the weakness of parties – a weakness that is rooted in a mismatch between the comparative depth of professionalisation within the legislature, and the attitudes and expectations of large swathes of their constituencies. All of this, we have suggested, may signal a degree of formalisation.

The reasons for a shift towards the affect and greater professionalism are complex, perhaps more so than within business organisations. Here, within the polity, we are dealing with a convergence of practices and representations from many directions such that, within a strongly personalistic context, hot-spots of attitudinal change and of informal-formal transformation are constantly emerging in the legislature and other institutional bodies. The sense of alienation created by an intensely personalistic atmosphere, and the practice of putting together and enabling complex institutions to work may comprise part of the explanation. The authoritarianism of Marcos's rule may have encouraged the development of the affect and brought clearer definition to the social sphere. Those members of both Houses who have about them a warm empathy and a genuine compassion for others (which seems to belong only to those who have themselves suffered) may be part of his legacy. The growing complexity of political institutions as democracy was re-introduced may be demanding greater professionalism, especially if those institutions are to work well enough to preserve the political life of their members. As it finds better synchronicity with the professional sphere, the affect, too, may begin to deepen further. If businesses are part of the problem (and it is clear that they can have an improper influence), then they are also part of the solution. As we noted in chapter 4 the practice of business and its professionalisation is associated with the deepening of the affect; and, for reasons that we have already set out, most legislators necessarily have some experience of running businesses, both large and small. The transmission of the professionalism and the affect from business to the polity, we might suggest, is therefore only a matter of time. Legislators educated in social sciences (which, we have suggested are often strongly imbued with the affect), the Church (through its strong emphasis on the primacy of social relationships among people and with God), and NGOs (with their concern with human rights, fairness, equality, and the probity of politicians and bureaucrats), may also be working to encourage the deepening of the affect and the strengthening of the professional sphere.

We have also noted that wider and more even transformation is constantly being frustrated by a lack of confidence. In this, too, social science analysis might have to bear some responsibility. We suggested in chapter 3 that scholarly analyses of the overseas Chinese may have helped to strengthen a sense that Filipinos are somehow less capable of running businesses and making money. But the dialectic between scholarly analyses, and the practice, of politics in the Philippines, may be even more vigorous. The channel for the transmission of ideas is open, clear, and direct. Many Senators and members of the Lower House, Executive and civil service are well read; and it is not unusual for scholar, politician, bureaucrat, or member of the judiciary to move to and from between these different professions. Those who practice are well aware of the academic and journalistic literature on the Philippines political economy. And they are, on the whole, within comparatively easy reach of journalists, academics, and voters. Their representations of the polity – at least those which have been well rehearsed – are often similar to those of the scholar, even in their vocabulary. Might the closeness of street and scholarship help to account for the structural emphasis in analyses, at least in comparison to the study of the overseas Chinese? Scholars are, perhaps, more at ease with the notion that English-speaking sophisticates are labouring within political institutions (with built-in inequalities in education, wealth, and influence) set up by a colonial power, and far less comfortable with their characterization as cultural products.

This is not to marginalise the kinds of structural and cultural analyses of the Philippines polity referred to in chapter 1. We might argue that patrimonial and institutional analyses, and their antecedents and variants, provide a sound interpretation of problems with the legislature noted above. The weakness of parties could be understood very usefully as a consequence of vertically-structured, patron-client relationships; and the influence of big business could also be set within patrimonialism. Moreover, patrimonialism and the broader academic debate suggest that we should be alert to change; and they provide some measure of explanation for change. For instance, the Senators' use of NGOs to promote legislation, the introduction and expansion of the party list system, and the stirrings of comparatively radical top-down reform, would seem to fit with both patrimonial and institutional analyses.

The apparent changes noted above might also be interpreted through those same prisms as *continuing* features of a personalistic state or a shallow democracy. In this view, the legislature can be described fairly as a shallow democratic institution; and the constraints on behaviour to which we have referred are no more than would be expected in a personalistic state. Unless the underlying cultural and structural features are dealt with first, institutional reform will amount to no more than ineffective tinkering, and will leave parties and the legislature weak. It would also be disingenuous to think other than that the influence of business interests is being hidden through the use of complex intermediaries and illicit practices by competing oligarchs who have suborned the judiciary and hired good lawyers. The apparent class war might simply indicate the long-standing and gradual turnover of the Philippines' socially mobile elite. The newer politicians who have broken into the establishment may themselves in time only reach down to pull up their own kind. Or it may be that those who appear to have replaced the dynasts, have done so only temporarily, or are their close allies. Alternatively, we might look at, say, Sidel's (1999, 1998, 1997) notion of bossism to help account for the apparent disjunction between those kinship links that run down from the Lower House into local government, and those which stretch upwards into the Senate and highest levels of public office.

Not only are such discussions interesting and revealing in themselves, but they may well inform the practice of politicians, NGOs, merchants, and sections of the electorate. However, if these representations are seen as something more than representations, if they take on an absolute quality, then there is the danger that they may entrench a sense of isolation and hopelessness in those who are more righteous, while encouraging those who are less mentally robust to join, rather than to fight, 'the system.' This could not happen at a worse time. There are reforms underway which, we have supposed, may lead to a further deepening of attitudinal change. There are, for instance, moves to strengthen parties; weaken the dynasts; bolster support for overseas Filipinos and small family businesses; shave away the 'pork'; and (if only to reduce the unrealistic pressures layered on the politicians) to encourage attitudinal shifts among the electorate. For the most part these reflect the visions, pet initiatives, and agendas, of legislators working either by themselves or in small groups; and without a coherent sense of purpose and direction nationally, it is doubtful whether these measures will have the momentum necessary to drive them home. In the light of these attempts at reform, and of what appear to be strong moves towards the affect, perhaps the time is right to consider the possibility that the weaknesses and problems of the polity, as much as they may be an expression of skeins of conspiratorial and personalistic relationships, may also reflect the somewhat haphazard working out of the beliefs, values, principles, and good intentions, of politicians, civil servants, and merchants, who, though weighed down by a sense of moral isolation, are honourable.

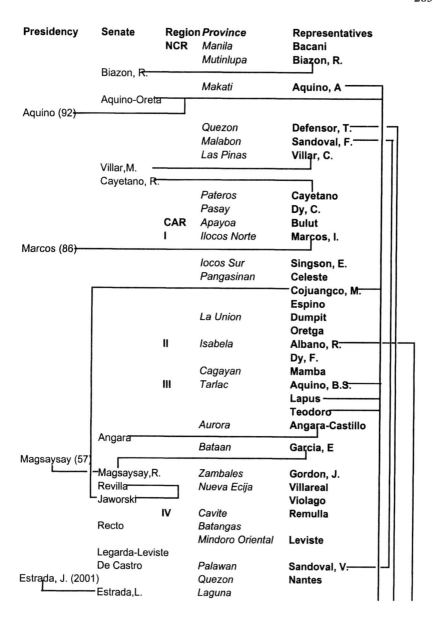

Figure 16. Kinship ties among elected politicians in central and local government, 12th Congress, 2001-2004. Set 1. *Source: see key.*

264

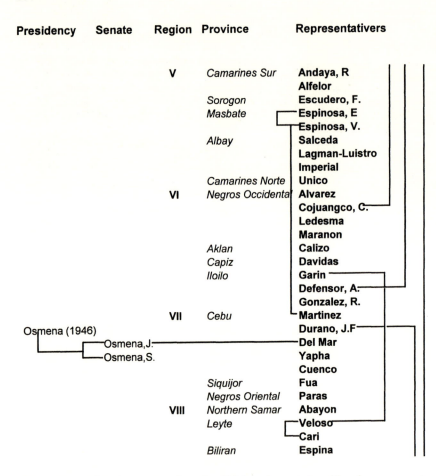

Presidency	Senate	Region	Province	Representativers

V — Camarines Sur — **Andaya, R / Alfelor**

Sorogon — **Escudero, F.**

Masbate — **Espinosa, E / Espinosa, V.**

Albay — **Salceda / Lagman-Luistro / Imperial**

Camarines Norte — **Unico**

VI — Negros Occidental — **Alvarez / Cojuangco, C. / Ledesma / Maranon**

Aklan — **Calizo**

Capiz — **Davidas**

Iloilo — **Garin / Defensor, A. / Gonzalez, R.**

VII — Cebu — **Martinez**

Osmena (1946) — Osmena, J. / Osmena, S. — **Durano, J.F / Del Mar / Yapha / Cuenco**

Siquijor — **Fua**

Negros Oriental — **Paras**

VIII — Northern Samar — **Abayon**

Leyte — **Veloso / Cari**

Biliran — **Espina**

Figure 17. Kinship ties among elected politicians in central and local government, 12th Congress, 2001-2004. Set 2. *Source: see key.*

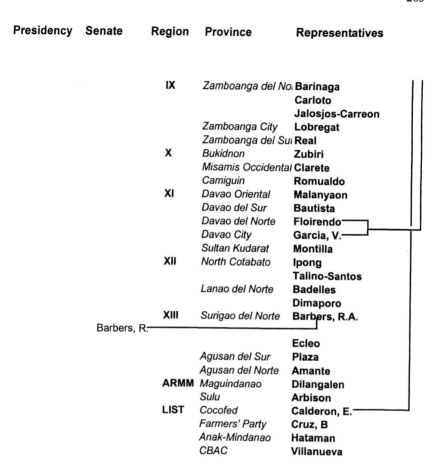

Presidency	Senate	Region	Province	Representatives
		IX	Zamboanga del No.	**Barinaga**
				Carloto
				Jalosjos-Carreon
			Zamboanga City	**Lobregat**
			Zamboanga del Su.	**Real**
		X	Bukidnon	**Zubiri**
			Misamis Occidental	**Clarete**
			Camiguin	**Romualdo**
		XI	Davao Oriental	**Malanyaon**
			Davao del Sur	**Bautista**
			Davao del Norte	**Floirendo**
			Davao City	**Garcia, V.**
			Sultan Kudarat	**Montilla**
		XII	North Cotabato	**Ipong**
				Talino-Santos
			Lanao del Norte	**Badelles**
				Dimaporo
		XIII	Surigao del Norte	**Barbers, R.A.**
	Barbers, R.			
				Ecleo
			Agusan del Sur	**Plaza**
			Agusan del Norte	**Amante**
		ARMM	Maguindanao	**Dilangalen**
			Sulu	**Arbison**
		LIST	Cocofed	**Calderon, E.**
			Farmers' Party	**Cruz, B**
			Anak-Mindanao	**Hataman**
			CBAC	**Villanueva**

Figure 18. Kinship ties among elected politicians in central and local government, 12th Congress, 2001-2004. Set 3. *Source: see key.*

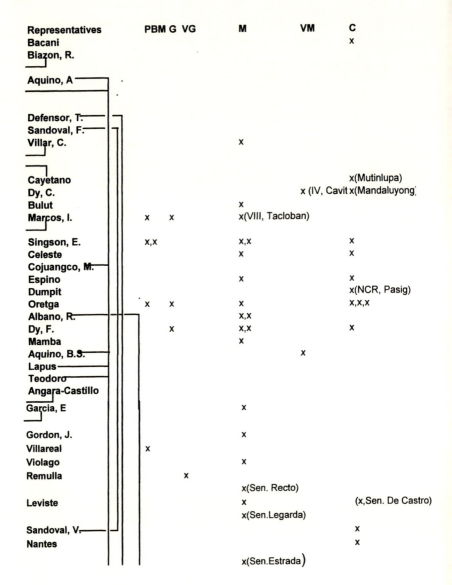

Representatives	PBM	G	VG	M	VM	C
Bacani						x
Biazon, R.						
Aquino, A						
Defensor, T.						
Sandoval, F.						
Villar, C.				x		
Cayetano						x(Mutinlupa)
Dy, C.					x (IV, Cavit	x(Mandaluyong)
Bulut				x		
Marcos, I.	x	x		x(VIII, Tacloban)		
Singson, E.	x,x			x,x		x
Celeste				x		x
Cojuangco, M.						
Espino				x		x
Dumpit						x(NCR, Pasig)
Oretga	x	x		x		x,x,x
Albano, R.				x,x		
Dy, F.		x		x,x		x
Mamba				x		
Aquino, B.S.					x	
Lapus						
Teodoro						
Angara-Castillo						
Garcia, E				x		
Gordon, J.				x		
Villareal	x					
Violago				x		
Remulla			x			
Leviste				x(Sen. Recto) x x(Sen.Legarda)		(x,Sen. De Castro)
Sandoval, V.						x
Nantes						x
				x(Sen.Estrada)		

Figure 19. Kinship ties among elected politicians in central and local government, 12th Congress, 2001-2004. Set 4. *Source: see key.*

Representatives	PBM	G	VG	M	VM	C
Andaya, R	x					
Alfelor	x			x		
Escudero, F.			x			
Espinosa, E			x	x		
Espinosa, V.	x					
Salceda				x		x
Lagman-Luistro				x		
Imperial						x
Unico				x		
Alvarez	x			x		
Cojuangco, C.						
Ledesma					x	
Maranon		x		x	x	
Calizo				x		
Davidas						x
Garin	x			x		
Defensor, A.						
Gonzalez, R.						x
Martinez						
Durano, J.F	x				x	x
Del Mar			x	x	x	x
Yapha				x		x,x,x
Cuenco						x
Fua		x		x		
Paras						x,x
Abayon						x
Veloso						x(NCR, Quezon
Cari		x		x		x
Espina		x		x		

Figure 20. Kinship ties among elected politicians in central and local government, 12th Congress, 2001-2004. Set 5. *Source: see key.*

268

Representatives	PBM	G	VG	M	VM	C
Barinaga	x,x					
Carloto				x,x,x		
Jalosjos-Carreon				x		
Lobregat				x		
Real	x					
Zubiri						x
Clarete				x		
Romualdo		x			x	
Malanyaon				x		
Bautista			x	x		
Floirendo						
Garcia, V.						
Montilla				x		
Ipong						x(VII, Bohol)
Talino-Santos				x		
Badelles						x
Dimaporo		x				
Barbers, R.A.		x				
Ecleo				x,x		
Plaza		x		x,		
Amante		x				
Dilangalen						x
Arbison				x		x
Calderon, E.						
Cruz, B			x(III, Bulacan)			x(III, Bulacan)
Hataman				x(IX, Basilan)		x(IX, Basilan)
Villanueva				x(III, Bulacan)		

Figure 21. Kinship ties among elected politicians in central and local government, 12th Congress, 2001-2004. Set 6. *Source: see key.*

PBM	Provincial Board Member
G	Governor
VG	Vice Governor
M	Mayor
VM	Vice Mayor
C	Councilor
———	kinship tie
x	relative holding post concurrently
(92)	year of presidential office

Key to Figures 16 – 21. *Sources: Material derived from the Philippines Center for Investigative Journalism (PCIJ), 2004; Securities of Exchange Commission, 2002-3, 2004. Thanks also to Ricky Castillo of the Congressional Staff for piecing together many of these links.*

RG Company	Representative 1
NCR Calatagan Golf and Country Club	**Cayetano**
Alabang Golf and Country Club	**Villar**
Manila Times (Owner)	**Jimenez**
Baguio Country Club Fortune Island Resort Club	**Gunigundo**
Central Azucarera de Tarlac (654) Fibreglass Inc	**Aquino, A.**
Fortune Island Resort Club Manila Yacht Club Subic Bay Yacht Club (SH) Tagaytay Highlands Golf and Country Club (SH)	**Dy, C.**
Delsan Industries (P.,Ch., SH)	**Sandoval, F.**
Eagle Ridge Golf and Country Club Fortune Island Resort Club Green Valley Golf and Country Club The Riviera Golf and Country Club (SH) (2417)	**Zialcita**
Air Philippines International Waterfront Philippines Inc. (VCh) **CAR**	**Gatchalian**
I Agus Resort and Development Luzon Loggers (P.)	**De Venecia**
San Miguel Corp (ch.) 2 Northern Cement Corp (Owner) (275) Paniqui Sugar Central (Owner) Plantations	**Cojuangco, M.** 21ch
The Riviera Golf and Country Club (SH) (2417)	**Tulagan**

Figure 22. Business Interests within The Lower House (12th Congress), Set 1.

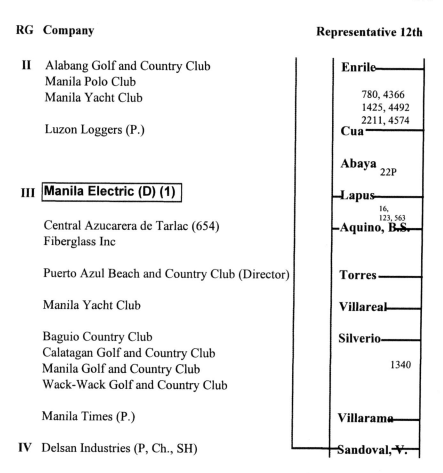

Figure 23. Business Interests within The Lower House (12th Congress), Set 2.

RG	Company	Representative 12th

IV | Petron Corp. (SH) (5) |

Baguio Country Club
Calatagan Golf and Country Club
Makati Sports Club
Manila Polo Club
Manila Yacht Club
| PLDT (SH) 7 |
Puerto Azul Beach and Country Club (SH)

Alaska Milk Corp. (147)

Wack-Wack Golf and Country Club

| PLDT (SH) 7 |

| PLDT (SH) 7 |
| San Miguel Corp (SH) 2 |

V | Petron Corp (SH) (5) |
| San Miguel Corp. (SH) (2 |

VI Negros Navigation (D.) (247)

| San Miguel Corp (Ch) (2) |
Northern Cement Corp (Owner) (275)
Paniqui Sugar Central (Owner)
Plantations

Equitable PCI Bank (SH) (27)
Fairways and Bluewater
Manila Golf and Country Club
Manila Polo Club
Tagaytay Highlands Golf and Country Club (SH)

Wack-Wack Golf and Country Club

Representatives column:
Gozos — 2885
Suarez — 177
Rodriguez, L
Duavit
Chipeco
Reyes, E.
Andaya, R.
Ledesma — 21Ch
Cojuangco, C.
Syjuco
Monfort

Figure 24. Business Interests within The Lower House (12th Congress), Set 3.

RG	Company	Representative 12th

VII   Alabang Golf and Country Club   **Teves** ────────

       Agus Resort and Development   **Del Mar** ────────

VIII   Green Valley Golf and Country Club   **Saludo** ────────
       Manila Polo Club
       The Riviera Golf and Country Club (SH) (2417)

       Subic Bay Yacht Club (SH)   **Abayon, H.** ────────

IX   Air Philippines International   **Lobregat** ────────
       Alabang Golf and Country Club   503, 833
       Alaska Milk Corp. (147)   850, 876
       Equitable PCI Bank (SH) (27)   2501, 107
       Manila Electric (SH) (1)   145, 219
       Negros Navigation (SH) (247)   255, 306
       Petron Corp (SH) (5)   100SH
       Waterfront Philippines Inc. (SH)   67SH

X   Fairways and Bluewater   **Jaraula** ────────
                                             1817

       Makati Sports Club   **Zubiri** ────────

       Petron Corp (SH) (5)   **Baculio** ────────

XI   Alabang Golf and Country Club   **Chiongbian** ────────
       Manila Golf and Country Club   117BM/SH
       Puerto Azul Beach and Country Club (SH)
       Tagaytay Highlands Golf and Country Club (SH)

       Manila Electric (SH) (1)   **Floirendo** ────────
                                             1866, 3382
                                             6658, 5130
                                             192 Owner

LIST Eagle Ridge Golf and Country Club   **Velarde** ────────

       Petron Corp (SH) (5)   **Sarenas** ────────
                                             13SH

Figure 25. Business Interests within The Lower House (12th Congress), Set 4.

274

Key to Figures 21 – 25
Business Interests within the 12th Congress (Lower House)

RG	region
List	Member of party list system
Ch	chairman of company
SH	shareholder in company
P	president of company
D	director of company
BM	company board member

_____   mutual business interests

▪▪▪▪▪   kinship ties

| 24 | company's national ranking |

25   additional interests (company's national ranking)

Sources: Material derived from the Philippines Center for Investigative Journalism (PCIJ), 2004; Securities of Exchange Commission, 2002-3, 2004. Thanks also to Ricky Castillo of the Congressional Staff for piecing together many of these links.

Chapter 7
Conclusions

1.0 Representations

At the start of this book, in chapters 1 and 2, we centred our attention on what we held to be the few certainties in our knowledge about the world: our social relationships; our attitudes to our relationships; and our representations of the social and natural worlds. We set out what we believe to be the play between our attitudes, representations and relationships. And we suggested that by reformulating our representations through a constant cycling of particular instances, the simple commonalities which underlie the complexities and surface differences of the social world soon become apparent. The representations which have emerged from previous chapters may be thought to comprise a number of layers.

(i) We start with a broad statistical outline of domestic trade networks and of links with China (though no claim is made that this amounts to anything more than a representation), emanating from the city of Davao. Here the figures seem to show that the marketplaces' principal source of dry and manufactured goods were wholesalers. These wholesalers are found in a part of the city commonly if loosely described as Chinese. And indeed some 54% of all establishments (sole proprietorships and corporations) are pure Chinese; and another 11% are predominantly Chinese. These wholesalers (Chinese or otherwise) commonly obtain their goods from suppliers in Binondo (an area loosely equated with Manila's Chinatown) or from marketplaces in Manila whose traders buy their goods from suppliers in Binondo. However, if we look in more detail at the wholesale sector in Davao we find that whilst two-thirds are Chinese, only a quarter (of the total) speak Chinese, and one-third of establishments are not Chinese. And, if we look more closely at the marketplaces, we find that the proportion of Chinese traders operating there is unexpectedly large (at around 16%) while only 1% speak Chinese.

These observations create an interesting pattern when set alongside what appears to be the diminution of the Chinese among the larger and more important companies in the Philippines dominating the domestic economy and trade with China. In Davao, most exports to and from Greater China are accounted for by companies with dominant Chinese interests. If we consider direct trade with mainland China only (and exclude trade with Hong Kong and Taiwan), the pre-eminence of Chinese-owned companies is even more pronounced. Some 60% of exports rests with just two companies that are predominantly Chinese; and again some 60% of imports rests with two, predominantly Chinese, companies. When we take the national view, however, and even though we concentrate on the Philippines' trade axis with mainland China (along which we would expect the overseas Chinese to show a strong presence), the balance of interests - Chinese, Filipino and International - appears to be almost the exact reverse of that which is found in Davao. Only around 11% of those companies dominating exports to China are predominantly Chinese (and are primarily Taiwanese, Singaporean or American Chinese). Some 22% of exporters are predominantly Filipino; and two-thirds are International.

These top exporters are set within their relationships of investment and board membership among the Philippines' strongest 120 companies (as measured by gross domestic sales). These 120 account for more than 40% of the nation's gross domestic sales, and for similar or larger shares of net income, assets and equity. Among these 120 companies the proportions dominated by Chinese and Filipinos rise to 25% and 31% respectively, whilst the proportion of Internationals falls correspondingly to 42%. Whilst there is some fit between these companies and the strongest exporters, most exporters are not ranked among the strongest 120 companies, nor are they linked into those 120 companies' networks of mutual investments and board memberships.

As in Davao, imports from China create a more complex picture. Nevertheless, it is clear that whilst there are in Binondo more companies engaged in importing goods from China than in any other administrative division in the Philippines, this is not matched proportionally by Binondo's weak share of the value of imports. Another observation (and one that is particularly interesting in view of the fact that it is from southeast China that most overseas Chinese originate) is that the origin of imports (and also the destination for exports) is strongly concentrated in Shanghai (a little over 40%).

As we trace links through to China - where we find a concentration of links in central east China (most especially Shanghai) and, to a lesser extent, in northeast China (Shandong and Tianjin) – three further observations emerge. First, as in the Philippines where International companies dominate trade with China, so it is that foreign companies figure most strongly in Shanghai's trade with the Philippines. We also find that these companies sit in a broader context of webs of investment and ownership that dominate the economy. Whilst foreign companies are more closely integrated within that complex than in the Philippines, some of the stronger importers and exporters also tend to lie outside that complex. A similar pattern is to be found in Davao where companies with a national and international reach dominate the local economy but lie outside the networks of investment and ownership among local companies.

Secondly, the organisation of industry in Shanghai appears to takes on a sharper and more deliberate form. If we trace the investment flows of the strongest fifty industrial groups and 500 enterprises (which together account for 3% of the number of enterprises and two-thirds of sales), we find that investments cascade down from state agencies in their various forms, into loose combines of companies, each combine being defined in part by the tendency of its members to invest in one another and by the operation of its members within the same or similar or closely related sector. The investments traced also appear to indicate that the Municipality's coalitions are parochial in their view of the rest of China, though heavily dependent upon foreign concerns and strategically connected to the centre by a shared interest in foreign money and markets.

Thirdly, connexions traced from the Philippines to China, and from Shanghai to the Philippines, are comparatively insulated from the rest of China in that backward linkages stemming from importers and exporters in Shanghai are limited. Trade networks associated with marketplaces are extensive (particularly between Shanghai and the south and southeast of the country). But the relative importance of marketplaces, and of domestic private enterprises as a whole, in an economy dominated by much larger state-local-foreign coalitions, has, if anything, declined in recent years. These marketplace traders are also insulated from those core enterprises trading with the Philippines. There are split-family businesses operating between China and Manila; but these do not begin to compare with the main channels of foreign trade between the two countries.

(ii) Upon this, further descriptions and interpretations of political support and business organisation are layered. It is suggested that in the Philippines the significance of ethnicity and kinship diminishes, while the cosmopolitan strengthens, with the importance of firms within the national economy and in trade with China. There exist inherent similarities in practices, attitudes and relationships among even the smaller and supposedly more traditional and distinctive businesses, regardless of ethnicity. It is argued that the significance of the Chinese in the economy as a whole has long since been exaggerated. Indeed, the role of individuals of Chinese descent may have increased in more recent times precisely because of the deliberate weakening of identity and the creation of a traditional antitype against which the modern could define themselves. These observations suggest a marked distancing of relationships as attitudes shift from the personalistic to affective, from informality to formality. What we are witnessing is not so much a convergence as a turning of common attitudes, relationships, and representations, such that commonalities become more apparent.

What is more surprising, perhaps, is that the significance of kinship and business interests among politicians is not easily squared with the characterisation of the Philippines' polity as one whose priorities, policies, and legislation are frequently distorted by those interests. Whilst kinship is undoubtedly used to secure political bases in the provinces, it is not a precondition for doing so. Although there are exceptions, it appears that the larger political dynasties in the provinces tend not to propel their members into higher political office. And whilst there are again exceptions, it would also seem that political office and larger business empires do not translate easily one to the other (not at least while the politician holds office).

The significance of kinship, then, cannot be ignored; certain institutions (most especially political parties) are undeniably very weak; there is damaging and illegitimate political interference in the lower levels of the bureaucracy; and even the most pro-business technocrats would not claim that businesses are purer than, and never seek to corrupt, politicians. Even so, practices, procedures, and institutions (both formal and informal) are strengthening. Indeed, it may be that the problems with the polity derive in some measure from the strengthening of professionalism within political institutions in Manila, while among large swathes of the politicians' constituencies, attitudes are more often strongly personalistic. The result is weak parties unable to exert a restraining influence on the cut and thrust of everyday democratic politics.

In Shanghai, more intimate connexions appear to exist between government, party, and enterprise. Permitted more autonomy and set against each other, bureaucrats, party officials, and enterprise managers in China, formed personalistic alliances. Yet the most striking quality of the organisation of industry in Shanghai is the strongly institutional appearance of investment flows. One possible explanation is that this reflects an attempt by comparatively impermeable and rigid sets of relationships and expectations (those of local and central governments, and of Party and enterprise managers) to hide their competing interests behind a facade of institutional channels (Shanghai's coalitions and those investment networks). However, the fact that there is now available data on investments might be indicative of greater openness. If so, then it may be more than coincidental that there are also underway what are regarded by many writers as the professionalisation of the polity, bureaucracy, and enterprise management; a move towards the rule of law; and, throughout Chinese society, a weakening of obligatory particularism. The institutional quality of Shanghai's industrial investments could, perhaps, be read as but part of the emergence more generally of professionalised, genuinely corporate, entities that are sharply focussed on economic matters in themselves, and treated less as extensions of political and bureaucratic interest.

(iii) At a still lower resolution there have also emerged from the previous chapters representations of transformation. We have argued that while often thought of as interpretative or conceptual, too much clarity and strength is imposed upon the distinction between, on the one hand, terms such as 'cultural', 'networked', 'relationships', 'informal', 'personalistic' and 'irregular', and, on the other hand, the 'institutional' (the structural, formal, deep, legal-rational, regularized, and bureaucratic). A slightly different 'take' on this distinction is to view it as an indication of shifts in attitude towards social relationships. On the one hand there is an attitude which may be described as personalistic, and through which social relationships are regarded and treated more as instruments. On the other hand there is an attitude through which relationships are viewed as being important in their own right, and their affective content emphasized.

Important qualifications have accompanied these descriptions. The affective and personalistic are not mutually exclusive. Both attitudes may colour all our relationships at all times. But a shift in the emphasis of these attitudes may be enough to imbue our social relationships with certain qualities such that we can define particular sets of relationships as being 'institutional'. As relationships are moved into the social sphere, and as their instrumental quality becomes less acceptable and less prominent, they come to be viewed and treated as important in their own right, their affective quality now idealized. As a consequence, economic and political institutions may become less permeable, more sharply defined and better focussed; and it is more likely that rules, practices and procedures will be observed without the need for authoritarianism or heavy monitoring. And rather than create an intrinsically impersonal atmosphere, their affective dimension, now cultivated in the social sphere is, through our masquerade, introduced more easily to help oil, rather than clog, the wheels of professional life.

In sum, formal institutions, procedures, and practices, are moulded from social relationships: the apparent distinction between the formal and informal reflects shifting attitudes rather than any material dichotomy (structural or cultural). When seen through an increasingly affective frame of mind, institutions only *appear* to precipitate out of the relationships they comprise. It is then that behaviour is altered such that it is *as if* a sense of corporeal structures and cultures are bearing down upon us. Thus attitudes and behaviour reinforce each other.

But when, where, and why might these shifts in attitude take place? One stimulus may be intrinsic to the human condition - the sense of alienation created by powerful constructs of self and by a strongly instrumental attitude. The intensification of trade (exchange for profit) and, by definition, unequal exchange - through its initial stimulation of instrumentalism and a sense of alienation - may also encourage the deepening of the affect and, as attempts are made to preserve the affective content of social relationships, the creation or sharpening of a social sphere of life.

A still more important stimulus may be the proliferation of businesses, most especially those built around the family. Making an enterprise work requires a conscious effort to distance family relationships (and the friction and emotions they generate) from the day-to-day running and longer-term planning of the business. As professionalisation and the deepening of the affect take hold, and as the scale of business increases, shifts in attitude may gather pace. In this way businesses, especially those founded on kinship, may strengthen rather than weaken broader institutional life. In China, the more conservative state and collective enterprises may also have some effect. They are commonly hierarchical and contained, in that each level is allowed by its superiors very limited information and responsibility; and there exist parallel lines of authority, often political and monitorial in nature. These restrictions are frequently countered by attempts to control and filter the flow of information upwards and to by-pass hierarchical and institutional boundaries such that they are in practice far more permeable than they might otherwise appear to be. This centralised and authoritarian quality, and the attempt to counter it, may encourage attitudinal change and provide lessons in the performance of the masquerade. But frustration (especially among younger employees and managers) with the limitations, policing, uncertainty, and lack of clarity within these state entities, is often heightened by their knowledge that, in foreign businesses, Chinese managers, even the most junior of them, find considerable release, relief, and stimulus in the trust and responsibility they are given, and in the distancing and differentiation of relationships they are expected to demonstrate. It is, then, foreign businesses, as well as China's own private family businesses, that may be the more important spark for change.

A further and equally pragmatic stimulus to attitudinal change may be the institutions of government itself. If they are to exist as more than brittle shells, authoritarian institutions and practices (which are often created in reaction to rip-tides of strongly personalistic relationships) may also stimulate the deepening of the affect and professionalisation. Authoritarianism, then, may carry the seeds of its own transformation.

In the case of the Philippines, another point of origin of attitudinal change may be moral teachings of the Catholic Church at whose heart lies a belief in the truth, and the affective content, of relationships with one another and with God. Associations, particularly those with a religious bent, may also help to promulgate a shift in attitude as part and parcel of their need for stability and organisational strength. From these various hot-spots (the family business, big business, political and bureaucratic institutions, schools, Church, and association), as well as from the spontaneity of the human condition, shifts in attitudes might begin to percolate more widely through society.

These arguments carry with them a number of implications concerning the manner of transformation. They suggest that informal-formal transformations are likely to be patchy, localised, and ambiguous. These patches of strengthening 'institutional' qualities may bubble up constantly through a political economy that is otherwise strongly personalistic. It follows that an understanding of what might block or neutralize the attainment of a critical mass of attitudinal change may be just as important to an understanding of how and why transformation takes place as an appreciation of the stimuli to transformation. One block may be the inertia created when representations of structure and culture - such as institutional and patrimonial descriptions of powerful family loyalties permeating state institutions, or, say, Confucianist explanations of Chinese economic success – are bound into thought and begin to inform behaviour. Another neutralizing influence may be the unevenness of transformation. The gap between the Congressional representatives' appreciation of the need for strong parties, and their constituencies' expectation of personal material reward for their political support, is but one example. A third neutralizing influence may be a lack of confidence in the polity. This may have been deepened and perpetuated by the fusion of street and scholarly representations of the Philippine polity and overseas Chinese.

Long periods of priming might therefore be expected in advance of widespread and thorough-going formalisation of the political economy. Only once patches of attitudinal change and informal-formal transformation have reached a critical mass, and a more pervasive atmosphere is established in which the affect and 'institutional' are accepted and regarded as proper, might we begin to see more radical and widespread change. At this point, more extensive and joined-up patterns of less permeable institutions emerge; and the compulsion to alter behaviour and distance relationships is felt more deeply. As a consequence, shifts in attitudes are further intensified, such that attitudes, representations, and practice begin to reinforce each other.

(iv) A fourth layer of representations describes how the complexity on the ground in the Philippines and China brings into question the certainty of our knowledge; and how our thought about the social world can have very real and often tragic consequences. The dialectic between attitudes and representations, between scholarly and street representations, between representations and practice, have inflated the economic significance of, and encouraged hostility towards, the overseas Chinese; masked the dimensionality, and the basic commonality, of trade and businesses organizations irrespective of ethnicity; and obscured instances of profound change in the Philippines' economy. Thus have scholarly representations contributed unintentionally to the erosion of the confidence of Filipinos. They are self-deprecating to a fault; and they see in their government only inefficiency and corruption. Seven million Filipinos work overseas and send money back home. In doing so they provide for their families a standard of living which could not be achieved otherwise, and confirm themselves in their view that their politicians are at best unnecessary, and at worst an obstacle to progress. This contrasts markedly with China where positive images of Chinese civilization - elaborated upon and romanticised by scholarship (of West and East), and now reinforced by economic success - have been of tremendous political value.

The consequences of this crisis of confidence in the Philippines are grave for the country, the region and the world. The Philippines occupies a vital strategic position, facing a true economic giant across sea lanes that run from the Pacific into the heart of southeast Asia; while to the north the islands flank the giant's reach to Taiwan and still further east into deep blue waters. Some within the Philippine Congress see in China no military threat. They believe that its economic power is likely to benefit all; that what is today described as 'globalisation' binds China into a mutually dependent community that precludes conflict. Others believe that they can see through China's bluster and into its many fragmented and shaky economies. Still others believe that the Philippines will awake to China's ambitions only when the Giant is sitting just off Palawan's coast. And it is they who fear that America will not be prepared to play the same stakes for the Philippines as for Taiwan. But what is certain is that if the Philippines is to fulfill its responsibilities to itself, to the region and to the world, then it must have the confidence to deal with all its neighbours on equal terms.

2.0 New beginnings?

These representations are not the end to which we are working: they are just the start of a subsequent cycle. They are part of the means to an understanding of the play of attributes and commonalities from which the social world is created. As we disaggregate and reformulate representations, attitudes, and relationships in the field, we consider whether we might need to revise our original representation of that play.

From these pages a number of questions that would seem to require elaboration in any subsequent cycle. These include a discussion of difference, imagination, and dreams; and a more thorough and specific attempt to elicit the detailed representations of those people in whom we are interested, and to do so over time as they age and as their circumstances alter. Just as essential, perhaps, is a consideration of the nature of what we might loosely term 'Western' society. We have, on a number of occasions, suggested that, within the social sciences, discussions on trade, business, and politics in the Philippines and China, often seem to be permeated with the absolute. This mutation of ideas into certainties may reflect attitudinal shifts towards the personal, and it may have very real effects on the lives of the people we study. But why should this shift in attitude, and towards thought more absolute in quality, be taking place? Since much of what is written on the Philippines and China by social scientists is either the denizen of 'the West', or follows the method, approaches, styles, and sentiments of social science practiced there, then it is to 'the West' that we must direct our attention.

It would seem that we must also form an understanding of the dialectic between representations, attitudes and relationships in those societies from which social science emerged. We could, perhaps, make the case that, initially, it was our treatment of relationships and representations *as if* absolute that allowed the segmentation of thought and, therefore, the segmentation of our lives. But the more categories we created, and the more we categorised our own lives, the further we moved those people who belonged to 'this' category away from those whom we placed in 'that' category. How could we now understand the links between these segments except as part of systems of cause and effect? Disciplines and specialisms now had to multiply; and as they did so, as thought and knowledge were fragmented and nested, as the distance between categories increased, and as differences between people were made absolute, truth was necessarily made relative. In an attempt to bring intellectual cohesion, batteries of statistics and universal systems have been replaced with reflexive processes which, though they share certain technical commonalities or *modus operandi*, are held to produce differences among us.

So clear and absolute now are the boundaries among the segments of our thought, and of our lives, that the social scientists' professional and social spheres appear to have detached themselves from each other entirely. Social scientists may acknowledge that they are part of what they study; and that through their studies they become part of the practice of the social world. Yet they permit themselves only the reflexivity of their own scholarly representations - especially those of culture and structure – and these are not subject to doubt. Indeed, it is precisely because these representations seem capable of both explaining the social world and the social scientist, that we are tempted to believe that our own representations have an interpretive or explanatory power well beyond those created by, and used to inform, the behaviour of those people whom we are studying. Thus, partly for this reason, do the ideas with which social scientists interpret themselves and others, come to be treated as certainties.

The suggestion we are leading to, then, is that while the affective began to move us towards the industrialisation of our thought, it was the absolute quality which we allowed our ideas to take on that finally completed this move. Through categorisation, fragmentation, nesting, separation, and the aura of certainty, thought became industrial in nature and made possible the industrialisation of our lives in practice. Even the language of social science now smells of machine oil and the lathe: what is held to be the truth – even the truth of relativity – is expressed in technical, specialised, machine-patterned sentences, machine-cut words (mechanism, function, discourse, factor, structure, system, process and product) and the suffixes of mass production (-isms, -ization, -ized and -graphic). Prompted by the growing certainty (or absolute quality) of thought (both within the social sciences, and on the street), the personal has strengthened, stimulating a desire for greater monitoring, measuring, and accounting, and making bureaucratic and political instruments of whatever it is that has had to be defined, measured, and monitored.

There is, however, another more important aspect to this tale; and it is one that may be seen more clearly from outside the social sciences. With our segmented thought and lives has come an intensity of experience of the natural and artistic world. When we look upon the rust-reddened Sinai desert at sun rise, the lakes of northern England in autumn, the purple dusk over the Celebes, or Cadiz in its own bright morning light, or when we listen to Bach's *St. John's Passion*, Debussy's *La Mer*, or Elgar's *Dream of Gerontius*, we find a beauty that is immediate. In Forster's *Passage to India*, or Powys' *Wolf Solent*, too, there is present between the words a kind of music. There is beauty here because the scene before us, and the sounds or words we experience, set up in our minds the conditions that allow us to open up lines to thought for ourselves*. It is through this beauty that we may catch glimpses into another world. This other world is altogether more vague. In this world we never really know or understand even the people closest to us. It is, as Forster puts it, a world of muddle. It is a world not of the general, but of the particular. The world we see, and make, is one of pure abstraction – of 'you', "I' and 'we', and of how 'you', 'I', and 'we', think about and treat each other. In this world the general is but a mental device, a way of arranging, fitting together, and working through particular relationships. Here in this world, beauty is the line to thought: to the thought that there is only our relationships - that our sense of 'self', 'you', and 'we', and of our place within the natural and social worlds, are matters intense interest *in themselves*. Here beauty is an appreciation of what we are in ourselves. It is found in our everyday relationships of our un-categorised and un-segmented lives. It is the pleasure and property of all, unencumbered by taste and intellect. But in this world, too, as in the artistic sphere of our industrial world, this truth

---

* See chapter 2, section 3.2.

must be hinted at, and discovered for oneself: presented boldly in clear, hard, and precise words, it is only flattened and dulled.

What this view from the outside world suggests, is that something more than a shift to the personal is going on within the industrial world. When we look from that outside world to our industrial existence we see that, in our industrial world, relationships – 'you' and 'I', and our thoughts and treatment of each other – and the beauty they hold, are confined to our own, small, private chambers; while on the street, where eyes rarely meet, we walk among ghosts. In its music, and in its art and literature, we hear the cries of souls unfulfilled. Its inhabitants have allowed the institutions, systems, and forces of society, polity, and economy, to become everything within their minds; the smallest nuances of behaviour and civility are, more and more, explicitly prescribed; non-contravention of the rules and roles of institutions is becoming the most important mark of righteousness and achievement; and commentary on this industrial world, and the language and written style through which this is expressed, are being homogenised. The absolute is coming to dominate; orthopraxy is sweeping all before it.

The move towards the personal, which we have argued would otherwise follow from the dominance of these absolutes, is being frustrated by a kind of Puritanism. There is a reluctance to make any admission - silent or explicit, public or private - of our rules' and roles' social quality and, therefore, of the instrumental nature of our relationships. Social relationships are now confined *only* to their own small sphere and are thus made absolute. The absolute quality of 'I' and 'we' is reconciled by 'I' the champion of 'we', the community; and because 'I' and the ideas which 'I' hold are absolute, then 'I' and my ideas are righteous. In this - in denying the personal and instrumental - the inhabitants of the industrial world deny the essential social quality of the world they create. In doing so they deny the affective. Confined within their own rare and idealised sphere and treated as absolute, the importance of social relationships in their own right is taken away from us. The importance and truth of relationships is merely presented to us complete and factual. We no longer have any choice about these qualities. And since these qualities no longer emanate from us, we cannot discover them for ourselves, nor therefore appreciate those qualities with any immediacy. The inhabitants of this world, it would seem, have forgotten that without the personal, the instrumental, the manipulative, and the selfish, the affective cannot be.

With this Puritanism grows disgust with any imperfection, any symptom of instrumentalism, in ourselves and in our roles, rules and institutions. Thus are we consumed gradually by an obsessive determination to eradicate the instrumental and imperfect, to impose orthopraxy, and, unknowingly, to remove from much of our lives compassion, consideration, and tolerance. In this frustration of the personal, in this outlawing of the instrumental, in this denial of what we are, in this confinement and degradation of the affect, in this intolerance of imperfection in ourselves and what we do, we run the risk of violent counter-action and sudden return to an intense and ruinous personalism. In all of this, we can, perhaps, sense Van der Post's 'Dark Eye', his *mata kelap*, strengthening.

These qualities – the industrial and those of the outside world, the Puritanical and the tolerant, the personal and the affective - do not describe East-West divisions. Inherent in each of us and in the world we create – and what a revised understanding of the play of attitudes, representations and relationships must consider and try to account for - is a conflict between Puritanism and tolerance, between a repugnance for our instrumental quality and an understanding of the beauty which that most essential quality brings. But there are times when too many of us give too much expression to particular attitudes or to our Puritanism; and perhaps such a time has been reached in the West.

These are arguments which caution social scientists, wherever we live, against the certainty with which we may hold our ideas, and against the steady professionalisation of our thought; and they suggest that we may do better to view ourselves occasionally from the outside world. These are arguments which also caution Filipinos from pursuing too strongly institutional and processual formality. The faults of Filipino society give expression to the strength of the personal; and in the wake of the personal, the affective is deepening. Filipino society is becoming more formal; and, up to now, it has done so without losing sight of the particular, the social, of what we are, of what it is that brings to our lives the qualities of tolerance and openness. This – the feel of the outside world that the Philippines has about it – is the hall mark of any true civilization.

BIBLIOGRAPHY

Agelasto, M. 1996. Cellularism, *guanxiwang* and corruption. *Crime, Law and Social Change* 25: 265-288

Amante, M. S. V. 1997. Converging and diverging trends in HRM: The Philippines' "Halo-Halo" approach. *Asia Pacific Business Review* 3:111–32

Amber, T., Styles, A. and Wang, X. C. 1999. The effect of channel relationships and *guanxi* on the performance of inter-province export ventures in the PRC. *International Journal of Research in Marketing* 16: 75–87

Anderson, B. 1994. Hard to Imagine: a puzzle in the history of Philippine nationalism. In Pertierra, R. and Urgarte, E.F. eds. *Cultures and Texts: representations of Philippine society.* UPP: Quezon

_____. 1995. Cacique democracy in the Philippines: origins and dreams. In Rafael, V.F. (ed) *Discrepant Histories: translocal essays on Filipino culture.* Temple University Press: Philadelphia

_____. 1998. *The Spectre of Comparisons: nationalism, southeast Asia, and the world* Verson: London

Ash, R.F. and He, L. 1998. Loss-making and the financial performance of China's industrial enterprises: data from the new accounting and statistical system. *Journal of Contemporary China* 7: 5-20

Bakken, B. 2000. *The Exemplary Society: human improvement, social controls and the dangers of modernity in China.* OUP: Oxford

Baofu, P. 2004. *The Future of Post-Human Consciousness.* Edwin Mellen: New York

Bastress-Dukehart, E. 2001. Family, property and feeling in early modern German noble culture: The Zimmerns of Swabia. *Sixteenth Century Journal* 32:1–19

Baum, E. 2004. *What is Thought?* MIT: Cambridge, Mass.

Bernal, V. 2004. Eritrea goes global: reflections on nationalism in a transnational era. *Cultural Anthropology* 19: 3-25

Bhatia, S. 2002. Acculturation, dialogical voices and the construction of the diasporic self. *Theory and Psychology* 12: 55-77

Bhatia, S. and Ram, A. 2001. Locating the dialogical self. *Culture and Psychology* 7: 297-309

Bian Yanjie, Shu Xiaoling and Logan, J.R. 2001. Communist Party membership and regime dynamics in China. *Social Forces* 79: 805-841

Birley, S., Ng, D., and Godfrey, A. 1999. The family and the business. *Long Range Planning* 32: 598-608

Blackburn, S. 1999. *Think.* OUP: Oxford

Blau, P. 1964. *Exchange and Power in Social Life.* John Wiley and Sons: New York

Bolongaita, E.P. 1995. Presidential versus parliamentary democracy. *Philippine Studies* 43: 105-23

Bond, M.H ed. 1986 *The Psychology of the Chinese People.* OUP: Hong Kong

Brentano, F. 1976. *Psychology from an Empirical Standpoint.* Volume 1. London. Edited by O. Kraus, and translated by L. McAlister *et al.*

Brødsgaard, K.E. 2002. The *bianzhi* system. *China Quarterly* 170: 361-386

Brown, D. E. 1991. *Human Universals.* Temple University Press: Philadelphia

Brown, David. 1994. *The State and Ethnic Politics in Southeast Asia.* Routledge: London

Brown, R.A. 2000. *Chinese Big Business and the Wealth of Asian Nations.* Palgrave: Basingstoke and New York

Buchanan, J.M., Tollison, R.D. and Tullock, G. 1980. *Toward a Theory of the Rent-Seeking Society.* Texas A & M Press: College Station, Texas

Budd, M. 1985. *Music and the Emotions: The Philosophical Theories.* Routledge & Kegan Paul: London

Bureau of Customs (Davao and Manila). Various Records (raw data) 2002-3. Republic of the Philippines

Callaghy, T.M. 1989. Toward state capability and embedded liberalism in the Third World: lessons for adjustment. In J.M. Nelson ed. *Fragile Coalitions: the politics of economic adjustment.* Transaction Books: New Jersey

Callis, H.G. 1942. *Foreign Capital in Southeast Asia.* New York

Carrithers, M. 1992. *Why Humans Have Cultures: explaining anthropology and social diversity.* OUP: Oxford

Casper, G. 1995 *Fragile Democracies: the legacies of authoritarian rule.* University of Pittsburg Press: Pittsburgh

Cavalli-Sforza, L. and F. 1995. *The Great Human Diasporas: the history of diversity and evolution.* Perseus: Cambridge MA

Celoza, A.F. 1997. *Ferdinand Marcos and the Philippines: the political economy of authoritarianism.* Praeger: London

Chalmers, D. 1996. *The Conscious Mind: in search of a fundamental theory.* OUP: Oxford

Chan Kwok Bun, ed. 2000. *Chinese Business Networks: state, economy and culture.* Pearson: Singapore

_____. 2000. State, economy and culture: Reflections on the Chinese business networks. In *Chinese Business Networks: state, economy and culture,* ed. Chan Kwok Bun. Pearson: Singapore

Chatterjee, K. 1996. *Merchants, Politics, and Society in Early Modern India: Bihar, 1730-1820.* Leiden: New York

Chee, K.T. and Yong, P.K. 1998. *Guanxi* bases, *xinrong* and Chinese business networks. *British Journal of Sociology* 49: 75-96

Chen, A. H. Y. 1999. Rational law, economic development, and the case of China. *Social and Legal Studies* 8: 97–120

Chen, Baizhu and Yi Feng. 2000. Determinants of economic growth in China: private enterprise, education and openness. *China Economic Review* 11: 1-15

Chen, Naixing 2002. 中国中小企业发展与预测 (*China's Small and Medium Enterprises: developments and predictions)* 经济管理出版社: 北京

Chen, Z. and Francesco, A. 2000. Employee demography, organisational commitment, and turnover intentions in China: do cultural differences matter? *Human Relations* 53: 869-887

Cheng, Y.S. and Lo, D. 2002. Explaining the financial performance of China's industrial enterprises: beyond the competition-ownership controversy. *China Quarterly* 170: 413-440

Child, J. 1994. *Management in China During the Age of Reform.* Cambridge University Press: Cambridge

Chirot, D. and A. Reid. 1997. *Essential Outsiders: Chinese and Jews in the modern transformation of Southeast Asia and central Europe.* University of Washington Press: Seattle

Chow, C. and Fung, M. 2000. Small businesses and liquidity constraints in financing business investment: evidence from Shanghai's manufacturing sector. *Journal of Business Venturing* 15: 363-383

Chow, C., Fung, M. and Ngo, H. 2001. Consumption patterns of entrepreneurs in the People's Republic of China. *Journal of Business Research* 52: 189-202

Chu, Richard T. 2002a. The "Chinese" and the "mestizos" of the Philippines: Towards a new interpretation *Philippine Studies* 50: 451–49.

_____. 2002b. Rethinking the Chinese mestizos of the Philippines. In *Beyond China: migrating identities,* ed. Shen Yuanfang and P. Edwards. Canberra: Centre for the Study of the Chinese Southern Diaspora, Australian National University.

Chua, A. 2003. *World on Fire.* London: Heinemann.

Chung, C. 2001. Markets, culture and institutions: the emergence of large business groups in Taiwan, 1950s-1970s. *Journal of Management Studies* 38: 719-745

Clark, H. 1991. *Community, Trade and Networks.* CUP: Cambridge

Clegg, S.R. and Redding, S.G. eds. 1990. *Capitalism in Contrasting Cultures* Walter de Gruyter: Berlin

CLFY 长江流域发展研究院 1999. *长江沿江主要城市投资环境评估* *(An Appraisal of the Investment Environment of Key Cities Along the Changjiang)* 长江开发沪港促进会研究项目: 上海

Clifford, J. 1997. *Routes: travel and translation in the late 20th Century* Harvard University Press: Cambridge, MA

Collingwood, R.G. 1946. *The Idea of History.* OUP: Oxford

_____. 1992. *The New Leviathan.* OUP: Oxford

Congressional Planning and Budget Department. 2004. *Towards a Robust and Broad-Based Growth: policy prescriptions fore the 13th Congress.* House of Representative: Republic of the Philippines

Corciño, E. 1945. *Davao, its Land, its People.* Davao

Cribb, R. 2000. Political structures and Chinese business connections in the Malay world: A historical perspective. In *Chinese Business Networks: state, economy and culture,* ed. Chan Kwok Bun. Pearson: Singapore

296

Crouch, H. 1979. Patrimonialism and military rule in Indonesia. *World Politics* 31: 571-87

———. 1985. *Economic Change, Social Structure, and Political Systems in Southeast Asia: Philippine development compared with other ASEAN countries.* ISEAS: Singapore

Csanyi, V. and Kampis, G. 1991. Modelling biological and social change. In *The New Evolutionary Paradigm*, ed. E. Laszlo (with a foreword by Prigogine, I.). Gordon and Breach: New York

Davis, P. and Stern, D. 1981. Adaptation, survival, and growth of the family business: an integrated systems perspective. *Human Relations* 34: 207-224

Davis, W. G. 1973. *Social Relations in a Philippine Market.* Berkeley: University of California Press: Berkeley

Dewey, A. 1962. *Peasant Marketing in Java.* Free Press of Glencoe: New York

Deyo, F. 1983. Chinese management practices and work commitment in comparative perspective. In *The Chinese in Southeast Asia*, eds. L. Lim and P. Gosling. Volume 2. Maruzen Asia: Singapore

Dilthey, W. 1976. *Selected Writings.* CUP: Cambridge. Edited and translated by H. Rickman

Ding, X.C. 2000. The illicit asset stripping of Chinese state firms. *China Journal* 43: 1-28

Dirlik, A. 1994. The postcolonial aura: Third World criticism in the age of global capitalism. *Critical Inquiry* 20: 328–66

———. 1997. Critical reflections on "Chinese capitalism" as a paradigm. *Identities* 3: 303–30

Dittmer, L. 1995. Chinese informal politics. *The China Journal* 34: 1-34

Dong, Jielin and Hu, Jie. 1995. Mergers and acquisitions in China. *Federal Reserve Book of Atlanta Economic Review* 80: 15-29

Drzewiecka, J.A and Halualani, R. 2002. The structural-cultural dialectic of diasporic politics. *Communication Theory* 12: 340-366

Duany, J. 2000. Nation on the move: the construction of cultural identities in Puerto Rico and the Diaspora. *American Ethnologist* 27: 5-30

Dunfee, T. W. and D. E. Warren. 2001. Is *guanxi* ethical? *Journal of Business Ethics* 32:191–204

Elias, N. 1994. *The Civilizing Process.* Basil Blackwell Ltd.: Oxford. Translated by Edmund Jephcott. Originally published in 1939, by Haus zum falker, Basel

Evans, P. 1989. Predatory, developmental and other apparatuses: a comparative political economy perspective on the Third World state. *Sociological Forum* 4: 561-587

———. 1992. The state as problem and solution: predation, embedded autonomy, and structural change. In *The Politics of Economic Adjustment*, eds. S. Haggard and R.R. Kaufman. Princeton University Press: Princeton

Fandy, M. 1999. CyberResistance: Saudi opposition between globalisation and localisation. *Comparative Studies in Society and History* 41: 124-147

Fernandez-Armesto, F. 2001. *Civilizations.* Macmillan: Basingstoke

_____. 2004. *So You Think You're Human?* Oxford University Press: Oxford

Fodor, J. 1987. *Psychosemantics: the problem of meaning in the Philosophy of Mind.* Cambridge, Mass.

Foley, S. and Powell, G. 1997. Re-conceptualising work-family conflict for business/marriage partners: a theoretical model. *Journal of Small Business management* 35: 36-47

Freud, S. 1991. *Civilization, Society and Religion.* Penguin: London. Translated by J. Strachey

_____. 1995. Totem and Taboo. In *The Freud Reader,* ed. P. Gay. Vintage: London

Fukuyama, F. 1995. *Trust: the social virtues and the creation of prosperity.* Hamish Hamilton: London

Gambe, A. R. 1999. *Overseas Chinese Entrepreneurship and Capitalist Development in Southeast Asia.* Munster: Lit Verlag

Gardella, R.O. 1982. Commercial bookkeeping in Ch'ing China and the West. *Modern China* IV: 56-72

Gardner, H. 1983. *Frames of Mind: The theory of multiple intelligences.* Basic Books: New York

_____. 1985. *The Mind's New Science: A history of the cognitive revolution.* Basic Books: New York

Gauci, P. 2001. *The Politics of Trade: the overseas merchant in state and society, 1660-1720.* OUP: Oxford

Geach, P. and Black, M. eds. 1960. *Philosophical Writings of Gottlob Frege.* OUP: Oxford

Geertz, C. 1965. The impact of the concept of culture on the concept of man. In *New Views of the Nature of Man,* ed. J. R. Platt. University of Chicago: Chicago

Gibbon, E. 1985. *The Decline and Fall of the Roman Empire.* Penguin Classics: London

Goffman, E. 1963. *Behaviour in Public Places.* The Free Press: Glencoe, Ill.

Goody, J. 1996. *The East in the West.* Cambridge University Press: Cambridge

Gore, L.L.P. 1998. *Market Communism: the institutional foundations of China's post-Mao hyper-growth* OUP: Hong Kong

Greenhalgh, S. 1994. De-orientalizing the Chinese family firm. *American Ethnologist* 21:746–75

Guthrie, D. 1999. *Dragon in a Three-Piece Suit: the emergence of capitalism in China.* Princeton University Press: Princeton

Haberlein, M. 1998. *Kinship, Gender and Business Failure: merchants' bankruptcies and social relations in Upper Germany, 1520-1620.* European University Institute: Florence

Hamilton, G. ed. 1996. *Asian Business Networks.* Walter de Gruyter: Berlin

_____. 1999. *Cosmopolitan Capitalists: Hong Kong and the Chinese diaspora at the end of the 20th century.* University of Washington Press: Seattle

Hertz, E. 1998. *The Trading Crowd: an enthnography of the Shanghai stock market.* CUP: Cambridge

HGZG 海关总署综合统计司, 中国对外经济贸易咨询公司 (2002) *中国主要进出口企业名录* (*A Directory of the Main Import and Export Enterprises in China*) 中国经济出版社: 北京

Hicks, G. and Mackie, J. 1994. A question of identity. *Far Eastern Economic Review* 14 July: 46-48

Hiscock, G. 2000. *Asia's New Wealth Club*. Nicholas Brealey: London

Hodder, R. 1996. *Merchant Princes of the East: cultural delusions, economic success, and the Overseas Chinese in Southeast Asia*. Wiley: London

———. 2000. *In China's Image: Chinese self-perception in Western thought*. Macmillan: London and New York

———. 2002. *Between Two Worlds: society, politics and business in the Philippines*. Routledge-Curzon: London

———. 2005. The study of the overseas Chinese in Southeast Asia: some comments on its political meanings with particular reference to the Philippines. *Philippine Studies* 53: 3-31

———. 2006. The Philippine legislature and social relationships: toward the formalization of the polity? *Philippine Studies* 53: 563-598

Holland, P. and Boulton, W. 1984. Balancing the family and the business in family. *Business Horizons* 27: 16-21

House of Representatives, Congressional Planning and Budget Department. 2004 (August 4th). *Highlights of the 96th LEDAC Meeting*. Quezon City

Hsing Y.T. 1998. *Making Capitalism in China: the Taiwan Connexion*. OUP: Oxford

Hu Bing. 1987. 上海工业系统企业集团发展中的几个问题 (Problems in the development of enterprise groups in Shanghai's industrial system) *工业经济 (Industrial Economics)* 8: 111-114

Huang, Y. H. 2000. The personal influence model and *gao guanxi* in Taiwan Chinese public relations. *Public Relations Review* 26:219–36

Huang, Y., Woo, W.T. and Duncan, R. 1999. Understanding the decline of China's state sector. *MOCT-MOST: Economic Policy in Transitional Economies* 9: 1-15

Hui, C. and Graen, G. 1997. *Guanxi* and professional leadership in contemporary Sino-American joint ventures in mainland China. *Leadership Quarterly* 8: 451–65

Hutchcroft, P. 1994. *Booty Capitalism: business-government relations in the Philippines*. In Business and government in industrializing Asia, ed. A. MacIntyre. Ithaca: Cornell University Press

———. 1998. *Booty Capitalism: the politics of banking in the Philippines*. Cornell University Press: Ithaca and London

———. 2001. Centralisation and decentralisation in administration and politics: assessing territorial dimensions of authority and power. *Governance* 14: 23-53

———. 1991. Oligarchies and cronies in the Philippine state: The politics of patrimonial plunder. *World Politics* 43:216–43

Hutchings, G. 2001. *Modern China*. Penguin: London

Huyssen, A. 2003. Diaspora and nation. *New German Critique* 88: 147-164

Hwang, K. 1990. Modernisation of the Chinese Family Business. *International Journal of Psychology* 25: 593-618

Iglesias Santos, M., ed. 1999. *Teoría de los polisistemas.* M. V. Dimic, I. Even-Zohar, J. Lambent, C. Robyns, Z. Shavit, R. Sheffy, G. Toury, and S. Yahalom. Madrid: Bibliotheca Philogica, Serie Lecturas.

Jacobs, B. 1979. A preliminary model of particularistic ties in Chinese political alliances. *The China Quarterly* 78: 236-73

Jahn, R. 2001. The challenge of consciousness. *Journal of Scientific Exploration* 15: 443-57

Jomo, K. S. 1997. A specific idiom of Chinese capitalism in Southeast Asia: Sino-Malaysian capital accumulation in the face of state hostility. In *Essential Outsiders: Chinese and Jews in the modern transformation of southeast Asia and central Europe,* ed. D. Chirot and A. Reid. Seattle: University of Washington Press: Seattle

Keister, L.A. 2000. *Chinese Business Groups: the structure and impact of inter-firm relations during economic development.* Oxford University Press: New York

Kerkvliet, B. J. 1995. Toward a more comprehensive analysis of Philippine politics: Beyond the patron-client, factional framework. *Journal of Southeast Asian Studies* 26:401–19

Khalil, E. and Boulding, K. 1996. *Evolution, Order and Complexity* Routledge: New York

King, A.Y.C. 1987. The transformation of Confucianism in the post-Confucian era: the emergence of rationalistic Confucianism in Hong Kong. Unpublished paper

_____. 1991. *Kuan-hsi* and network building. *Daedalus* 120:63–84

Kipnis, A. 1996. The language of gifts. *Modern China* 22: 285–314

_____. 1997. *Producing Guanxi: sentiment, self and subculture in a north China village.* Duke University Press: Durham, NC

Kotkin, J. 1993. *Tribes: how race, religion and identity determine success in the new global economy.* New York: Random House

Kraar, L. 1993 The importance of Chinese in Asian business. *Journal of Asian Business* 9:87–94

Lambent, J. 1997. Itamar Even-Zohar's polysystem studies: an interdisciplinary perspective on culture research. *Canadian Review of Comparative Literature/Revue Canadienne de Littérature Comparée* 24:7–14

Landé, C. H. 1965. *Leaders, Factions and Parties: the structure of Philippine politics.* Monograph 6. Yale University, Centre for Southeast Asian Studies: New Haven

_____. 1996. *Post-Marcos Politics: a geographical and statistical analysis of the 1992 presidential election.* St Martin's Press: New York

_____. 2001. The return of "People Power" in the Philippines. *Journal of Democracy* 12: 88-102

Laszlo, E. ed. 1991. *The New Evolutionary Paradigm.* Gordon and Breach: New York

Lau, S.K.   1978   From traditional familism to utilitarianistic familism: the metamorphosis of familial ethos among the Hong Kong Chinese. *Occasional Paper 78.* Social Research Centre: The Chinese University of Hong Kong

_____. 1982 *Society and Politics in Hong Kong.* The Chinese University Press: Hong Kong

Li Zhaowen ed. 2002. 新兰德2002投资手册 (*NewLand Investment Hand Book 2002),* 深圳新兰德证券投资咨询有限公司: 上海

Li, J., Lam, K. and Qian, G. 2001. Does culture affect behaviour and performance of firms? The case of joint ventures in China. *Journal of International Business Studies* 32: 115-131

Liang Yingming.   1993.   中国改革开放与东南亚华人 (China's opening and reform, and Southeast Asia's Chinese) 华侨华人历史研究 *(Overseas Chinese Historical Research)* 4: 16-21

Lim, L. 1992. The emergence of a Chinese economic zone in Asia? *Journal of Southeast Asian Business* 8: 41–46

Lim, L. and Gosling, P. eds. 1983 *The Chinese in Southeast Asia* (2 volumes). Maruzen Asia: Singapore

Lo, C. Wing-hung. 1995. *China's Legal Awakening.* Hong Kong University Press: Hong Kong.

Lo, D.and Chan, T.M.H.   1998. China's nexus of foreign trade and economic growth. *Journal of International Development* 10: 733-749

Logan, J.R. and Bian Fuqin. 1999. Family values and co-residence with married children in urban China. *Social Forces* 74: 1253-1252

Logan, J.R., Bian Fuqin, and Bian Yanjie. 1998. Tradition and change in the urban Chinese family: the case of living arrangements. *Social Forces* 76: 851-82

Lu Bingyan. 1999.   长江经济带发展战略研究 *(A Study of the Development Strategy of the Changjiang Economic Zone)* 华东师范大学出版社: 上海

Luo, J. D. 1997. The significance of networks in the initiation of small businesses in Taiwan. *Sociological Forum* 12: 297–317.

Mackie, J. 1992. Overseas Chinese entrepreneurship. *Asian-Pacific Economic Literature* 6: 41-64

_____. 2000. The economic roles of the Southeast Asian Chinese: Information gaps and research needs. In *Chinese Business Networks: state, economy and culture,* ed. Chan Kwok Bun. Pearson: Singapore

Mauss, M. 1969. *Essais de Sociologie.* Editions de Minuit: Paris

McCoy, A.W. ed. 1993. *An Anarchy of Families: state and family in the Philippines.* University of Wisconsin Press: Madison

McFadden, J. 2001. *Quantum Evolution.* Norton: New York

McVey, R. ed. 1992. *Southeast Asian Capitalists.* Cornell University: Ithaca

Mendoza, D. et al. 1999. *Politics and Governance: theory and practice in the Philippine context.* Office of Research and Publications, Ateneo de Manila University: Quezon City

Minority Rights Group, ed. 1992. *The Chinese in Southeast Asia.* Manchester: Manchester Free Press

Montuori, A. 2003. The complexity of improvisation and the improvisation of complexity: Social science, art and creativity. *Human Relations* 56: 237–55

Morin, E. 1994. *La complexité humaine (Human Complexity)*. Flammarion: Paris

Moscovici, S. 1981. On social representations. In *Social Cognition: perspectives on everyday understandings*, ed. J.P. Forgas. Academic Press: London

Mulder, N. 1997. Filipino images of the nation. *Philippine Studies* 45: 50–74

Mumford, L. 1956. *The Transformations of Man.* New York

Murphey, R. 1977 *The Outsiders: the Western Experience in India and China.* University of Michigan Press: Ann Arbor, Michigan

Naficy, H. 1993. *The Making of Exile Cultures: Iranian Television in Los Angeles.* Minneapolis

Nathan, A.J. and Tsai, K.S. 1995. Factionalism: a new institutionalist restatement. *The China Journal* 34: 157-92

Nee, V. 1996. The emergence of a market society: changing mechanisms of stratification in China. *American Journal of Sociology* 101: 908-49

Nee, V. and Su, Sijin 1998. Institutional foundations of robust economic performance: public sector industrial growth in China. In *Look East?* Eds. J. Henderson, K. Balaton and G. Lengyel. St Martin's Press: New York.

Ning Yuemin 2002. 世界著名高科技园区的营运和发展 (The operation and development of high-tech parks) 世界地理研究 *(World Regional Studies)* 11: 1-7

Nissé, J. 1999. Sony enters the next century. *Times (Business Life)* 13 March: 26-27

Nolan, P. 1996. Large firms and industrial reform in former planned economies: the case of China. *Cambridge Journal of Economics* 20: 1-29

North, D. 1990. *Institutions, Institutional Change, and Economic Performance.* CUP: Cambridge

Nowak, T.C. and Snyder, K.A. 1974. Clientelist politics in the Philippines: integration or instability. *American Political Science Review* 68: 1147-1170

Numazaki, I. 1991. The role of personal networks in the making of Taiwan's related enterprises. In *Business Networks and Economic Development in East and Southeast Asia*, ed. Hamilton G.G., Centre for Asian Studies, University of Hong Kong: Hong Kong

O'Connor, N., Luo, Y. and Lee, D. 2001. Self-selection, socialisation and budget control in the PRC. A study of a US-Sino joint venture and Chinese state-owned enterprise. *Journal of Business Research* 52: 135-148

Oi, J. 1985. Communism and clientelism: rural politics. *World Politics* 37: 238-66

Omohundro, J. T. 1977. Trading patterns of the Philippine Chinese: Strategies of sojourning middlemen. In *Economic Exchange and Social Interaction in Southeast Asia: perspectives from prehistory, history and ethnography*, ed. K. L. Hutterer. Michigan Papers on South and Southeast Asia, No. 13. Ann Arbor, Michigan: Center for South and Southeast Asian Studies, University of Michigan

_____. 1981. *Chinese Merchant Families in Iloilo: commerce and kin in a central Philippine city.* Quezon City: Ateneo de Manila University Press. Ohio: Ohio University Press

302

_____. 1983. Social networks and business success for the Philippine Chinese. In *The Chinese in Southeast Asia*, ed. L. Lim and L. Gosling. Vol. 1. Singapore: Maruzen

Ong, A. 1999. *Flexible Citizenship: the cultural logic of transnationality* Duke University Press, Durham

Palanca, E. H. 1997. The 1990 top corporations in the Philippines. *Philippine Studies* 45: 547–74

Pambansang Lupon sa Ugnayang Pang-Estadistika (Republika ng Pilipinas) 2002. *Philippines Statistical Yearbook 2002*. Manila

Pan, L., ed. 1999. *The Encyclopaedia of the Chinese Overseas*. Curzon: Richmond

Park, S. H. and Luo Y. D. 2001. *Guanxi* and organizational dynamics: organizational networking in Chinese firms. *Strategic Management Journal* 22: 455–77

Parsons, T. and Smelser, N. 1956. *Economy and Society.* The Free Press: New York

Pearson, M.M. 1997. *China's New Business Elite.* University of California Press: London

Peng, Daijin. 2000. Ethnic Chinese business networks and the Asia-Pacific economic integration. *Journal of African and Asian Studies* 35: 229–50

Pertierra, R. and Urgarte, E.F. 1994. *Cultures and Texts: representations of Philippine society.* UPP: Quezon

Philippine Center for Investigative Journalism. 2004. *Ties That Bind*. Manila

Pinches, M. 1997. Élite democracy, development and people power: contending ideologies and changing practices in Philippines politics. *Asian Studies Review* 21: 104-19

Pinker, S. 1994. *The Language Instinct.* Penguin

Polanyi, K. 1944. *The Great Transformation.* Holt, Rinehart and Winston: NewYork

Popper, K. and Eccles, J. 1977. *The Self and Its Brain.* Springer International: Berlin

Postan, D. L, Mao, M. X, and Yu, M. Y. 1994. The global distribution of the Overseas Chinese around 1990. *Population and Development Review* 20: 631–45

Purcell, V. 1965. *The Chinese in Southeast Asia.* Oxford University Press: London

Putzel, J. 1999. Survival of an imperfect democracy in the Philippines. *Democratization* 6: 198-223

Pye, L. 1995. Factions and the politics of *guanxi*: paradoxes in Chinese administrative behaviour. *China Journal* 34: 35-54

Rafael, V.L. 2003. The cell phone and the crowd. *Public Culture* 15: 399-425

Rao Meijiao. 1993. 东盟国家与中国之经济关系 (*Economic relations between China and the 'Eastern alliance'*) 中国经济协作系统论 (A Theory of China's Economic Cooperation): 137-163

Redding, S. G. 1990. *The Spirit of Chinese Capitalism.* Walter de Gruyter: Berlin

Régnier, P. 2000. *Small and Medium Enterprises in Distress.* Gower: Vermont

Reid, Anthony, ed. 1996. *Sojourners and Settlers.* St. Leonards NSW: Allen and Unwin

Reid, B. 2001. The Philippine democratic uprising and the contradictions of neo-liberalism: EDSA II. *Third World Quarterly* 22: 777-793

Reis, M. 2004. Theorising diaspora: perspectives on classical and contemporary Diaspora. *International Migration* 42: 41-60

Renfrew, C. 1972. *The Emergence of Civilization.* London

_____. ed. 1973. *The Explanation of Cultural Change: models in prehistory.* Duckworth: London

Rozelle, S., Huang, J.K. and Benziger, V. 2003. Continuity and change in China's rural periodic markets. *China Quarterly* 49: 89-115

Ruskola, T. 2000. Conceptualizing corporations and kinship: Comparative law and development theory in a Chinese perspective. *Stanford Law Review* 52:1599–1729

Sanjek, R. 2003. Rethinking migration: ancient to future. *Global Networks* 3: 315-336

Sawyer, R. K. 1999. Improvisation. In *Encyclopedia of Creativity,* ed. M. Runco and S. Pritzker. Vol. 2. Academic Press: San Diego

Scruton, R. 1997. *Modern Philosophy: an introduction and survey.* Arrow: London

SCXQFXB 上海市促进小企业发展协调办公室 (2002) *服务与发展上海市小企业发展报告 (Serve and Develop: a report on the development of small enterprises in Shanghai)* 上海

Securities and Exchange Commission (Manila), Various Records, 2003-2004

Securities and Exchange Commission (Republic of the Philippines) 2003 *Top Corporations 2003.* Manila

Senate Journal. 2002. Session No. 28, October 22. Republic of the Philippines. Pasay City

Senate Publications Bureau & the Legislative Bills and Index Service. 2002. *Rules of the Senate.* Pasay City

Senate, Republic of the Philippines. 2003 (June 4th). *Rules of the Commission on Appointments and Standing Committees.* Pasay City

Senate, the Legislative Bills and Index Division. 2004. *Legislative Histories (RAN8745-8758).* Pasay City

_____. 2004. *Legislative Histories (RAN9163-9298).* Pasay City

Senate, the Legislative Research Service. 1998. *The Performance of the Senate, Tenth Congress.* Pasay City

_____. 2001. *The Performance of the Senate, Eleventh Congress.* Pasay City

_____. 2004. *The Performance of the Senate, Twelfth Congress.* Pasay City

SGG (上海市工商管理局) [Industrial and Commercial Administration Bureau, Shanghai] Various Records 2002-3. Shanghai

Shen Yufang, Zhang Chao 2002 加入 WTO 后我国地区产业调控机制和模式的转型研究 (Changing models on the control and form of China's regional industries)*世界地理研究 (World Regional Studies)* 11: 15-23

304

SHHG (上海海关) 2001. *上海海关统计年鉴 (Shanghai Statistical Almanac)*. 上海社会科学院出版社: 上海

SHHG (上海海关综合统计处) (Shanghai Customs, Comprehensive Statistics Department). Various Records 2002-3. Shanghai

SHRZ (上海荣正投资咨询有限公司). 2002. *中国企业家价值报告 (White Paper on Chinese Entrepreneur Value)* 百家出版社: 上海

Sidel, J. T. 1997. Philippines politics in town, district and province: Bossism in Cavite and Cebu. *Journal of Asian Studies* 56: 947–66

————. 1998. The underside of progress: land, labor and violence in two Philippine growth zones, 1985–95. *Bulletin of Concerned Asian Scholars* 30: 3–12

————. 1999. *Capital, Coercion and Crime: bossism in the Philippines*, Stanford University Press: Stanford

Silliman, G., and Noble, L. eds. 1998. *Organising for Democracy: NGOs, civil society, and the Philippine state.* University of Hawaii Press: Honolulu

Sison, A. J. G and A. Palma-Angeles. 1997. Business ethics in the Philippines. *Journal of Business Ethics* 16:1519–28

Siu, W. S. 2001. Small firm marketing in China: a comparative study. *Small Business Economics* 16: 279–92

Skene, C. 2003. Authoritarian practices in new democracies. *Journal of Contemporary Asia* 33: 189-214

Skinner, G. W. 1996. Creolised Chinese societies in Southeast Asia. In *Sojourners and Settlers*, ed. A. Reid. St. Leonards NSW: Allen and Unwin

Slobin, G. 2001. Theorising diaspora: the homecoming of the first wave diaspora and its cultural legacy. *Slavic Review* 60: 513-529

Smart, A and Smart J. 1998. Transnational social networks and negotiated identities in interactions between Hong Kong and China. In *Transnational Networks from Below* , eds. M.P. Smith and L.E. Guarnizo. Transaction Publishers: New Brunswick

SNBW 上海年鉴编纂委员会. 2002. *上海年间 (Shanghai Almanac, 2002)* 上海年鉴社:上海

Spengler, O. 1959. *The Decline of the West*. George Allen and Unwin: London. Translated by C.F. Atkinson

SSTJJ 上海市统计局 2002. *上海统计年间 (Shanghai Statistical Yearbook, 2002)* 中国统计出版社: 上海 (in Chinese and English)

Standifird, S. S. and R. S. Marshall. 2000. The transaction cost advantage of *guanxi*-based business practices. *Journal of World Business* 35: 21–42

Suryadinata, L. 1985. *China and the ASEAN States*. Institute of Southeast Asian Studies: Singapore

Tao Zhigang and Zhu Tian. 2001. An agency theory of transactions without contract enforcement: the case of China. *China Economic Review* 12: 1-14

Thompson, M. R. 1995. *The Anti-Marcos Struggle: personalistic rule and democratic transition in the Philippines.* New Haven: Yale University Press.

Toloyan, K. 1996. Rethinking diaspora: stateless power in the transnational movement. *Diaspora* 5: 14-36

Toynbee, A. 1949. *Civilization on Trial.* London: Oxford University Press.

Valins, O. 2003. Stubborn identities and the construction of socio-spatial boundaries: ultra-orthodox Jews living in contemporary Britain. *Transactions, Institute of British Geographers* 28:158–75

Walder, A. 1986. *Communist Neo-Traditionalism, Work and Authority in Chinese Industry.* University of California Press: Berkeley

Wang G. W. 2000. *The Chinese Overseas: from earthbound China to the quest for autonomy.* London: Harvard University Press

_____. 1999. Introduction. In *The Encyclopedia of the Chinese Overseas,* ed. Lynn Pan. Curzon: Richmond

_____. 1995 *The Chinese Way: China's position in international relations.* Norwegian Nobel Institute Lecture Series. Scandinavian University Press: Oslo

Wank, D. 1999. *Commodifying Communism: business, trust and politics in a Chinese city.* Cambridge University Press: Cambridge

Weber, M. 1958. *The Protestant Ethic and the Spirit of Capitalism.* Scribner: New York

_____. 1968. *Economy and Society: an outline of interpretive sociology.* New York: Bedminster Press

_____. 1981. *General Economic History*, Transaction Books: New Jersey

White III, Lynn T. 1989. *Shanghai Shanghaied? Uneven taxes in reform China.* Centre of Asian Studies, University of Hong Kong, Occasional papers and Monographs No. 84: Hong Kong

Wickberg, E. 1962. Early Chinese economic influence in the Philippines, 1850-98. *Pacific Affairs* XXXV (3).

_____. 1988. Chinese organizations and ethnicity in Southeast Asia and North America since 1945: A comparative analysis. In *Changing Identities of the Southeast Asian Chinese Since World War II,* ed. J. Cushman and G.W. Wang. Hong Kong University Press: Hong Kong

_____. 1999. Ethnicity. In *The Encyclopaedia of the Chinese Overseas.* Richmond: Curzon, ed. L. Pan. Curzon: Richmond

_____. 2000. *The Chinese in Philippine Life, 1850–1898.* Reprint edition of 1965. Ateneo de Manila University Press: Quezon City

Wong S. L. 1999. Deciding to stay, deciding to move, deciding not to decide. In *Cosmopolitan Capitalists: Hong Kong and the Chinese diaspora at the end of the 20th century,* ed. G. Hamilton. University of Washington Press: Seattle

_____. 1985 The Chinese family firm: a model. *British Journal of Sociology* 36: 58-72

_____. 1988. *Emigrant Entrepreneurs: Shanghai industrialists in Hong Kong.* OUP: Hong Kong

Wong, Y. H. and Chan, R. Y. K. 1999. Relationship marketing in China: *Guanxi,* favoritism and adaptation. *Journal of Business Ethics* 22:107–18

306

Wu Hanfei. 2002. 中国公开选拔领导干部制度研究 *(The System for the Public Selection and Appointment of Cadres in China)* 中国社会科学出版社: 北京 (with an abstract in English)

Wu, J. M. 2001. State policy and *guanxi* network adaptation in China: Local bureaucratic rent-seeking. *Issues and Studies* 37:20–48.

Wurfel, D. 1988. *Filipino Politics: development and decay.* Cornell University Press: Ithaca

XJJ 新经济 (New Economy). 2002. 市场经济的黑与白 (The "black and white" of a market economy). November: 60-70

Yan, Y.N. 2000. *International Joint Ventures in China.* Macmillan: Basingstoke

Yang Chengxun. 1984. 城市经济体制改革应以发达的社会主义商品经济为基点 (Reform of the urban economic system should regard a developed socialist commodity economy as its vital point) *经济研究 (Economic Research)* 11: 17-21

Yang Wanzhong. 2001. *上海及长江流域地区经济协调发展 (The Coordinated Development of the Economies of Shanghai and the Changjiang Valley)* 华东师范大学出版社: 上海

Yang, Mayfair. 2000. Putting global capitalism in its place: economic hybridity, bataille and ritual expenditure. *Current Anthropology* 41: 477-509

————. 2002. The resilience of *guanxi* and its new deployments: a critique of some new *guanxi* scholarship. *China Quarterly* 170: 459–76

————. 1994. *Gifts, Favors and Banquets: the art of social relationships in China.* Cornell University Press: Ithaca

Yao Souchou. 1984. Why Chinese voluntary associations: structure or function? *Journal of the South Seas Society* 39: 75-99

————. 2002. *Confucian Capitalism: discourse, practice and the myth of Chinese enterprise.* Routledge-Curzon: London and New York

Yeun-Tsang, A.W.K., Ho, D., and Ku, A. 2001. The changing support strategies of Chinese families in the midst of rapid social and economic transitions. *Asia Pacific Journal of Social Work* 10: 55-72

ZCZP 中国诚信证券评估有限公司, 中诚信国际信用评级有限责任公司 2002. *中国上市公司基本分析 (An Analysis of China's Listed Companies)* 中国财政经济出版社: 北京

Zhang Zhaozhong. 1999. *战争离我们有多远 (How Far the War from Us?)* 解放军出版社: 北京

ZQLH (中国企业联合会) 2003. *中国企业管理年间编委会 (China Enterprise Management Annual).* 企业管理出版社: 北京

ZQLZQX 中国企业联合会, 中国企业家协会 2002. *中国企业发展报告 (A Report on the Development of Chinese Enterprises)* 企业出版社: 北京

INDEX

308

community, 5, 10, 27, 28, 33, 38, 63,
64, 70, 79, 99, 131, 153, 196, 222,
224, 285, 289
companies, 20, 83, 84, 85, 86, 87, 88,
89, 90, 94, 97, 103, 111, 112, 124,
125, 127, 130, 133, 134, 140, 144,
146, 147, 148, 151, 153, 158, 159,
162, 163, 164, 165, 166, 169, 170,
171, 175, 176, 177, 178, 181, 182,
183, 185, 186, 187, 188, 194, 195,
197, 200, 201, 202, 204, 221, 230,
233, 237, 239, 240, 250, 251, 276,
277, 278
complexity, 21, 34, 45, 46, 47, 48, 51,
53, 62, 65, 68, 69, 76, 82, 97, 100,
104, 123, 134, 149, 151, 166, 170,
172, 173, 259, 284
computers, 39
confidence, 2, 22, 41, 42, 77, 78, 119,
130, 178, 201, 221, 242, 255, 256,
257, 259, 284, 285
Confucian, 32, 122, 125, 174
Confucianism, 7, 12, 13, 41, 77, 97
consciousness, 25, 26, 45, 46, 50, 52,
53, 56, 70 *(see also awareness)*
Contractual agreements, 178
corruption, 180, 221, 234, 239, 240,
247, 284
cultural-structural accommodation,
10, 101, 102
cultural-structural representations,
78, 80, 100, 101, 119, 120
culture, 2, 6, 8, 10, 11, 12, 13, 18, 23,
25, 26, 33, 38, 39, 40, 42, 44, 64,
72, 77, 78, 79, 80, 100, 101, 102,
104, 107, 124, 174, 181, 287

D

'Dark Eye', 290
Davao, 83, 85, 86, 88, 89, 91, 92, 95,
96, 103, 105, 108, 109, 111, 112,
120, 125, 127, 129, 130, 131, 140,
143, 155, 162, 164, 166, 173, 222,
275, 276, 277

death, 50, 53, 127, 157
decentralization, 133, 151
Defensor-Santiago, 234, 252
democracy, 16, 180, 205, 246, 251,
259, 261
democratic, 17, 175, 180, 194, 203,
204, 205, 206, 258, 261, 279
diasporas, 98, 99
DNA, 39

E

electoral fraud, 234, 238, 241, 242,
257
Elgar, 57, 288
emotion, 44, 49, 53, 54, 55, 58, 59,
60, 62, 64, 71
emotions, 27, 32, 59, 133, 143, 282
empathy, 29, 30, 32, 33, 35, 71, 95,
138, 147, 150, 152, 168, 259
Enrile, 237, 239, 240, 245, 252
equal temperament, 57
Estrada, 230, 238, 242, 252
ethnicity, 1, 7, 9, 14, 25, 82, 91, 95,
96, 108, 109, 111, 112, 124, 152,
158, 159, 162, 168, 171, 173, 174,
175, 278, 284
Europe, 2, 10, 42, 43, 100, 124, 148,
205, 237
Executive, 223, 224, 225, 226, 227,
229, 230, 231, 232, 234, 235, 236,
238, 239, 240, 243, 245, 247, 260

F

factions, 14, 15, 18, 28, 200
family, 6, 7, 11, 12, 15, 20, 32, 41,
91, 95, 120, 122, 125, 126, 127,
130, 133, 140, 142, 143, 144, 148,
151, 156, 157, 164, 169, 171, 172,
194, 195, 197, 199, 200, 201, 202,
204, 237, 238, 241, 243, 252, 254,
255, 261, 278, 282, 283
fear, 41, 54, 56, 59, 136, 143, 204,
231, 237, 242, 285
formality., 1, 14, 279, 290

masquerade, 131, 139, 153, 159, 161,
167, 168, 175, 178, 179, 197, 281,
282
media, 229, 239, 242, 247, 252
monitoring, 29, 30, 43, 134, 135, 139,
146, 161, 281, 287
morality, 41, 45, 53, 205
music, 35, 41, 43, 57, 58, 59, 60, 71,
288, 289

N

natural reason, 45, 48, 49, 52, 53, 55,
59, 60, 62, 64, 70, 72
natural selection, 26, 39, 40, 44, 45,
54, 55, 64, 65, 66, 67, 68, 69, 70
NGOs, 229, 259, 260, 261
nothingness, 51

O

Ombudsman, 233, 234, 235, 256
Orientalism, 7
overseas Chinese, 1, 2, 5, 6, 10, 12,
13, 17, 21, 22, 23, 77, 80, 86, 99,
103, 171, 172, 176, 177, 181, 182,
193, 259, 276, 277, 284

P

paradox, 49, 50, 51, 53
parties, 14, 226, 230, 235, 236, 238,
242, 243, 244, 254, 256, 258, 260,
261, 279, 284
Party Development Act, 244
patron-client, (and patrimonial
analysis) 14, 15, 16, 22, 252, 260
personal, (attitude) 14, 15, 19, 20, 27,
28, 29, 72, 83, 120, 123, 124, 134,
146, 150, 151, 167, 168, 178, 229,
233, 239, 241, 242, 246, 251, 252,
253, 255, 284, 286, 287, 289, 290
PLLO, 226, 228, 244
political dynasties, 237, 244, 245,
247, 248, 249, 279
'pork', 224, 225, 254, 257, 262

P

Presidential-Legislative Liaison
Officers (PLLO), 226
professionalisation, 124, 128, 137,
138, 150, 159, 166, 167, 169, 170,
171, 174, 180, 195, 196, 202, 203,
204, 221, 252, 259, 280, 282, 283,
290
psychology, 25, 33, 39, 43
Puritanism, 2, 289, 290

R

Ramos, 234
reason, (see natural reason)

representations, 1, 2, 26, 27, 29, 30,
31, 32, 33, 34, 35, 37, 38, 45, 48,
56, 58, 59, 60, 61, 62, 63, 64, 70,
71, 72, 75, 76, 78, 79, 80, 92, 94,
95, 96, 97, 98, 99, 100, 102, 119,
120, 122, 123, 124, 128, 131, 132,
135, 136, 144, 147, 149, 152, 166,
167, 169, 171, 172, 173, 174, 175,
181, 196, 199, 204, 205, 206, 221,
223, 258, 260, 261, 275, 279, 280,
283, 284, 285, 286, 287, 290
rule of law, 16, 195, 201, 203, 280

S

Senate, 224, 227, 228, 229, 230, 232,
235, 236, 237, 238, 243, 245, 247,
248, 249, 250, 252, 253, 261
Shanghai, 19, 20, 89, 90, 108, 109,
134, 137, 143, 145, 146, 148, 153,
158, 163, 169, 171, 172, 173, 176,
177, 178, 181, 182, 183, 184, 185,
187, 188, 189, 190, 192, 193, 194,
197, 198, 199, 201, 207, 208, 209,
210, 211, 212, 213, 214, 215, 216,
217, 218, 221, 277, 278, 279
Shenzhen, 89, 109, 183, 187, 188,
198
Singapore, 6, 100, 128, 162
social capital, 16, 179